Le Monde

THE JANUS LIBRARY

Lorenzo Valla, DE VOLUPTATE (ON PLEASURE).
Maristella Lorch and A. Kent Hieatt
* * *
Rene Descartes, LE MONDE (THE WORLD).
Michael Sean Mahoney,
* * *
Immanuel Kant, DER STREIT DER FAKULTÄTEN
(THE CONFLICT OF THE FACULTIES). Mary J.
Gregor and Robert E. Anchor
* * *
Thomas Hobbes, DE CORPORE (PART FIRST).
Aloysius Patrick Martinich; with an inquiry into
Hobbes' Theory of Language, Speech and Reason-
ing by Isabel C. Hungerland and George R. Vick
* * *
Immanuel Kant, DER EINZIG MÖGLICHE BEWEIS-
GRUND (THE ONE POSSIBLE BASIS FOR A
DEMONSTRATION OF THE EXISTENCE OF
GOD). Gordon Treash
* * *
Etienne Bonnot de Condillac, LA LOGIQUE (LOGIC).
W. R. Albury
* * *
Nicholas de Cusa, IDIOTA DE MENTE. Clyde Lee
Miller
* * *
Johannes Reuchin, DE ARTE CABBALISTICA. Martin
Goodman
* * *
Johannes Kepler, MYSTERIUM COSMOGRAPHICUM,
E. J. Aiton and A. M. Duncan
* * *
Marsilio Ficino, DE VITA. Carol Kaske
* * *
Immanuel Kant, FORTSCHRITTE DER METAPHYSICK
(PROGRESS IN METAPHYSICS). Ted B. Humphrey
* * *

RENE DESCARTES • Le Monde, ou Traité de la lumière

TRANSLATION AND INTRODUCTION BY MICHAEL SEAN MAHONEY

ABARIS BOOKS, INC. • NEW YORK

Copyright © 1977 by Abaris Books, Inc.
International Standard Book Number 0-913870-35-8
Library of Congress Card Number 77-086236
First published 1977 by Abaris Books, Inc.
24 West 40th Street, New York, New York
Printed in the United States of America

Contents

Introduction

I. *The Composition of* The World

In 1629, at the age of thirty-three, René Descartes quit his native France to settle permanently in Holland.[1] There he hoped to pursue his philosophical investigations without interruption or distraction. But no sooner had he settled in his new surroundings than he received, from two different sources, requests for an explanation of the phenomenon of *parhelia,* or "false suns," observed by Christoph Scheiner at Frascati, near Rome, in March 1629.[2] He apparently made short work of the problem, for in October, within two months of first hearing about it, he wrote to Marin Mersenne[3] that he could "give some account of it." In fact, dropping what he had been working on (early drafts of what became the *Meditations on First Philosophy*), he had decided

> to make of it a small treatise which will contain an explanation of the colors of the rainbow—which have given me more trouble than all the rest—and generally of all sublunary phenomena.[4]

Within a week Descartes had expanded his design even farther:

> Instead of explaining only one phenomenon, I have resolved
> to explain all the phenomena of nature, that is to say, all of
> physics. And the design I have satisfies me more than any
> other I have ever had, for I think I have found a means for
> setting out all my thoughts in such a way that they will
> satisfy some and that others will have no occasion to
> contradict them. [5]

The World, or a Treatise on Light was underway.

It remained underway for the next four years and reached
completion only to be withdrawn from publication for reasons to
be discussed presently. Subsequently Descartes redistributed its
contents, often heavily revised, among other writings. The extant
version, published posthumously from an incomplete manuscript
copy, does not seem to contain the entire treatise as Descartes
planned and wrote it. Several internal references, together with
passages from his correspondence over the period 1629 to 1634,
form a picture of the work quite close to that drawn by Descartes
in Part V of the *Discourse on Method* (1637). Originally he
intended

> to set out there rather fully what I conceived about light,
> and then at that occasion to add something about the sun
> and the fixed stars, because light proceeds almost entirely
> from them; about the heavens because they transmit it;
> about the planets, comets, and the earth, because they
> reflect it; and in particular about all the bodies that are on
> the earth, because they are colored, or transparent, or
> luminous; and finally about man, because he is the spectator
> of light. [6]

The treatise Descartes had in mind, then, included not only the
text published here, but also the separately published *Meteors*
(1637) and *Man* (1662). In addition it may have included the
Dioptrics (1637), which fitted closely with it. *The World* set out
the real mechanism of light only hinted at in the opening
paragraphs of the *Dioptrics* and depended on the laws of optics
derived and applied therein.[7] Most important, however, as the

subtitle of *The World* implies, light was to be the keystone of Descartes's cosmology. How it was produced and how it behaved would not only account for the observed phenomena but would also provide the criteria for judging what caused those phenomena.

In addition to conveying details of the original treatise and of the order in which Descartes worked them out, the correspondence for the period reveals his gradually waning enthusiasm for the undertaking. What in 1629 had "satisfi[ed] me more than anything I have ever done," in November 1630 still "pleas[ed] me too much for me to fail to complete it," though he had come to doubt that he could meet his three-year deadline with anything more than an abridgment.[8] By 1633, only his promise to Mersenne drove him to complete even that revised plan.[9] Judging from his letters, one senses that Descartes would have welcomed almost any excuse to drop the project.

Two main problems caused him difficulty and concern. First, the transition from flash of insight to coherent exposition involved him in a clamor of details that threatened to get out of hand. Convinced though he was of the intuitive certainty of his scheme, he became increasingly anxious about how to share that intuition and about where the scheme was leading him. The cosmology made sense as a whole. Indeed, it formed a tightly woven unit, as Descartes insisted when writing to Mersenne in April 1630:

> all these problems of physics, touching which I have told you I have taken a position, are so linked together and depend so heavily one on the other that it would be impossible for me to demonstrate one of them without demonstrating all of them together, and I cannot do that any sooner nor more succinctly than in the treatise I am preparing.[10]

He was finding it difficult to pick out the proper strand by which to unravel the whole without losing the reader. For every strand was new and, taken separately, could provoke strong dissent. "I

have a thousand different things to consider all together,'' he told Mersenne in December 1630,

> in order to find an approach [*biais*] by means of which I might speak the truth without stunning anyone's imagination or shocking commonly received opinions. That is why I wish to take a month or two to think about nothing else.[11]

The task of organizing the argument of *The World* led directly to the second main problem. Resolution of the details was drawing him inexorably toward questions of metaphysics and theology that he had not yet worked out and that he was far from ready to make public. Publication of *The World,* promised by Mersenne from the outset of the project, would commit Descartes to metaphysical and theological positions he was not yet sure he could defend. Throughout the correspondence of 1629 and 1630 his growing anxiety on this count sounds a counterpoint to his litany of organizational woes.

In October 1629, when parhelia and other atmospheric phenomena still constituted the main theme, Descartes described the work to Mersenne as ''a sample of my philosophy'' and proposed after publishing it ''to hide behind the drapes to listen to what people say.''[12] As the scope of the project grew, so too did his worries. By December 1629 the joking allusion to anonymity had become a firm resolve ''not to put my name to it'' and to have the work thoroughly examined by people he trusted. ''I desire this principally because of theology, which has been so subjected to Aristotle that it is almost impossible to set out another philosophy without its appearing at first contrary to faith.''[13] More and more, *The World* became for Descartes a test of his ability to set out his new philosophy without provoking censorship midway in his presentation. For *The World* involved fundamental theological insights that he feared to publish without suitable preparation. He announced to Mersenne in May 1630, for example, that all truths—even the truths of mathematics—depended on God. ''You also ask,'' he added,

what necessitated God to create these truths, and I say that He was as free to make it not true that all lines drawn from the center [of a circle] to the circumference are equal as not to create the world.[14]

By November 1630 he had decided on a strategy. For the moment he would avoid theology:

> I shall find out in the *Dioptrics* whether I am capable of explaining my conceptions and of persuading others of a truth after I have persuaded myself of it. I do not really think I can. But, if I should find by experience that such is the case, I do not say that someday I shan't complete a small treatise on metaphysics that I began when in Frisia and of which the principal points are to prove the existence of God and that of our souls when they are separated from the body, whence follows their immortality.[15]

In Descartes's mind at least, physics and theology were two sides of the same coin.[16] Two fears began to haunt him: either that an error in the physics would undermine his theology or that the theology implied by his physics would be deemed heretical and thereby sap the foundations of his reform of philosophy.

To counter the first fear, Descartes began sending out portions of his research early in 1632, beginning with the first part of the *Dioptrics* dealing with refraction. Toward the end of 1632 he asked Mersenne to tell him more about Galileo's theory of the tides as presented in the recently published *Dialogues Concerning the Two Great World Systems,* "for that is one of the things that has given me the most trouble to find, and, although I think I have got around it, there are nevertheless circumstances about which I am not clear."[17] In the same letter he spoke of the minor differences between his physiological theories—he had decided during the fall to add a final section on man[18] —and those of William Harvey. Both references have the tone of reconnaissance forays feeling out the strength of any possible opposition. Once committed publicly, he could not afford to lose an argument about his physics.

On 22 July 1633 Descartes announced to Mersenne that

> My treatise is just about finished, although I still must
> correct and recopy it. Because there is nothing new left to
> seek, I find it so hard to work on it that, if I had not
> promised you three years ago to send it to you by the end of
> this year, I do not believe I could finish it for a long time.
> But I want to try to keep my promise.[19]

He did not keep it. A month earlier, his second fear had been
realized in Rome, though he did not yet know it. By November
1633 he had heard the news:

> I was at that point when I received your last of the eleventh
> of this month, and I wanted to do what bad debtors do who
> go ask their creditors to give them a short extension when
> they feel the term of their debt approaching. In fact, I had
> proposed to send you my *World* as a New Year's gift; less
> than two weeks ago I was still resolved to send you at least a
> part of it if the whole could not be transcribed in that time.
> But I shall say to you that, having inquired over the last few
> days in Leiden and Amsterdam whether there was a copy of
> Galileo's *System of the World* (because I seem to have heard
> that it had been published in Italy last year), I was told that
> it was true that it had been published but that all copies of it
> had been burned at Rome at the same time and he
> condemned to some punishment. This has so astonished me
> that I am almost resolved to burn all my papers, or at least
> not to let anyone see them. For I cannot imagine that he,
> who is an Italian and even well loved by the Pope, as I
> understand, could have been made a criminal for anything
> other than having wanted to establish beyond doubt the
> motion of the earth, which I know well to have been once
> censured by some cardinals. But I thought I had heard it
> said that since then one had not stopped teaching it publicly,
> even in Rome. I confess that, if it is false, all the
> foundations of my philosophy are also. For they clearly
> demonstrate it. It is so linked to all parts of my treatise that I
> cannot detach it without rendering the rest completely
> defective.
> But, since I would not for all the world want a discourse
> to issue from me that contained the least word of which the

Church would disapprove, so I would prefer to suppress it than to have it appear crippled. I have never had a drive aimed at producing books, and if I had not engaged myself by a promise to you and several others of my friends, so that the desire to keep my word to you obliged me all the more to study, I would never have finished it.

But, after all, I am sure you will not send a sergeant after me to force me to acquit myself of my debt and that you will perhaps be happy to be freed of the pain of reading bad material. There are already so many opinions in philosophy that have some plausibility and that can be sustained in debate that, if mine have nothing more certain about them and cannot be proved without controversy, I do not want ever to publish them.

Relenting somewhat, Descartes concluded by asking for another year to look the treatise over again; in the meantime, Mersenne was to send more detailed word about the Galileo affair.

It did not alleviate Descartes's fears to learn that this letter never reached its destination.[21] In a letter of April 1634 he discussed his now firm decision in more measured tones:

I shall say to you that everything I have set out in my treatise among which was also this opinion of the earth's motion, so depend on one another that it is enough to know that there is one of them that is false in order to know that all of the arguments I have used have no force. Even if I thought they were supported by very certain and very evident demonstrations, I would nevertheless not want for anything in the world to sustain them against the authority of the Church. I well know that one could say that everything the Inquisitors of Rome have decided is not thereby automatically an article of faith and that it is first necessary for a Council to pass it. But I am not so enamored of my ideas to want to use such excuses in order to have means to maintain those ideas. The desire that I have to live in repose and to continue the life I began by taking as my motto *bene vixit, bene qui latuit* ["He has lived well who has hid well"] makes me happier to be delivered from the fear I have of acquiring by means of my work more acquaintances than I desire that it makes me angry at having lost the time and trouble I took to write it.[22]

Having already convinced himself by the difficulties of organizing his treatise that its contents were inextricably interwoven, and having already conjured up the fear of censorship, Descartes reacted to the news of Galileo's condemnation in a wholly predictable way. Whatever the time, trouble, and pride he had invested in *The World,* he had never meant it to be more than a sample of his philosophy, a foretaste of a larger system he was convinced would rout scepticism and establish orthodox theology on unshakeable foundations. He knew the dangers of premature exposure. He had worried about them even before the Galileo affair revealed their full extent. He would not sacrifice his main mission for the sake of a preliminary sketch. He had important things to say. For the moment, however, he would say nothing.

The Mechanistic Universe

The World demands close attention, especially from the modern reader. Often what at first seems obvious rests in fact on profound analysis, and what seems implausible turns out to be an ingenious solution to a subtle problem. Yet, for all that, it is easy, as even Descartes's firmest supporters admitted, to find fault with the details of the mechanistic universe of *The World,* or even with the lack of details. From the first samples in his correspondence of the early 1630s, through the veiled references in the *Dioptrics* and *Meteors* of 1637, to the expanded version in the *Principles of Philosophy* of 1644, the system set forth in *The World* provided unsolved problems for his followers and critical handholds for his opponents. The mechanism of light, the laws of motion and of impact, the mechanics of vortices, the existence of the vacuum all became central concerns of seventeenth-century science, unleashing controversies that continued over decades.

Yet those very controversies, and the vehemence with which they were carried on, attest to the historical importance of Descartes's system and make its earliest exposition in *The World* especially interesting to historians and philosophers. Even

though unpublished at that time, it is one of those rare works that, regardless of whether it is ultimately right or wrong, signals a new epoch in human thought. As the first attempt to construct an entire physical universe on mechanistic foundations, it captured the thrust of contemporary creative thought and showed where it could lead. What had previously been a set of isolated experiments in mechanical explanation became the constituents of a unified program of natural philosophy. Thenceforth scientists might differ over precisely how the machine of the world worked or was put together, but they all agreed it was a machine and could be explained mechanically.[23]

The idea itself of a world-machine dated back to the Middle Ages. The imitation of planetary motion in armillary spheres and planetaria by means of clockwork mechanisms—the motions conformed, of course, to the Ptolemaic system—suggested by reverse metaphor an analogous mechanism governing the real heavens. Few, if any, took the comparison as more than metaphorical or analogical. The perfection of uniform circular motion and the guiding influence of celestial intelligences continued to move the planets about an earth sealed by its very nature in a sphere beneath that of the moon and governed by a different code of natural behavior. Within the terrestrial sphere, elements strove by their nature to attain their natural place, earth and water moving downward, air and fire upward. At an analytically more complex level, all substances, animate and inanimate, similarly strove toward the perfection (in the sense of "completion") of their essences which, when apprehended by the mind, corresponded to their real definitions. Those motions of striving toward perfection could be countered by force. Then heavy bodies rose upward, animals threw off monstrous progeny, people got sick, and so on. Nature followed habits, not laws. The unnatural, because it was unusual, offered no insight into the natural. But machines by their very essence "overcame the disadvantages of nature" and brought unnatural results. Hence, to the traditional medieval mind the machine of the world could only be a metaphor.[24]

It first became more than that in the sixteenth century. As the engineer emerged from the anonymity and secrecy of the guild to claim for his art the status of discipline and for himself the rank of mathematician and philosopher, he laid increasing emphasis on the laws by which nature limited his art. He gradually changed from a trickster overcoming nature to her most obedient servant. In this shift of role he drew assistance from his sometime allies, the natural magician, the alchemist, and the hermetic philosopher, all of whom also insisted with growing fervor that one controlled nature only by obeying her laws.[25] The machine thereby became a reflection or even exemplar of nature, promising insight into her own structure and operations.

Within this setting, Copernicus took the metaphor of the world-machine seriously enough to posit for the earth an annual countermotion in order to maintain the fixed direction of its axis. That motion only makes sense if one is indeed thinking of an actual physical mechanism transferring motion from one sphere of the heavens to another. Later, Kepler explicitly set forth the notion of a celestial mechanism. Having entertained and then abandoned the concept of a motive spirit [*anima motrix*] overseeing the variation of orbital speed with changing distance from the sun, he looked for a machine to transmit motive force [*vis motrix*]. So, he wrote to Herwart von Hohenburg in February 1605,

> I mean to say here that the celestial machine is not like a divine animal but like a clock (he who thinks the clock to be animate glorifies the work of the artisan), so that in the machine almost all variety of motion depends on one most simple, corporal magnetic force, just as in a clock all motions depend on the most simple one.[26]

But the mechanism did not fit the model well enough for Kepler to develop his suggestion very far. Moreover, when seeking to understand the reflection and refraction of light, he chose a very different mechanism.

Other contemporaries followed this piecemeal pattern in their investigations. Eschewing any causal explanation of the

accelerated free fall of bodies, Galileo could establish no mechanical links between local phenomena of motion and the grand motions of heavenly bodies. Instead, he fell back on the basically metaphysical, even spiritual notion of the perfection and privileged being of the circle and of uniform motion. Similarly, his tantalizing references in the *Assayer* (1624) to primary and secondary qualities and to corpuscular mechanisms lack substantial ties to any laws of motion that could produce a unified system.

Beeckman's corpuscular theories of sound and of fluid mechanics, Bacon's theory of heat as the motion of corpuscles, and various other corpuscular and atomist theories[27] shared with Galileo's *Assayer* the conviction that only machines could be fully and exactly understood. Ultimately they consisted of matter of a certain shape and dimension, arranged in a certain way and moving according to a definite pattern. They demanded no belief in intangible entities, vague concepts, or unverifiable agents. To know how a machine worked was to be able to construct it and to use it; its successful construction and application guaranteed one's certain knowledge of it.

Here one converges on the themes informing Descartes's *World*. He brought them together into a single system. If that system did not yet work, it nonetheless gave promise of doing so. More important, it was successful enough to undermine any traditional alternative, at least in the minds of those outside the scholastic university. Combined with the doctrines of Bacon in the thought of the young Robert Boyle, it became a foundation of the "mechanical philosophy." To Christiaan Huygens it was the common ground linking his investigations into mechanics, optics, and cosmology. To Isaac Newton it was the basis of a rival theory of optics and a challenge to provide a more precise and coherent system of the world. At the same time, it set Newton's parameters of matter and motion and of force as their conjoint action.[28]

An historian of seventeenth-century mechanics once summed up Descartes's achievement in the following terms:

> The essential message that Descartes would carry to his century lies not in the solution of concrete problems that then occupied scientists, but rather in the construction of a complete system that he meant to see substituted entirely for the doctrine of the School and in which all substantial qualities and forms were banished in favor of a universal mechanism explaining all the phenomena of this visible world with the aid of only three concepts, to wit, extension, shape, and motion . . . .
>
> The model was admirable for the simplicity of its premises, if not for that of its methods [*voies*], and filled in a great number of minds the need for an explanatory account of physical phenomena. [29]

Where it did not fill that need, it stimulated similar attempts. That, perhaps, is the most important measure of its place in the history of science.

The Text of the World

Clearly Descartes was right when he told Mersenne in 1633 that the Copernican hypothesis could not be separated from his cosmology. By common consent the sun and stars emitted light, and the earth, moon, and planets reflected it. If the matter that produced light differed essentially from the matter that reflected it, reason and order dictated that the one body consisting of the first sort be at the center of the many bodies made up of the second. It would be hard to imagine a Ptolemaic sun of the first element swirling in a small, contained vortex in the fourth of seven orbits otherwise occupied by large bodies of the third element, all within a vortex of the second element rotating about a stationary earth of the third element. Nor could any body caught up in such a vortex avoid rotating about its own axis as a result of the differential of speeds on the inside and outside edges. Descartes's cosmology was not, and could not be, astronomically neutral. It fitted only one system. If Copernicus fell, Descartes fell with him.

So Descartes suppressed *The World*. However, still wishing to give the learned public a "sample of my philosophy," he

polished the *Dioptrics,* which he had already completed and sent to Jakob Gool in 1632.[30] Concentrating on the laws of reflection and refraction and on the theory of lenses (and hence of vision) derivable from them, he began the work with only the vaguest hint of an underlying cosmology from which he meant to take his real model of light. At the same time, he gathered together his explanations for such atmospheric phenomena as rainbows, halos, and *parhelia* and composed a work to which he gave the traditional title *Meteors.*[31] The mechanisms at work here bore little relation to the imperceptible particles of *The World.* Instead, fragments of ice and drops of rain acted as miniature prisms to reflect and refract light. Finally, he composed his *Geometry,* which by tying plane curves to indeterminate equations in two unknowns brought the theory of equations to bear on geometry and made short work of determining the shape of lenses.

To these three *Essays,* ready for publication in 1637, Descartes added by way of introduction a short *Discourse on the Method of Rightly Directing the Reason.* Besides condensing the essentials of his *Rules for the Direction of the Mind* and outlining his method of doubt, he held before his readers the prospect of a complete cosmology based on light. If he meant thereby to provoke demands for that cosmology, he met instead with criticism of his metaphysics and his science. Not until 1644 in the *Principles of Philosophy* did he finally publish the substance of *The World,* greatly expanded at some points (especially in regard to the laws of motion) and slightly "crippled" at another: the earth's vortex, combined with a hastily concocted theory of the relativity of motion, became now a device for maintaining the stability of the earth even as it moved about the sun. For whatever reason, the fear of offending orthodox sensibilities by espousing Copernicanism still held Descartes in thrall.

In the midst of this revision and redistribution of material, the single treatise on the *World* was separated into two works, one bearing the original title and the other, the long final chapter, the title *Man. Man* was the first to be published in 1662 in a Latin

translation made from two copies of the French original. Two years later, a Parisian bookseller put out an edition of *The World,* based on a copy of the original and accompanied by two small treatises—on local motion and on fevers—not by Descartes. Also in 1664, Claude Clerselier, Descartes's literary executor and editor of his *Letters* (3 vols., 1657-67), published an edition of *Man* based on the French original and with revised illustrations. Although in his preface he decried the haste that had led to publication of *The World* without reference to the original in his possession, he waited—probably for the sake of his publisher's investment—another thirteen years before bringing out a new version of the 1664 *Man* together with *The World* from the original.[32]

Clerselier also pointed out in his preface that the original manuscripts clearly linked the two works as parts of a single treatise. The opening words of *Man* that Florenz Schuyl, the editor of the 1662 version, found puzzling made complete sense when read as the beginning of Chapter 18 of *The World.* Yet, knowing this, Clerselier still did not publish the work in its intended form. In 1677, *The World* dangled at the end of a series of works concerned with *Man,* which by title and position had become the main treatise. So it is that the text and translation to follow begin on p. 405 and run to p. 511; following the lead of Charles Adam and Paul Tannery, the editors of the *Oeuvres de Descartes,* the translation is based on the 1677 version of *The World,* according to Clerselier the original version.[33]

Michael Sean Mahoney

Notes

1. Biographies of Descartes abound. The most readable to appear recently in English is Jack R. Vrooman, *René Descartes: A Biography* (New York, 1970). Descartes's early years are the most difficult to reconstruct. Few records or papers survive, and Descartes's own later statements cannot be wholly trusted. He tended to remember the development of his thought as it should have taken place rather than as it did. Two recent studies that take account of previous scholarship while offering new interpretations are Geneviève Rodis-Lewis, *L'Oeuvre de Descartes* (Paris, 1971) and John A. Schuster, "Descartes and the Scientific Revolution, 1618-1634" (Ph.D. dissertation, Princeton, 1977).

The study of Descartes begins and ends with the magisterial national edition of his *Oeuvres,* edited by Charles Adam and Paul Tannery (13 vols., Paris, 1897-1913; new edition with additions and corrections, Paris, 1964-), which includes Adam's critical biography in Vol. XII. References to this edition below will be abbreviated in the form AT.XI.36 to denote Vol. XI, p. 36; references to correspondence are abbreviated 15.IV.30 to indicate a letter of 15 April 1630. Gregor Sebba's *Bibliographia Cartesiana:* (The Hague, 1964) is indispensable; the "Equipe Descartes" of the Centre National de la Recherche Scientifique has taken up Sebba's task for the literature since 1970 in yearly "Bulletins cartesiens" in *Archives de philosophie,* 1972-. The notes to the Introduction and to the text below cite only the works consulted for their preparation or directly pertinent to the points being discussed. In most cases those works lead in turn to further literature.

What follows derives in part and benefits as a whole from discussion with John A. Schuster who, first as student and then as colleague, pursued some of my suggestions and shared with me his own ideas concerning the development of Descartes's philosophical and scientific thought. As is so often the case when people work together on the same or closely related topics, Schuster and I now find it difficult to assign precise credit for the ideas and interpretations we have discussed; they have simply bounced back and forth between us for too long. Instead, I readily and gratefully acknowledge our long and pleasant collaboration, at the same time that I take full responsibility for any errors here committed. For Schuster's own, fuller account of *The World* and its immediate background, see chapters 6 and 8 of his dissertation cited above.

2. Cardinal Barberini in Rome sent a description of Scheiner's observations to the French astronomer Nicolas Peiresc, who in turn distributed copies to his associates, among them Pierre Gassendi. Gassendi published his explanation in two works, *Phaenomenon rarum Romae observatum 20 Martij et eius causarum explicatio* (Amsterdam, 1629) and *Parhelia seu soles IV spurij qui circa verum apparuerunt Romae die 20 Martij 1629 . . .* (Paris, 1630). In anticipation of Gassendi's promised solution, a Dr. Wassenaer and Henry Reneri solicited Descartes's explanation of the phenomenon so as to compare the two. Descartes then received a second request from Mersenne, who surely had received one of Peiresc's copies of the original report (information taken from AT.1.29, note). For a description of the phenomenon and Descartes's account of it see his *Meteors,* Discourse X.

3. A member of the Minim order (*Ordo fratrum minimorum*) founded by St. Francis de Paul, Mersenne (1588-1648) began his scholarly career as an apologist for orthodoxy. His *Quaestiones in Genesim* (1623) was directed against naturalistic interpretations of the creation, while his *L'Impiété des déistes, athées et libertins de ce temps* (1624) and *La vérité des sciences, contre les sceptiques ou pyrrhoniens* (1625) took aim at other opponents of the Roman Catholic faith. After the mid-twenties Mersenne increasingly directed his efforts toward the sciences themselves. His interest in music theory and sound made him an ardent supporter of the mathematical, mechanical approach to nature, and the various versions of his *Harmonie universelle* (1627-1636) range over the newest results in mathematics, mechanics, optics, and cosmology. Through personal meetings in his Paris convent, through journeys to Italy and the Low Countries, and through correspondence embracing almost the entire European philosophical world, Mersenne kept himself and others informed of the most recent investigations in science. He was in particular the conduit through which the work of Galileo, Descartes, Fermat, Hobbes, and others reached the Parisian learned community. On Mersenne, see Robert Lenoble, *Mersenne, ou la naissance du mécanisme* (Paris, 1943); C. de Waard, et al., eds., *Correspondance de Mersenne* (Paris, 1932-); Richard H. Popkin, *The History of Scepticism from Erasmus to Descartes* (New York, 1964), chapter 6; and A.C. Crombie, *Dictionary of Scientific Biography* (Scribner's, 1970-), IX, 316-322.

4. Descartes to Mersenne, 8.X.29, AT.I.23.

5. Descartes to Mersenne, 13.X.29, AT.I.70.

6. *Discours de la méthode*, AT.VI.42.

7. From the outset the two texts were almost inseparable in Descartes's mind. Together they formed an interlocked whole. He described their interrelation to Mersenne in November 1630. He asked that Mersenne not broadcast Descartes's plans to publish the *Dioptrics*, "for the way I work, it will not be ready for a long time. I want to insert in it a discourse in which I shall try to explain the nature of colors and of light. That has held me up for six months and is not yet half-finished. But also, it will be longer than I thought and will contain just about a complete new Physics; in that way I hope it will serve to discharge me of the promise I made to you to have completed my *World* in three years, for it will be like an abridgment of it . . . . I think I shall send you this discourse on Light as soon as it is done and before sending you the rest of the *Dioptrics*." (AT.I.178-180) Although letters to Mersenne and Gool in 1632 speak of the *Dioptrics* as a wholly independent treatise, as do references to it in *The World* (see in particular chapter 14), the works apparently remained interwoven. In autumn 1635 Descartes told Mersenne: "As regards lenses, I shall tell you that since the condemnation of Galileo I have reviewed and wholly completed the treatise I started earlier and, having entirely separated it from my *World*, I propose shortly to have it printed alone" (AT.I.322). Perhaps only at this point did *The World* begin to point "elsewhere" for explanations of such phenomena as reflection and refraction.

8. Descartes to Mersenne, 25.XI.1630, AT.I.179; see also the passage quoted first in the preceding note.

9. Descartes to Mersenne, 22.VII.33, AT.I.268, and XI.33, AT.I.271; see also the earlier letter of 15.IV.30, AT.I.136ff., and below.

10. Descartes to Mersenne, 15.IV.30, AT.I.140.

11. Descartes to Mersenne, 23.XII.30, AT.I.194.

12. Descartes to Mersenne, 8.X.29, AT.I.23.

13. Descartes to Mersenne, 18.XII.29, AT.I.85.

14. Descartes to Mersenne, 27.V.30, AT.I.152.

15. Descartes to Mersenne, 25.XI.30, AT.I.182.

16. Descartes to Mersenne, 15.IV.30, AT.I.143-144: "As for your question of Theology, even though it goes beyond the capacity of my mind, it does not seem to me beyond my calling, because it does not touch on what depends on Revelation, which is what I properly call Theology. Rather, it is metaphysics and should be examined by human reason. Now I think that everyone to whom God has given the use of that reason is obligated to use it principally in trying to know Him and to know himself. That is how I have tried to begin my studies; and I will say to you that I could not have found the foundations of Physics if I had not sought them in that way." Mersenne and Descartes were both educated by the Jesuits of La Flèche. The Minim needed no lessons on the distinction between theology and philosophy unless Descartes meant to redefine it.

17. Descartes to Mersenne, XI or XII.32, AT.I.261-262.

18. See note 15. Descartes spoke about his plans in the December letter just cited: "I shall speak a bit more than I thought [I would] about man in my *World,* for I am undertaking to explain all his principal functions. I have already written [about] those that pertain to life, such as digestion of food, the beating of the pulse, distribution of nourishment, etc., and the five senses. I am now dissecting the heads of various animals to uncover [*expliquer*] in what imagination, memory, etc. consist. I have seen the book *On the Motion of the Heart,* of which you once spoke to me, and find myself differing a bit from his opinion, although I did not see it until after having finished writing on this matter" (AT.I.263).

19. AT.I.268.

20. AT.I.270-272.

21. Descartes to Mersenne, IV.34, AT.I.285.

22. *Ibid.,* 285-286; see *Discourse on Method,* Part VI.

23. For a concise account of the new mechanistic science of the seventeenth century, see Richard S. Westfall, *The Construction of Modern Science: Mechanisms and Mechanics* (New York, 1971).

24. Paolo Rossi, in chapter I of his *Philosophy, Technology, and the Arts in the Early Modern Era* (New York, 1970; Italian original Milan, 1962), probes the medieval attitude toward the mechanical arts through

attacks on them by sixteenth-century writers. For a more extensive, philosophical account, see Franco Alessio, "La filosofia e le *artes mechanicae* nel secolo XII," *Studi medievali,* 3a ser., 6(1965), 71-161.

25. See Paolo Rossi, *Francesco Bacone: Dalla magia alla scienza* (Bari, 1957; Engl. trans. Chicago, 1968) and *Philosophy, Technology and the Arts in the Early Modern Era* (New York, 1970); and Frances Yates, "The Hermetic Tradition in Renaissance Science", *Art, Science, and History in the Renaissance* (ed. C.S. Singleton, Baltimore, 1967), 255-274. As straightforward engineers, both Galileo in his *Meccaniche* (1593-1600) and Simon Stevin in his *Beghinseln der Weghkonst* (1586) insisted on the lawlike behavior of machines; they could not cheat nature and they did not perform wondrous acts.

26. *Gesammelte Werke* (ed. W. von Dyck and M. Caspar, Munich, 1937-), XV, 146.

27. Isaac Beeckman (1588-1637) was Descartes's earliest scientific collaborator during the period 1619 to 1623. His training as an engineer, with special interest in water flow, was probably the source of his steadfast commitment to mathematics as the proper tool of physics and to mechanical corpuscularism as its proper foundation. He published nothing in his lifetime but kept a scientific diary (*Jornael,* first published by C. de Waard, The Hague, 1939-1953). It contains, among other things, attempts at a mechanistic cosmology similar to Descartes's and set down just before the latter began working on *The World.* It is uncertain whether Descartes saw that material. Francis Bacon's corpuscular philosophy stands out most clearly in Book II of his *New Organon* (London, 1620), though it also underlies the epistemology of Book I. Ancient atomism, though revived at the turn of the seventeenth century and intellectually related to the corpuscularism of the time, seems to have had little direct influence on the latter. See Robert H. Kargon, *Atomism in England from Hariot to Newton* (Oxford, 1966).

28. See the massive account of Richard S. Westfall, *Force in Newton's Physics* (London, 1972).

29. Rene Taton, ed., *Histoire générale des sciences* (Paris, 1957-64), II, 252, 255.

30. AT.I.234-5.

31. At least since Aristotle, *meteora* included all phenomena occuring "up there" between the surface of the earth and the sphere of the moon.

32. The editions referred to are in, order:

RENATUS DESCARTES DE HOMINE, figuris & latinitate donatus a Florentio Schuyl . . . Leyden: Franciscus Moyardus & Petrus Leffen, 1662.

LE MONDE DE Mr. DESCARTES, ou LE TRAITTÉ DE LA LUMIERE, & des autres principaux objets des Sens. Avec un Discours de Mouvement Local & un autre des Fièvres, composez selon les principes du même Auteur. Paris: Jacques Le Gras, 1664.

L'HOMME DE RENÉ DESCARTES, & un TRAITÉ DE LA FORMATION DU FOETUS du mesme Autheur. Avec les remarques de Louys de la Forge, Docteur en Medecine, demeurant à la Fleche, sur le Traitté de l'Homme de René Descartes, & sur les Figures par luy inuentées. Paris: Théodore Girard, 1664.

L'HOMME de RENÉ DESCARTES, et la FORMATION DU FOETUS, avec les Remarques de Louis de la Forge. A quoy l'on a ajouté LE MONDE, ou TRAITÉ DE LA LUMIERE, du mesme Autheur. Paris: Michel Bobin & Nicolas Le Gras, 1677.

The various prefaces to these editions, together with the bibliographical information from which the above was taken, are contained in AT.XI.i-xxiv.

33. The editors of AT, while accepting Clerselier's word and taking the 1677 edition as the basis of their own, nonetheless add a caveat (AT.XI.v-vi): the text that Clerselier presents as taken from the original manuscript contains phrases and orthography postdating Descartes and disagreeing with his established habits. According to the preface to the 1664 edition, written by an unidentified "D.R.," the manuscript copy of the text had been divided into chapters, presumably by Descartes, although "looking at the way the author sometimes begins them, I judge that his design was to carry on an uninterrupted discourse . . . " (AT. XI.ix). Clerselier, in his preface to the 1664 *Man* and the 1677 *Man* and *World,* confirmed the chapter division *ex silentio* but in the text itself significantly altered the chapter headings. Hence, it would seem that the division stems from Descartes, the headings by contrast from the copyists or early editors. The translation below, in keeping with the reproduced text, gives the 1677 headings; for the earlier version, see AT.XI.ix-x.

LE MONDE DE Mr DESCARTES,

ou LE TRAITÉ DE LA LVMIERE

ET DES AVTRES PRINCIPAVX objets des Sens.

Avec un Discours de l'Action des Corps, & un autre des Fiévres, composez selon les principes du même Auteur.

A PARIS,

Chez Michel Bobin & Nicolas le Gras, au troisiéme pillier de la grand'Salle du Palais, à l'Esperance & à L. Couronnée.

M. DC. LXIV.

Avec Privilege du Roy.

Title page of the first edition of Descartes' *Le Monde*, written between 1629 and 1633 but withheld from publication until 1664.

LE MONDE

DE
RENE' DESCARTES,
OU TRAITE'
DE LA LUMIERE.

CHAPITRE PREMIER.

*De la difference qui est entre nos sentimens & les
choses qui les produisent.*

E proposant de traiter icy de la Lumiere, la
premiere chose dont je veux vous avertir, est,
qu'il peut y avoir de la difference entre le sentiment que nous en avons, c'est à dire l'idée
qui s'en forme en nostre imagination par l'entremise de
nos yeux, & ce qui est dans les objets qui produit en nous
ce sentiment, c'est à dire ce qui est dans la flâme ou dans
le Soleil qui s'appelle du nom de Lumiere. Car encore
que chacun se persuade communément que les idées que
nous avons en nostre pensée sont entierement sembla-

THE WORLD

BY

RENÉ DESCARTES

OR TREATISE

ON LIGHT

CHAPTER I

*On the Difference Between our Sensations and
the Things That Produce Them*

In proposing to treat here of light, the first thing
I want to make clear to you is that there can be a
difference between our sensation[1] of light (i.e., the
idea that is formed in our imagination through the
intermediary of our eyes) and what is in the objects
that produces that sensation in us (i.e., what is in
the flame or in the sun that is called by the name of
"light"). For, even though everyone is commonly
persuaded that the ideas that are the objects of our
thought are wholly like

1

406   LE MONDE DE RENE' DESCARTES,

bles aux objets dont elles procedent, je ne vois point toutesfois de raifon qui nous affure que cela foit ; mais je remarque au contraire plufieurs experiences qui nous en
doivent faire douter.

Vous fçavez bien que les paroles n'ayant aucune reffemblance avec les chofes qu'elles fignifient ne laiffent
pas de nous les faire concevoir, & fouvent mefme fans
que nous prenions garde au fon des mots, ny à leurs fyl-
labes ; en forte qu'il peut arriver qu'aprés avoir ouy vn difcours dont nous aurons fort bien compris le fens, nous ne
pourrons pas dire en quelle langue il aura efté prononcé.
Or fi des mots qui ne fignifient rien que par l'inftitution
des hommes, fuffifent pour nous faire concevoir des chofes avec lefquelles ils n'ont aucune reffemblance ; pourquoy la Nature ne pourra-t'elle pas auffi avoir eftably
certain figne qui nous faffe avoir le fentiment de la
Lumiere, bien que ce figne n'ait rien en foy qui foit femblable à ce fentiment ? Et n'eft-ce pas ainfi qu'elle a eftably les ris & les larmes, pour nous faire lire la joye & la
trifteffe fur le vifage des hommes ?

Mais vous direz, peut-eftre, que nos oreilles ne nous
font veritablement fentir que le fon des paroles, ny nos
yeux que la contenance de celuy qui rit ou qui pleure, &
que c'eft noftre Efprit, qui ayant retenu ce que fignifient
ces paroles & cette contenance, nous le reprefente en
mefme temps. A cela je pourrois répondre que c'eft
noftre Efprit tout de mefme, qui nous reprefente l'idée
de la Lumiere, toutes les fois que l'action qui la fignifie
touche noftre œil. Mais fans perdre le temps à difputer,
j'auray plutoft fait d'apporter vn autre exemple.

Penfez-vous, lors mefme que nous ne prenons pas garde à la fignification des paroles, & que nous oyons feule-

2

the objects from which they proceed, nevertheless I can see no reasoning that assures us that this is the case. On the contrary, I note many experiences that should cause us to doubt it.

You well know that words bear no resemblance to the things they signify, and yet they do not cease for that reason to cause us to conceive of those things, indeed often without our paying attention to the sound of the words or to their syllables. Thus it can happen that, after having heard a discourse, the sense of which we have very well understood, we might not be able to say in what language it was uttered.[2] Now, if words, which signify nothing except by human convention, suffice to cause us to conceive of things to which they bear no resemblance, why could not nature also have established a certain sign that would cause us to have the sensation of light, even though that sign in itself bore no similarity to that sensation? Is it not thus that she has established laughter and tears, to cause us to read joy and sorrow on the faces of men?

But perhaps you will say that our ears in fact cause us to hear only the sound of the words, or our eyes to see only the countenance of him who laughs or cries, and that it is our mind that, having remembered what those sounds and that countenance signify, represents their meaning to us at the same time.[3] To that I could respond that it is nonetheless our mind that represents to us the idea of light each time the action that signifies it touches our eye. But, rather than lose time in disputation, I would do better to adduce another example.

Do you think that, even when we do not pay attention to the meaning of words and hear only

3

OU TRAITE' DE LA LUMIERE.

ment leur son, que l'idée de ce son qui se forme en nostre pensée, soit quelque chose de semblable à l'objet qui en est la cause? Vn homme ouvre la bouche, remuë la langue, pousse son haleine, je ne vois rien en toutes ces actions qui ne soit fort different de l'idée du son qu'elles nous font imaginer. Et la plûpart des Philosophes asseurent que le son n'est autre chose qu'vn certain tremblement d'air qui vient frapper nos oreilles; En sorte que si le sens de l'oüie rapportoit à nostre pensée la vraye image de son objet, il faudroit, au lieu de nous faire concevoir le son, qu'il nous fist concevoir le mouvement des parties de l'Air qui tremble pour lors contre nos oreilles. Mais parce que tout le monde ne voudra peut-estre pas croire ce que disent les Philosophes, j'apporteray encore vn autre exemple.

L'attouchement est celuy de tous nos sens que l'on estime le moins trompeur & le plus asseuré; de sorte que si je vous montre que l'attouchemét mesme nous fait concevoir plusieurs idées qui ne ressemblent en aucune façon aux objets qui les produisent, je ne pense pas que vous deviez trouver estrange si je dis que la veuë peut faire le semblable. Or il n'y a personne qui ne sçache que les idées du chatoüillement & de la douleur qui se forment en nostre pensée à l'occasion des corps de dehors qui nous touchent, n'ont aucune ressemblance avec eux. On passe doucement vne plume sur les lévres d'vn enfant qui s'endort, & il sent qu'on le chatoüille, pensez-vous que l'idée du chatoüillement qu'il conçoit, ressemble à quelque chose de ce qui est en cette plume ? Vn Gendarme revient d'vne mélée; pendant la chaleur du combat il auroit pû estre blessé sans s'en appercevoir ; mais maintenant qu'il commence à se refroidir il sent de la douleur, il

4

their sound, the idea of that sound, which forms in our thought, is anything like the object that is the cause of it? A man opens his mouth, moves his tongue, forces out his breath: in all these actions I see nothing that is not very different from the idea of the sound that they cause us to imagine. Also, most philosophers assure us that sound is nothing other than a certain vibration of air striking against our ears. Thus, if our sense of hearing were to report to our mind the true image of its object, then, instead of causing us to conceive of sound, it would have to cause us to conceive of the motion of the parts of air that then vibrate against our ears. But, because not everyone will perhaps want to believe what the philosophers say, I will adduce another example.

Of all our senses, touch is the one thought least misleading and most certain, so that, if I show you that even touch causes us to conceive many ideas that in no way resemble the objects that produce them, I do not think you will find it strange if I say that sight can do the same. Now, there is no one who does not know that the ideas of tickling and of pain, which are formed in our thoughts when bodies from without touch us, bear no resemblance whatever to those bodies. One passes a feather lightly over the lips of a child who is falling asleep, and he perceives that someone is tickling him.[4] Do you think the idea of tickling that he conceives resembles anything in this feather? A soldier returns from battle; during the heat of combat he could have been wounded without being aware of it. But now that he begins to cool off, he feels pain and

5

4c8   LE MONDE DE RENE' DESCARTES;

croit eftre bleffé, on appelle vn Chirurgien, on ofte fes
armes, on le vifite, & on trouve enfin que ce qu'il fentoit
n'eftoit autre chofe qu'vne boucle ou vne courroye qui
s'eftant engagée fous fes armes le preffoit & l'incommo-
doit. Si fon attouchement, en luy faifant fentir cette courroye, en eût imprimé l'image en fa penfée, il n'auroit
pas eu befoin d'vn Chirurgien pour l'avertir de ce qu'il
fentoit.

Or je ne vois point de raifon qui nous oblige à croire,
que ce qui eft dans les objets d'où nous vient le fentiment
de la Lumiere, foit plus femblable à ce fentiment, que les
actions d'vne plume & d'vne courroye le font au chatoüillement & à la douleur. Et toutesfois je n'ay point
apporté ces exemples pour vous faire croire abfolument
que cette Lumiere eft autre dans les objets que dans nos
yeux, mais feulement afin que vous en doutiez; & que
vous gardant d'eftre préoccupé du contraire, vous puiffiez maintenant mieux examiner avec moy ce qui en eft.

CHAPITRE II.

En quoy confifte la Chaleur & la Lumiere du feu.

JE ne connois au monde que deux fortes de corps dans
lefquels la Lumiere fe trouve, à fçavoir les Aftres, & la
Flâme ou le Feu. Et parce que les Aftres font fans doute
plus éloignez de la connoiffance des hommes, que n'eft
le feu ou la flâme, je tâcheray premierement d'expliquer
ce que je remarque touchant la Flâme.

Lors qu'elle brûle du bois, ou quelqu'autre femblable
matiere, nous pouvons voir à l'œil qu'elle remuë les petites parties de ce bois, & les fepare l'yne de l'autre, trans-
formant

6

believes he has been wounded. A surgeon is called, the soldier's armor is removed, and he is examined. In the end, one finds that what he felt was nothing but a buckler or a strap, which was caught under his armor and was pressing on him and making him uncomfortable. If, in causing him to feel this strap, his sense of touch had impressed the image on his thought, there would have been no need of a surgeon to show him what he was feeling.

Now, I see no reason forcing us to believe that what is in the objects from which the sensation of light comes to us is any more like that sensation than the actions of a feather and of a strap are like tickling and pain. Nevertheless, I have not adduced these examples to make you believe absolutely that this light is something different in the objects from what it is in our eyes, but only so that you will doubt it and so that, forbearing from being preoccupied by the contrary, you can now better examine with me what light is.

CHAPTER 2

In What the Heat and Light of Fire Consists

I know of only two sorts of bodies in the world in which light is found; to wit, the stars and flame or fire.[5] And, because the stars are without a doubt farther from human knowledge than is fire or flame, I shall try first to explicate what I observe regarding flame.

When flame burns wood or some other similar material, we can see with our eyes that it moves the small parts of the wood and separates them from one another, thus trans-

7

formant ainſi les plus ſubtiles en feu, en air, & en fumée,
& laiſſant les plus groſſieres pour les cendres. Qu'vn autre
donc imagine s'il veut en ce bois la forme du feu, la qualité de la chaleur, & l'action qui le brûle, comme des choſes toutes diverſes, pour moy qui crains de me tromper ſi
j'y ſuppoſe quelque choſe de plus que ce que je vois neceſſairement y devoir eſtre, je me contente d'y concevoir le mouvement de ſes parties. Car mettez-y du feu,
mettez-y de la chaleur, & faites qu'il brûle tant qu'il vous
plaira, ſi vous ne ſuppoſez point avec cela qu'il y ait aucune de ſes parties qui ſe remuë, ny qui ſe détache de ſes
voiſines, je ne me ſçaurois imaginer qu'il reçoive aucune
alteration ny changement. Et au contraire, oſtez-en le
feu, oſtez-en la chaleur, empeſchez qu'il ne brûle, pourveu ſeulement que vous m'accordiez qu'il y a quelque
puiſſance qui remuë violemment les plus ſubtiles de ſes
parties, & qui les ſepare des plus groſſieres, je trouve que
cela ſeul pourra faire en luy tous les meſmes changemens qu'on experimente quand il brûle.

Or dautant qu'il ne me ſemble pas poſſible de concevoir qu'vn corps en puiſſe remuër vn autre, ſi ce n'eſt en
ſe remuant auſſi ſoy-meſme, je conclus de cecy, que le
corps de la flâme qui agit contre le bois, eſt compoſé de
petites parties qui ſe remuent ſeparément l'vne de l'autre
d'vn mouvement tres-prompt & tres-violent, & qui ſe remuant en cette ſorte, pouſſent & remuent avec ſoy les
parties des corps qu'elles touchent, & qui ne leur font
point trop de reſiſtance. Je dis que ſes parties ſe remuent
ſeparément l'vne de l'autre : car encore que ſouvent elles
s'accordent & conſpirent pluſieurs enſemble pour faire
vn meſme effet, nous voyons toutesfois que chacune d'elles agit en ſon particulier contre les corps qu'elles tou-
Fff

forming the subtler parts into fire, air, and smoke, and leaving the grosser parts as ashes. Hence, someone else may, if he wishes, imagine the form of "fire," the quality of "heat," and the action that "burns" it to be completely different things in this wood.[6] For my part, afraid of misleading myself if I suppose anything more than what I see must of necessity be there, I am content to conceive there the motion of its parts. For, posit "fire" in the wood, posit "heat" in the wood, and make the wood "burn" as much as you please. If you do not suppose in addition that some of its parts are moved or detached from their neighbors, I cannot imagine that it would undergo any alteration or change. By contrast, remove the "fire," remove the "heat," prevent the wood from "burning": provided only that you grant me that there is some power that violently removes the subtler of its parts and separates them from the grosser, I find that that alone will be able to cause in the wood all the same changes that one experiences when it burns.

Now, insofar as it does not seem to be possible to conceive that one body could move another unless it itself were also moving,[7] I conclude from this that the body of the flame that acts against the wood is composed of small parts, which move independently of one another with a very fast and very violent motion. Moving in this way, they push and move with them the parts of the body that they touch and that do not offer them too much resistance. I say that its parts move independently of one another because, even though several of them often act in accord and conspire together to bring about the same effect, we see nonetheless that each of them acts on its own against the bodies they touch.

410 LE MONDE DE RENE' DESCARTES,

chent. Je dis auſſi que leur mouvement eſt tres-prompt & tres-violent : car eſtant ſi petites que la veuë ne nous les ſçauroit faire diſtinguer, elles n'auroient pas tant de force qu'elles ont pour agir contre les autres corps, ſi la promptitude de leur mouvement ne recompenſoit le défaut de leur grandeur.

Je n'adjoute point de quel coſté chacune ſe remuë : car ſi vous conſiderez que la puiſſance de ſe mouvoir, & celle qui détermine de quel coſté le mouvement ſe doit faire, ſont deux choſes toutes diverſes, & qui peuvent eſtre l'vne ſans l'autre (ainſi que j'ay expliqué en la Dioptrique) vous jugerez aiſément que chacune ſe remuë en la façon qui luy eſt renduë moins difficile par la diſpoſition des corps qui l'environnent ; & que dans la meſme flâme il peut y avoir des parties qui aillent en haut, & d'autres en bas, tout droit, & en rond, & de tous coſtez, ſans que cela change rien de ſa nature. En ſorte que ſi vous les voyez tendre en haut preſque toutes, il ne faut pas penſer que ce ſoit pour autre raiſon, ſinon parce que les autres corps qui les touchent ſe trouvent preſque toûjours diſpoſez à leur faire plus de reſiſtance de tous les autres coſtez.

Mais aprés avoir reconnu que les parties de la flâme ſe remuent en cette ſorte, & qu'il ſuffit de concevoir ſes mouvemens, pour comprendre comment elle a la puiſſance de conſumer le bois, & de brûler ; examinons, je vous prie, ſi le meſme ne ſuffiroit point auſſi, pour nous faire comprendre comment elle nous échauffe, & comment elle nous éclaire : Car ſi cela ſe trouve, il ne ſera pas neceſſaire qu'il y ait en elle aucune autre qualité, & nous pourrons dire que c'eſt ce mouvement ſeul, qui ſelon les differens effets qu'il produit, s'appelle tantoſt **Chaleur,** & tantoſt **Lumiere.**

I say also that their motion is very fast and very violent because, being so small that we cannot distinguish them by sight, they would not have the force they have to act against other bodies if the quickness of their motion did not compensate for their lack of size.[8]

I add nothing concerning the direction in which each moves. For, if you consider that the power to move and the power that determines in what direction the motion should take place are two completely different things and can exist one without the other (as I have set out in the *Dioptrics*),[9] you will easily judge that each part moves in the manner made least difficult for it by the disposition of the bodies surrounding it.[10] Moreover, in the same flame there can be some parts going upward, and others downward, some in straight lines, and others in circles; indeed, they can go in all directions, without changing anything of the flame's nature. Thus, if you see almost all of them tending upward, you need not think that this is for any reason other than that the other bodies touching them are almost always disposed to offer them greater resistance in any other direction.

But, having recognized that the parts of the flame move in this manner, and that it suffices to conceive of their motions in order to understand how the flame has the power to consume the wood and to burn, pray let us examine if the same will not also suffice to make us understand how the flame heats us and how it sheds light for us. For, if that is the case, it will not be necessary for the flame to possess any other quality, and we will be able to say that it is this motion alone that is called now "heat" and now "light" according to the different effects it produces.

OÛ TRAITE' DE LA LUMIERE. 411

Or pour ce qui eſt de la Chaleur, le ſentiment que nous
en avons peut ce me ſemble eſtre pris pour vne eſpece de
douleur, quand il eſt violent, & quelquefois pour vne eſpece de chatoüillement, quand il eſt moderé. Et comme
nous avons déja dit qu'il n'y a rien hors de noſtre penſée
qui ſoit ſemblable aux idées que nous concevons du chatoüillement & de la douleur, nous pouvons bien croire
auſſi qu'il n'y a rien qui ſoit ſemblable à celle que nous
concevons de la Chaleur ; mais que tout ce qui peut remuer diverſement les petites parties de nos mains, ou de
quelqu'autre endroit de noſtre corps, peut exciter en
nous ce ſentiment. Meſmes pluſieurs experiences favori-
ſent cette opinion, car en ſe frottant ſeulement les mains
on les échauffe; & tout autre corps peut auſſi eſtre échauf-
fé ſans eſtre mis auprés du feu, pourveu ſeulement qu'il
ſoit agité, & ébranlé en telle ſorte que pluſieurs de ſes
petites parties ſe remuent, & puiſſent remuer avec ſoy
celles de nos mains.

Pour ce qui eſt de la Lumiere, on peut bien auſſi concevoir que le meſme mouvement qui eſt dans la flâme ſuffit
pour nous la faire ſentir. Mais parce que c'eſt en cecy que
conſiſte la principale partie de mon deſſein, je veux tâ-
cher de l'expliquer bien au long, & reprendre mon Diſcours de plus haut.

CHAPITRE III.

De la Dureté, & de la Liquidité.

JE conſidere qu'il y a vne infinité de divers mouvemens
qui durent perpetuellement dans le Monde. Et aprés
avoir remarqué les plus grands, qui font les jours, les

Now, as regards heat, the sensation that we have of it can, it seems to me, be taken for a type of pain when it is violent, and sometimes for a type of tickling when it is moderate.[11] Since we have already said that there is nothing outside our thought that is similar to the ideas we conceive of tickling and pain, we can well believe also that there is nothing that is similar to that which we conceive of as heat; rather, anything that can move the small parts of our hands, or of any other part of our body, can arouse this sensation in us. Indeed, many experiences favor this opinion. For merely by rubbing our hands together we heat them, and any other body can also be heated without being placed close to a fire, provided only that it is shaken and rubbed in such a way that many of its small parts are moved and can move with them those of our hands.

As regards light, one can also well imagine that the same motion that is in the flame suffices to cause us to sense light. But, because it is in this that the main part of my design consists, I want to try to explain it at some length and to take up my discourse from anew.

CHAPTER 3

On Hardness and Liquidity

I consider that there is an infinity of diverse motions that endure perpetually in the world. After having noted the greatest of these (i.e., those that bring about the days,

412 LE MONDE DE RENE' DESCARTES,

mois, & les années, je prens garde que les vapeurs de la Terre ne cessent point de monter vers les nuées & d'en descendre, que l'air est toujours agité par les vents, que la mer n'est jamais en repos, que les fontaines & les rivieres coulent sans cesse, que les plus fermes bâtimens tombent enfin en décadence, que les plantes & les Animaux ne font que croître ou se corrompre, bref qu'il n'y a rien en aucun lieu qui ne se change. D'où je connois evidemment que ce n'est pas dans la flâme seule qu'il y a quantité de petites parties qui ne cessent point de se mouvoir; mais qu'il y en a aussi dans tous les autres corps, encore que leurs actions ne soient pas si violentes, & qu'à cause de leur petitesse elles ne puissent estre apperceuës par aucun de nos sens.

Je ne m'arreste pas à chercher la cause de leurs mouvemens: car il me suffit de penser qu'elles ont commencé à se mouvoir, aussi-tost que le Monde a commencé d'estre; Et cela estant, je trouve par mes raisons qu'il est impossible que leurs mouvemens cessent jamais, ny mesme qu'ils changent autrement que de sujet. C'est à dire que la vertu ou la puissance de se mouvoir soy-mesme, qui se rencontre dans vn corps, peut bien passer toute ou partie dans vn autre, & ainsi n'estre plus dans le premier, mais qu'elle ne peut pas n'estre plus du tout dans le Monde. Mes raisons, dis-je, me satisfont assez là dessus, mais je n'ay pas encore occasion de vous les dire; Et cependant vous pouvez imaginer si bon vous semble, ainsi que font la pluspart des Doctes, qu'il y a quelque premier mobile, qui roulant autour du Monde avec vne vîtesse incomprehensible, est l'origine & la source de tous les autres mouvemens qui s'y rencontrent.

Or en suite de cette consideration, il y a moyen d'ex-

months, and years), I take note that the vapors of the earth never cease to rise to the clouds and to descend from them, that the air is forever agitated by the winds, that the sea is never at rest, that springs and rivers flow ceaselessly, that the strongest buildings finally fall into decay, that plants and animals are always either growing or decaying; in short, that there is nothing anywhere that is not changing. Whence I know clearly that it is not in the flame alone that there are a number of small parts never ceasing to move, but that there are also such parts in every other body, even though their actions are not as violent and they cannot, due to their smallness, be perceived by any of our senses.

I do not stop to seek the cause of their motion, for it is enough for me to think that they began to move as soon as the world began to exist. And that being the case, I find by my reasoning that it is impossible that their motions should ever cease or even that those motions should change in any way other than with regard to the subject in which they are present. That is to say, the virtue or power in a body to move itself can well pass wholly or partially to another body and thus no longer be in the first; but it cannot no longer exist in the world. My arguments, I say, are enough to satisfy me as to the above, but I have not yet had occasion to relate them to you. In the meantime, you can imagine if you choose, as do most of the learned, that there is some first mover which, rolling about the world at an incomprehensible speed, is the origin and source of all the other motions found therein.

Now, in consequence of this consideration, there is a way of ex-

OU TRAITE' DE LA LUMIERE. 413

pliquer la caufe de tous les changemens qui arrivent dans le monde, & de toutes les varietez qui paroiffent fur la Terre; mais je me contenteray icy de parler de celles qui fervent à mon fujet.

La difference qui eft entre les corps durs & ceux qui font liquides, eft la premiere que je defire que vous re-marquiez; & pour cét effet, penfez que chaque corps peut eftre divifé en des parties extrémement petites. Je ne veux point déterminer fi leur nombre eft infiny ou non; mais du moins il eft certain qu'à l'égard de noftre connoiffan-ce il eft indéfiny, & que nous pouvons fuppofer qu'il y en a plufieurs millions dans le moindre petit grain de fable qui puiffe eftre apperceu de nos yeux.

Et remarquez que fi deux de ces petites parties s'entre-touchent, fans eftre en action pour s'éloigner l'vne de l'autre, il eft befoin de quelque force pour les feparer, fi peu que ce puiffe eftre: Car eftant vne fois ainfi pofées, elles ne s'aviferoient jamais d'elles-mefmes de fe mettre autrement. Remarquez auffi qu'il faut deux fois autant de force pour en feparer deux, que pour en feparer vne; & mille fois autant pour en feparer mille. De forte que s'il en faut feparer plufieurs millions tout à la fois, comme il faut peut-eftre faire pour rompre vn feul cheveu, ce n'eft pas merveille s'il y faut vne force affez fenfible.

Au contraire, fi deux ou plufieurs de ces petites parties fe touchent feulement en paffant, & lors qu'elles font en action pour fe mouvoir l'vne d'vn cofté, l'autre de l'autre, il eft certain qu'il faudra moins de force pour les feparer, que fi elles eftoient tout à fait fans mouvement; Et mef-me qu'il n'y en faudra point du tout, fi le mouvement avec lequel elles fe peuvent feparer d'elles-mefmes, eft égal ou plus grand que celuy avec lequel on les veut feparer. Or

Fff iij

16

plaining the cause of all the changes that take place in the world and of all the variety that appears on the earth. However, I shall be content here to speak of those that serve my purpose.

The difference between hard bodies and those that are liquids is the first thing I would like you to note. To that end, consider that every body can be divided into extremely small parts. I do not wish to determine whether their number is infinite or not; at least it is certain that, with respect to our knowledge, it is indefinite and that we can suppose that there are several millions in the smallest grain of sand our eyes can perceive.

Note also that, if two of these small parts are touching one another, without being in the act [12] of moving away from one another, some force is necessary to separate them, however small it may be. For, once so placed, they would never be inclined to dispose themselves otherwise. Note also that twice as much force is necessary to separate two of them than to separate one of them, and a thousand times as much to separate a thousand of them. Thus, if it is necessary to separate several millions of them all at once, as is perhaps necessary in order to break a single hair, it is not surprising that a rather sensible force is necessary.

By contrast, if two or more of these small parts touch one another only in passing and while they are in the act of moving, one in one direction and the other in another, certainly it will require less force to separate them than if they were in fact without motion. Indeed, no force at all will be required if the motion with which they are able to separate themselves is equal to or greater than that with which one wishes to separate them. Now,

17

414 LE MONDE DE RENE' DESCARTES,

je ne trouve point d'autre difference entre les corps durs & les corps liquides , finon que les parties des vns peuvent eftre feparées d'enfemble beaucoup plus aifément que celles des autres. De forte que pour compofer le corps le plus dur qui puiffe eftre imaginé , je penfe qu'il fuffit fi toutes fes parties fe touchent, fans qu'il refte d'efpace entre deux, ny qu'aucunes d'elles foient en action pour fe mouvoir : Car quelle colle ou quel ciment y pourroit-on imaginer outre cela pour les mieux faire tenir l'vne à l'autre ?

Je penfe auffi que c'eft affez pour compofer le corps le plus liquide qui fe puiffe trouver , fi toutes fes plus petites parties fe remuent le plus diverfement l'vne de l'autre & le plus vifte qu'il eft poffible ; encore qu'avec cela elles ne laiffent pas de fe pouvoir toucher l'vne l'autre de tous coftez, & fe ranger en auffi peu d'efpace que fi elles eftoiét fans mouvement. Enfin je croy que chaque corps approche plus ou moins de ces deux extremitez , felon que fes parties font plus ou moins en action pour s'éloigner l'vne de l'autre. Et toutes les experiences fur lefquelles je jette les yeux me confirment en cette opinion.

La flàme dont j'ay déja dit que toutes les parties font perpetuellement agitées, eft non feulement liquide, mais auffi elle rend liquide la plufpart des autres corps ; Et remarquez que quand elle fond les métaux, elle n'agît pas avec vne autre puiffance que quand elle brûle du bois ; Mais parce que les parties des métaux font à peu prés toutes égales, elle ne les peut remuer l'vne fans l'autre, & ainfi elle en compofe des corps tout liquides : au lieu que les parties du bois font tellement inégales, qu'elle en peut feparer les plus petites & les rendre liquides, c'eft à dire les faire voler en fumée, fans agiter ainfi les plus groffes.

18

I find no difference between hard bodies and liquid bodies other than that the parts of the one can be separated from the whole much more easily than those of the other. Thus, to constitute the hardest body imaginable, I think it is enough if all the parts touch each other with no space remaining between any two and with none of them being in the act of moving. For what glue or cement can one imagine beyond that to hold them better one to the other?

I think also that to constitute the most liquid body one could find, it is enough if all its smallest parts are moving away from one another in the most diverse ways and as quickly as possible, even though in that state they do not cease to be able to touch one another on all sides and to arrange themselves in as small a space as if they were without motion. Finally, I believe that every body more or less approaches these extremes, according as its parts are more or less in the act of moving away from one another. All the phenomena on which I cast my eye confirm me in this opinion.

Since, as I have already said, all the parts of flame are perpetually agitated, not only is it liquid, but it also renders most other bodies liquid. Note also that, when it melts metals, it acts with no other power than when it burns wood. Rather, because the parts of metals are just about all equal, the flame cannot move one part without moving the other, and hence it forms completely liquid bodies from them. By contrast, the parts of wood are unequal in such a way that the flame can separate the smaller of them and render them liquid (i.e., cause them to fly away in smoke) without agitating the larger parts.

OU TRAITE' DE LA LUMIERE. 415

Aprés la flâme il n'y a rien de plus liquide que l'air, &
l'on peut voir à l'œil que ses parties se remuent separé-
ment l'vne de l'autre : Car si vous daignez regarder ces
petits corps qu'on nomme communément des atomes,
& qui paroissent aux rayons du Soleil, vous les verrez, lors
mesme qu'il n'y aura point de vent qui les agite, voltiger
incessamment çà & là, en mille façons differentes. On
peut aussi éprouver le semblable en toutes les liqueurs les
plus grossieres, si l'on en mesle de diverses couleurs l'vne
parmy l'autre, afin de mieux distinguer leurs mouvemens.
Et enfin cela paroist tres-clairement dans les eaux fortes,
lors qu'elles remuent & separent les parties de quelque
métal.

Mais vous me pourriez demander en cet endroit-cy,
pourquoy, si c'est le seul mouvement des parties de la flâme qui fait qu'elle brûle & qu'elle est liquide, le mouvement des parties de l'air, qui le rend aussi extrémement
liquide, ne luy donne-t'il pas tout de mesme la puissance
de brûler, mais qu'au contraire, il fait que nos mains ne
le peuvent presque sentir. A quoy je répons, Qu'il ne faut
pas seulement prendre garde à la vitesse du mouvement,
mais aussi à la grosseur des parties ; & que ce sont les plus
petites, qui font les corps les plus liquides ; mais que ce
sont les plus grosses, qui ont le plus de force pour brûler,
& generalement pour agir contre les autres corps.

Remarquez en passant, que je prens icy, & que je pren-
dray toûjours cy-aprés pour vne seule partie, tout ce qui
est joint ensemble, & qui n'est point en action pour se
separer ; encore que celles qui ont tant soit peu de grosseur, puissent aisément estre divisées en beaucoup d'autres plus petites : Ainsi, vn grain de sable, vne pierre, vn
rocher, & toute la Terre mesme, pourra cy-aprés estre

After flame, there is nothing more liquid than air, and one can see with the eye that its parts move separately from one another. For, if you take the effort to watch those small bodies that are commonly called "atoms" and that appear in rays of sunlight, you will see them flutter about incessantly here and there in a myriad of different ways, even when there is no wind stirring them up. One can also experience the same sort of thing in all the grosser liquids if one mixes them together in different colors, in order better to distinguish their motions. Finally, the phenomenon appears very clearly in acids[13] when they move and separate the parts of some metal.

But you could ask me here at this point why, if it is only the motion of the parts of flame that cause it to burn and make it liquid, the motion of the parts of air, which also make it extremely liquid, do not at all give it the power to burn but, on the contrary, make it such that our hands can hardly feel it? To this I reply that one must take into account not only the speed of motion, but also the size of the parts. It is the smaller ones that make the more liquid bodies, but it is the larger ones that have more force to burn and in general to act on other bodies.

Note in passing that here, and always hereafter, I take a single part to be everything that is joined together and is not in the act of separation, even though the smallest parts could easily be divided into many other smaller ones. Thus, a grain of sand, a stone, a rock, indeed the whole earth itself, may hereafter be

416 LE MONDE DE RENE' DESCARTES,
prife pour vne feule partie, entant que nous n'y confide-
rerons qu'vn mouvement tout fimple & tout égal.

Or entre les parties de l'air, s'il y en a de fort groffes en
comparaifon des autres, comme font ces atomes qui s'y
voyent, elles fe remuent auffi fort lentement ; & s'il y en
a qui fe remuent plus vifte, elles font auffi plus petites.
Mais entre les parties de la flâme, s'il y en a de plus petites que dans l'air, il y en a auffi de plus groffes, ou du
moins il y en a vn plus grand nombre d'égales aux plus
groffes de celles de l'air, qui avec cela fe remuent beaucoup plus vifte ; & ce ne font que ces dernieres qui ont la
puiffance de brûler.

Qu'il y en ait de plus petites, on le peut conjecturer de
ce qu'elles penetrent au travers de plufieurs corps dont
les pores font fi étroits que l'air mefme n'y peut entrer.
Qu'il y en ait ou de plus groffes, ou d'auffi groffes en plus
grand nombre, on le voit clairement en ce que l'air feul
ne fuffit pas pour la nourrir. Qu'elles fe remuent plus
vifte, la violence de leur action nous le fait affez éprouver. Et enfin que ce foient les plus groffes de ces parties
qui ont la puiffance de brûler, & non point les autres, il
paroift en ce que la flâme qui fort de l'eau de vie, ou des
autres corps fort fubtils, ne brûle prefque point, & qu'au
contraire celle qui s'engendre dans les corps durs & pefans eft fort ardente.

CHAP.

taken as a single part insofar as we are there considering only a completely simple and completely equal motion.[14]

Now if, among the parts of air, there are some that are very large in comparison with the others (as are the "atoms" that are seen there), they also move very slowly; and, if there are some that move more quickly, they are also smaller. If, however, among the parts of flame there are some smaller than in air, there are also larger ones, or at least there is a larger number of parts equal to the largest of those of air. In addition, these larger parts of flame move much more quickly, and hence it is they alone that have the power to burn.

That there are smaller parts may be conjectured from the fact that they penetrate many bodies of which the pores are so narrow that even air cannot enter. That there are larger parts, or equally large parts in greater number, is seen clearly from the fact that air alone does not suffice to nourish flame. That they move more quickly is sufficiently shown to us by the violence of their action. Finally, that it is the largest of these parts that have the power to burn, and not the others, is apparent from the fact that the flame that issues from brandy, or from other very subtle bodies, hardly burns at all, while on the contrary that which is engendered in hard and heavy bodies is very hot.

CHAPITRE IV.

Du vuide ; Et d'où vient que nos sens n'apperçoivent pas certains corps.

MAIS il faut examiner plus particulierement pourquoy l'Air estant vn corps aussi bien que les autres, ne peut pas aussi bien qu'eux estre senty ; & par mesme moyen nous délivrer d'vne erreur dót nous avons tous
esté préoccupez dés nostre enfance, lors que nous avons
crû qu'il n'y avoit point d'autres corps autour de nous,
que ceux qui pouvoient estre sentis : Et ainsi que si l'Air
en estoit vn, parce que nous le sentions quelque peu, il ne
devoit pas au moins estre si materiel ny si solide que ceux
que nous sentions davantage.

Touchant quoy je desire premierement que vous re-
marquiez que tous les corps tant durs que liquides sont
faits d'vne mesme matiere, & qu'il est impossible de concevoir que les parties de cette matiere composent jamais
vn corps plus solide, ny qui occupe moins d'espace,
qu'elles font lors que chacune d'elles est touchée de tous
costez par les autres qui l'environnent ; D'où il suit, ce
me semble, que s'il peut y avoir du vuide quelque part, ce
doit plûtost estre dans les corps durs que dans les liquides : Car il est évident que les parties de ceux-cy se peuvent bien plus aisément presser & agencer l'vne contre
l'autre, à cause qu'elles se remuent, que ne font pas celles
des autres, qui sont sans mouvement.

Si vous mettez, par exemple, de la poudre en quelque
vase, vous le secoüez, & frapez contre, pour faire qu'il y
en entre davantage ; mais si vous y versez quelque liqueur,

Ggg

24

CHAPTER 4

On the Void, and How it Happens that Our Senses Are Not Aware of Certain Bodies

But we must examine in greater detail why air, although it is as much a body as the others, cannot be sensed as well as they. By doing so, we will free ourselves from an error with which we have been preoccupied since childhood, when we believed that there were no other bodies around us except those that could be sensed and thus that, if air were one of them, then, because we sensed it so faintly, it at least could not be as material nor as solid as those we sense more clearly.[14a]

On this subject, I would first like you to note that all bodies, both hard and liquid, are made from the same matter, and that it is impossible to conceive of the parts of that matter ever composing a more solid body, or one occupying less space, than they do when each of them is touched on all sides by the others surrounding it. Whence it seems to me to follow that, if there can be a void anywhere, it ought to be in hard bodies rather than liquid ones; for it is evident that the parts of the latter can much more easily press and arrange themselves against one another (because they are moving) than can those of the former (which are without motion).

For example, if you are placing powder in a jar, you shake the jar and pound against it to make room for more powder. But, if you are pouring some liquid into it,

418 LE MONDE DE RENE' DESCARTES;
elle fe range incontinent d'elle-mefme en auffi peu de
lieu qu'on la peut mettre. Et mefme fi vous confiderez fur
ce fujet quelques-vnes des experiences dont les Philofophes ont accoûtumé de fe fervir pour montrer qu'il n'y a
point de vuide en la Nature, vous connoiftrez aifément
que tous ces efpaces que le peuple eftime vuides, & où
nous ne fentons que de l'air, font du moins auffi remplis,
& remplis de la mefme matiere, que ceux où nous fentons
les autres corps.

Car dites-moy, je vous prie, quelle apparence y auroit-
il que la Nature fift monter les corps les plus pefans, &
rompre les plus durs, ainfi qu'on experimente qu'elle fait
en certaines machines, plûtoft que de fouffrir qu'aucunes
de leurs parties ceffent de s'entretoucher, ou de toucher
à quelques autres corps; & qu'elle permift cependant que
les parties de l'Air, qui font fi faciles à plier & à s'agencer
de toutes manieres, demeuraffent les vnes auprés des autres fans s'entretoucher de tous coftez, ou bien fans qu'il
y eût quelqu'autre corps parmy elles auquel elles tou-
chaffent. Pourroit-on bien croire que l'eau qui eft dans
vn puys duft monter en haut contre fon inclination naturelle, afin feulement que le tuyau d'vne pompe foit
remply, & penfer que l'eau qui eft dans les nuës ne duft
point defcendre, pour achever de remplir les efpaces qui
font icy bas, s'il y avoit tant foit peu de vuide entre les
parties des corps qu'ils contiennent?

Mais vous me pourriez propofer icy vne difficulté qui
eft affez confiderable; c'eft à fçavoir que les parties qui
compofent les corps liquides, ne peuvent pas, ce femble,
fe remuer inceffamment, comme j'ay dit qu'elles font, fi
ce n'eft qu'il fe trouve de l'efpace vuide parmy elles, au
moins dans les lieux d'où elles fortent à mefure qu'elles

the liquid spontaneously arranges itself in as small a place as one can put it. By the same token, if you consider in this regard some of the experiments the philosophers have been wont to use in showing that there is no void in nature,[15] you will easily recognize that all those spaces that people think to be empty, and where we feel only air, are at least as full, and as full of the same matter, as those where we sense other bodies.

For pray tell me what reason would there be to think that nature would cause the heaviest bodies to rise and the most solid to break—as one experiences her doing in certain machines, rather than to suffer that any of their parts should cease to touch one another or to touch some other bodies—and yet permit the parts of air—which are so easy to bend and to be arranged in all manners— to remain next to one another without being touched on all sides, or even without there being another body among them that they touch? Could one really believe that the water in a well should mount upward against its natural inclination merely in order that the pipe of a pump may be filled and [yet] think that the water in clouds should not fall in order that the spaces here below be filled, if there were even some little void among the parts of the bodies that they contain?[16]

But you could propose to me here a rather considerable problem, to wit, that the parts composing liquid bodies cannot, it seems, move incessantly, as I have said they do, unless there is some empty space among them, at least in the places from which they depart and to the extent that they

27

OU TRAITE' DE LA LUMIERE.

fe remuent. A quoy j'aurois de la peine à répondre, fi je n'avois reconnu par diverfes experiences, que tous les mouvemens qui fe font au Monde font en quelque façon circulaires; c'eft à dire que quand vn corps quitte fa place, il entre toujours en celle d'vn autre, & celuy-cy en celle d'vn autre, & ainfi de fuitte jufques au dernier, qui occupe au mefme inftant le lieu délaiffé par le premier; en forte qu'il ne fe trouve pas davantage de vuide parmy eux, lors qu'ils fe remuent, que lors qu'ils font arreftez. Et remarquez icy qu'il n'eft point pour cela neceffaire, que toutes les parties des corps qui fe remuent enfemble, foient exactement difpofées en rond comme vn vray cercle, ny mefme qu'elles foient de pareille groffeur & figure; car ces inégalitez peuvent aifément eftre compenfées par d'autres inégalitez qui fe trouvent en leur vîteffe.

Or nous ne remarquons pas communément ces mouvemens circulaires quand les corps fe remuent en l'air, parce que nous fommes accoûtumez de ne concevoir l'air que comme vn efpace vuide. Mais voyez nager des poiffons dans le baffin d'vne fontaine; s'ils ne s'approchent point trop prés de la furface de l'eau, ils ne la feront point du tout branler, encore qu'ils paffent deffous avec vne tres-grande vîteffe. D'où il paroift manifeftement que l'eau qu'ils pouffent devant eux, ne pouffe pas indifferemment toute l'eau du baffin; mais feulement celle qui peut mieux fervir à parfaire le cercle de leur mouvement, & rentrer en la place qu'ils abandonnent.

Et cette experience fuffit pour montrer combien ces mouvemens circulaires font aifez & familiers à la Nature; Mais j'en veux maintenant apporter vne autre, pour montrer qu'il ne fe fait jamais aucun mouvement qui ne foit circulaire. Lors que le vin qui eft dans vn tonneau ne cou-

Ggg ij

are moving. I would have trouble responding to this, had I not recognized through various experiences that all the motions that take place in the world are in some way circular. That is to say, when a body leaves its place, it always enters into that of another, and the latter into that of still another, and so on down to the last, which occupies in the same instant the place left open by the first.[17] Thus, there is no more of a void among them when they are moving than when they are stopped. And note here that it is not thereby necessary that all the parts of bodies that move together be exactly disposed in the round, as in a true circle, nor even that they be of equal size and shape; for these inequalities can easily be compensated for by other inequalities to be found in their speed.

Now, when bodies move in the air, we do not usually notice these circular motions, because we are accustomed to conceiving of the air only as an empty space. But look at fish swimming in the pool of a fountain: if they do not approach too near to the surface of the water, they cause no motion whatever in it, even though they pass below it at a very great speed. Whence it clearly appears that the water they push before them does not push indifferently all the water of the pool, but only that which can best serve to perfect the circle of fishes' motion and return to the place they leave behind.[18] This experience suffices to show how these circular motions are easy for nature and familiar to her.

Now, however, I want to adduce another experience to show that no motion ever takes place that is not circular. When the wine in a cask does not flow

420   LE MONDE DE RENE' DESCARTES,

le point par l'ouverture qui eſt au bas, à cauſe que le deſſus eſt tout fermé, c'eſt parler improprement, que de dire,
ainſi que l'on fait d'ordinaire, que cela ſe fait, crainte du
vuide. On ſçait bien que ce vin n'a point d'eſprit pour
craindre quelque choſe ; Et quand il en auroit, je ne ſçay
pour quelle occaſion il pourroit apprehender ce vuide,
qui n'eſt en effet qu'vne chimere. Mais il faut dire plû-
toſt, qu'il ne peut ſortir de ce tonneau, à cauſe que dehors
tout eſt auſſi plein qu'il peut eſtre, & que la partie de l'air
dont il occuperoit la place s'il deſcendoit, n'en peut trouver d'autre où ſe mettre en tout le reſte de l'Vnivers, ſi on
ne fait vne ouverture au deſſus du tonneau, par laquelle
cét air puiſſe remonter circulairement en ſa place.

Au reſte, je ne veux pas aſſurer pour cela qu'il n'y a
point du tout de vuide en la Nature ; j'aurois peur que
mon Diſcours ne devinſt trop long ſi j'entreprenois d'expliquer ce qui en eſt ; & les experiences dont j'ay parlé ne
ſont point ſuffiſantes pour le prouver , quoy qu'elles le
ſoient aſſez, pour perſuader que les eſpaces où nous ne
ſentons rien ſont remplis de la meſme matiere , & contiennent autant pour le moins de cette matiere, que ceux
qui ſont occupez par les corps que nous ſentons. En ſorte
que lors qu'vn vaſe par exéple eſt plein d'or ou de plomb,
il ne contient pas pour cela plus de matiere, que lors que
nous penſons qu'il ſoit vuide : Ce qui peut ſembler bien
eſtrange à pluſieurs, dont la raiſon ne s'eſtend pas plus
loin que les doigts, & qui penſent qu'il n'y ait rien au
Monde que ce qu'ils touchent. Mais quand vous aurez vn
peu conſideré ce qui fait que nous ſentons vn corps, ou
que nous ne le ſentons pas, je m'aſſure que vous ne trouverez en cela rien d'incroyable. Car vous connoiſtrez évidemment, que tant s'en faut que toutes les choſes qui

30

through an opening at the bottom because the top is completely closed, it is improper to say (as one ordinarily does) that this takes place owing to *horror vacui.* One well knows that the wine has no mind to fear anything; and, even if it had one, I do not know for what reason it might fear that void, which is in fact nothing but a chimera. Rather, one should say that the wine cannot leave the cask because outside everything is as full as it can be and that the part of the air, whose place the wine would occupy should it descend, cannot find another place to put itself anywhere in the rest of the universe unless one makes an opening in the top of the cask, through which this air can rise circularly to its place.

Nevertheless, I do not want to say for certain that there is no void at all in nature. I fear my discourse would become too long if I undertook to unfold the whole story, and the experiences of which I have spoken are not sufficient to prove it, although they are enough to persuade us that the spaces where we sense nothing are filled with the same matter, and contain at least as much of that matter, as those occupied by the bodies that we sense. Thus, for example, when a vessel is full of gold or lead, it nonetheless contains no more matter than when we think it is empty. This may well seem strange to many whose [powers of] reasoning do not extend beyond their fingertips and who think there is nothing in the world except what they touch. But when you have considered for a bit what makes us sense a body or not sense it, I am sure you will find nothing incredible in the above. For you will know clearly that, far from all the things

font autour de nous puiffent éftre fentics, qu'au contraire ce font celles qui y font le plus ordinairement qui le peuvent eftre le moins, & que celles qui y font toujours ne le peuvent eftre jamais.

La Chaleur de noftre cœur eft bien grande, mais nous ne la fentons pas, à caufe qu'elle eft ordinaire. La pefanteur de noftre corps n'eft pas petite, mais elle ne nous incommode point. Nous ne fentons pas mefme celle de nos habits, parce que nous fommes accoûtumez à les porter. Et la raifon de cecy eft affez claire : Car il eft certain que nous ne fçaurions fentir aucun corps, s'il n'eft caufe de quelque changement dans les organes de nos fens, c'eft à dire s'il ne remuë en quelque façon les petites parties de la matiere dont ces organes font compofez. Ce que peuvent bien faire les objets qui ne fe prefentent pas toujours, pourveu feulement qu'ils ayent affez de force : Car s'ils y corrompent quelque chofe pendant qu'ils agiffent, cela fe peut reparer après par la Nature lors qu'ils n'agiffent plus. Mais pour ceux qui nous touchent continuellement, s'ils ont jamais eu la puiffance de produire quelque changement en nos fens, & de remuer quelques parties de leur matiere, ils ont dû à force de les remuer, les feparer entierement des autres dés le commencement de noftre vie, & ainfi ils n'y peuvent avoir laiffé que celles qui refiftent tout à fait à leur action, & par le moyen defquelles ils ne peuvent en aucune façon eftre fentis. D'où vous voyez que ce n'eft pas merveille qu'il y ait plufieurs efpaces autour de nous où nous ne fentons aucun corps, encore qu'ils n'en contiennent pas moins que ceux où nous en fentons le plus.

Mais il ne faut pas penfer pour cela, que cét air groffier que nous attirons dans nos poumons en refpirant, qui

Ggg iij

32

around us being sensible, it is on the contrary those that are there most of the time that can be sensed the least, and those that are always there that can never be sensed at all.

The heat of our heart is quite great, but we do not feel it because it is always there. The weight of our body is not small, but it does not discomfort us. We do not even feel the weight of our clothes because we are accustomed to wearing them. The reason for this is clear enough; for it is certain that we cannot sense any body unless it is the cause of some change in our sensory organs, i.e., unless it moves in some way the small parts of the matter of which those organs are composed. The objects that are not always present can well do this, provided only that they have force enough; for, if they corrupt something there while they act, that can be repaired afterward by nature, when they are no longer acting. But if those that continually touch us ever had the power to produce any change in our senses, and to move some part of their matter, in order to move them they had perforce to separate them entirely from the others at the beginning of our life, and thus they can have left there only those that completely resist their action and by means of which they cannot be sensed in any way. Whence you see that it is no wonder that there are many spaces about us in which we sense no body, even though they contain bodies no less than those in which we sense them the most.

But one need not therefore think that the grosser air that we draw into our lungs while breathing, that

422   LE MONDE DE RENE' DESCARTES,

ſe convertit en vent quand il eſt agité , qui nous ſemble dur quand il eſt enfermé dans vn balon, & qui n'eſt compoſé que d'exhalaiſons & de fumées , ſoit auſſi ſolide que l'eau ny que la Terre. Il faut ſuivre en cecy l'opinion commune des Philoſophes , leſquels aſſurent tous qu'il eſt plus rare. Et cecy ſe connoiſt facilement par experience: car les parties d'vne goutte d'eau eſtant ſeparées l'vne de l'autre par l'agitation de la chaleur, peuvent compoſer beaucoup plus de cét air, que l'eſpace où eſtoit l'eau n'en ſçauroit contenir. D'où il ſuit infailliblement qu'il y a grande quantité de petits intervales entre les parties dont il eſt compoſé ; car il n'y a pas moyen de concevoir autrement vn corps rare. Mais parce que ces intervales ne peuvent eſtre vuides , ainſi que j'ay dit cy-deſſus , je conclus de tout cecy qu'il y a neceſſairement quelques autres corps, vn ou pluſieurs, mélez parmy cét air, leſquels rempliſſent auſſi juſtement qu'il eſt poſſible les petits intervales qu'il laiſſe entre ſes parties. Il ne reſte plus maintenant qu'à conſiderer quels peuvent eſtre ces autres corps: & aprés cela j'eſpere qu'il ne ſera pas mal-aiſé de comprendre quelle peut eſtre la nature de la Lumiere.

CHAPITRE V.

Du nombre des Elemens , & de leurs qualitez.

LEs Philoſophes aſſurent qu'il y a au deſſus des nuées vn certain air beaucoup plus ſubtil que le noſtre, & qui n'eſt pas compoſé des vapeurs de la Terre comme luy, mais qui fait vn Element à part. Ils diſent auſſi qu'au deſſus de cét air il y a encore vn autre corps beaucoup plus ſubtil, qu'ils appellent l'Element du Feu. Ils ajoûtent de-

is converted into wind when agitated, that appears solid when enclosed in a balloon, and that is composed only of exhalations and smoke is as solid as water or earth. Here one should follow the common opinion of the philosophers, who all assure us that it is rarer, as one also easily recognizes from experience. For the parts of a drop of water, separated from one another by the agitation of heat, can make up much more of this air than the space that held the water can contain. Whence it follows most certainly that there is a great quantity of small intervals among the parts of which the air is composed; for there is no other way to conceive of a rare body. But, because these intervals cannot be empty, as I have said above, I conclude from all this that of necessity there are mixed with the air some other bodies, either one or several, which fill as exactly as possible the small intervals left among its parts. Now there remains to consider only what these other bodies can be; thereafter I hope it will not be difficult to understand what the nature of light can be.

CHAPTER 5

On the Number of Elements and on Their Qualities

The philosophers assure us that there is above the clouds a certain air much subtler than ours. That air is not composed of vapors of the earth as it is, but constitutes an element in itself. They say also that above this air there is still another, much subtler body, which they call the element of fire. They add, more-

OU TRAITE' DE LA LUMIERE. 423

plus, que ces deux Elemens font mélez avec l'Eau & la Terre en la compofition de tous les corps inferieurs. Si bien que je ne feray que fuivre leur opinion, fi je dis que cét Air plus fubtil & cét Element du Feu rempliffent les intervales qui font entre les parties de l'air groffier que nous refpirons ; en forte que ces corps entre-lacez l'vn dás l'autre compofent vne maffe qui eft auffi folide qu'aucun corps le fçauroit eftre.

Mais afin que je puiffe mieux vous faire entendre ma penfée fur ce fujet, & que vous ne penfiez pas que je veüille vous obliger à croire tout ce que les Philofophes nous difent des Elemens, il faut que je vous les décrive à ma mode.

Je conçoy le premier, qu'on peut nommer l'Element du Feu, comme vne liqueur la plus fubtile & la plus penetrante qui foit au Monde. Et en fuite de ce qui a efté dit cy-deffus touchant la nature des corps liquides, je m'imagine que fes parties font beaucoup plus petites, & fe remuent beaucoup plus vifte, qu'aucune de celles des autres corps. Ou plûtoft, afin de n'eftre pas contraint d'admettre aucun vuide en la Nature, je ne luy attribuë point de parties qui ayent aucune groffeur ny figure déterminée ; mais je me perfuade que l'impetuofité de fon mouvement eft fuffifante pour faire qu'il foit divifé en toutes façons & en tous fens par la rencontre des autres corps, & que fes parties changent de figure à tous momens, pour s'accommoder à celle des lieux où elles entrent ; En forte qu'il n'y a jamais de paffage fi étroit ny d'angle fi petit, entre les parties des autres corps, où celles de cét Element ne penetrent fans aucune difficulté, & qu'elles ne rempliffent exactement.

Pour le fecond, qu'on peut prendre pour l'Element de

over, that these two elements are mixed with water and earth in the composition of all the inferior bodies. Thus, I am only following their opinion if I say that this subtler air and this element of fire fill the intervals among the parts of the grosser air we breathe, so that these bodies, interlaced with one another, compose a mass as solid as any body can be.

But, in order better to make you understand my thought on this subject, and so that you will not think I want to force you to believe all the philosophers tell us about the elements, I should describe them to you in my fashion.

I conceive of the first, which one may call the element of fire, as the most subtle and penetrating fluid there is in the world. And in consequence of what has been said above concerning the nature of liquid bodies, I imagine its parts to be much smaller and to move much faster than any of those of other bodies. Or rather, in order not to be forced to admit any void in nature, I do not attribute to this first element parts having any determinate size or shape; but I am persuaded that the impetuosity of their motion is sufficient to cause it to be divided, in every way and in every sense, by collision with other bodies and that its parts change shape at every moment to accommodate themselves to the shape of the places they enter. Thus, there is never a passage so narrow, nor an angle so small, among the parts of other bodies, where the parts of this element do not penetrate without any difficulty and which they do not fill exactly.[19]

As for the second, which one may take to be the element of

424 LE MONDE DE RENE' DESCARTES,

l'Air, je le conçois bien auſſi comme vne liqueur tres-
ſubtile, en le comparant avec le troiſiéme ; Mais pour le
comparer avec le premier, il eſt beſoin d'attribuer quelque groſſeur & quelque figure à chacune de ſes parties, &
de les imaginer à peu prés toutes rondes, & jointes enſemble, ainſi que des grains de ſable & de pouſſiere. En ſorte
qu'elles ne ſe peuvent ſi bien agencer, ny tellement preſ-
ſer l'vne contre l'autre, qu'il ne demeure toujours autour
d'elles pluſieurs petits intervales, dans leſquels il eſt bien
plus aiſé au premier Element de ſe gliſſer, que non pas à
elles de changer de figure tout exprés pour les remplir. Et
ainſi je me perſuade que ce ſecond Element ne peut eſtre
ſi pur en aucun endroit du Monde, qu'il n'y ait toujours
avec luy quelque peu de la matiere du premier.

Aprés ces deux Elemens je n'en reçois plus qu'vn troiſiéme, à ſçavoir celuy de la Terre, duquel je juge que les
parties ſont d'autant plus groſſes & ſe remuent d'autant
moins viſte à comparaiſon de celles du ſecond, que ſont
celles-cy à comparaiſon de celles du premier. Et meſme
je croy que c'eſt aſſez de le concevoir comme vne ou pluſieurs groſſes maſſes, dont les parties n'ont que fort peu
ou point du tout de mouvement qui leur faſſe changer de
ſituation à l'égard l'vne de l'autre.

Que ſi vous trouvez eſtrange que pour expliquer ces
Elemens, je ne me ſerve point des qualitez qu'on nomme
Chaleur, Froideur, Humidité, & Sécher</ſſe, ainſi que
font les Philoſophes, je vous diray que ces qualitez me
ſemblent avoir elles-meſmes beſoin d'explication; & que
ſi je ne me trompe, non ſeulement ces quatre qualitez,
mais auſſi toutes les autres, & meſme toutes les formes
des corps inanimez, peuvent eſtre expliquées, ſans qu'il
ſoit beſoin de ſuppoſer pour cét effet aucune autre choſe
en

38

air, I conceive of it also as a very subtle fluid in comparison with the third; but in comparison with the first there is need to attribute some size and shape to each of its parts and to imagine them as just about all round and joined together like grains of sand or dust. Thus, they cannot arrange themselves so well, nor so press against one another that there do not always remain around them many small intervals into which it is much easier for the first element to slide than for the parts of the second to change shape expressly in order to fill them. And so I am persuaded that this second element cannot be so pure anywhere in the world that there is not always some little matter of the first with it.

Beyond these two elements, I accept only a third, to wit, that of earth. Its parts I judge to be as much larger and to move as much less swiftly in comparison with those of the second as those of the second in comparison with those of the first. Indeed, I believe it is enough to conceive of it as one or more large masses, of which the parts have very little or no motion that might cause them to change position with respect to one another.

If you find it strange that, in setting out these elements, I do not use the qualities called "heat," "cold," "moistness," and "dryness," as do the philosophers, I shall say to you that these qualities appear to me to be themselves in need of explanation.[20] Indeed, unless I am mistaken, not only these four qualities, but also all the others (indeed all the forms of inanimate bodies) can be explained without the need of supposing for that purpose anything

OU TRAITE' DE LA LUMIERE.   425

en leur matiere, que le mouvement, la groffeur, la figure, & l'arrangement de fes parties. En fuite dequoy je vous pourray facilement faire entendre pourquoy je ne reçoy point d'autres Elemens que les trois que j'ay décris ; Car la difference qui doit eftre entre-eux & les autres corps que les Philofophes appellent mixtes, ou mélez & com-pofez, confifte, en ce que les formes de ces corps mélez contiennent toujours en foy quelques qualitez qui fe contrarient & qui fe nuifent, ou du moins qui ne tendent point à la confervation l'vne de l'autre ; Au lieu que les formes des Elemens doivent eftre fimples, & n'avoir au-cunes qualitez qui ne s'accordent enfemble fi parfaite-ment, que chacune tende à la confervation de toutes les autres.

Or je ne fçaurois trouver aucunes formes au monde qui foient telles, excepté les trois que j'ay décrites. Car celle que j'ay attribuée au premier Element, confifte, en ce que fes parties fe remuent fi extremement vifte, & font fi petites, qu'il n'y a point d'autres corps capables de les arrefter ; & qu'outre cela elles ne requierent aucune grof-feur, ny figure, ny fituation déterminées. Celle du fe-cond, confifte, en ce que fes parties ont vn mouvement & vne groffeur fi mediocre, que s'il fe trouve plufieurs caufes au Monde qui puiffent augmenter leur mouve-ment & diminuer leur groffeur, il s'en trouve juftement autant d'autres qui peuvent faire tout le contraire ; En forte qu'elles demeurent toujours comme en balance en cette mefme mediocrité. Et celle du troifiéme confifte, en ce que fes parties font fi groffes, ou tellement jointes enfemble, qu'elles ont la force de refifter toujours aux mouvemens des autres corps.

Examinez tant qu'il vous plaira toutes les formes que
Hhh

40

in their matter other than the motion, size, shape, and arrangement of its parts. In consequence whereof I shall easily be able to make you understand why I do not accept any other elements than the three I have described. For the difference that should exist between them and the other bodies that the philosophers call "mixed" or "composite" consists in the forms of these mixed bodies always containing in themselves some qualities that are contrary and that counteract one another, or at least do not tend to the conservation of one another, whereas the forms of the elements should be simple and not have any qualities that do not accord with one another so perfectly that each tends to the conservation of all the others.

Now I could not find any such forms in the world except the three I have described. For the form I have attributed to the first element consists in its parts moving so extremely fast and being so small that there are no other bodies capable of stopping them. Beyond that, they require no determinate size or shape or position. The form of the second consists in its parts having such a middling motion and size that, if there are in the world many causes that could increase their motion and decrease their size, there are just as many others that can do exactly the opposite. Thus, they always remain balanced as it were in the same middling condition. And the form of the third consists in its parts being so large or so joined together that they have the force always to resist the motions of the other bodies.

Examine as much as you please all the forms that

426   LE MONDE DE RENE' DESCARTES ;
les divers mouvemens, les diverſes figures & groſſeurs, &
le different arrangement des parties de la matiere peuvent donner aux corps mélez, & je m'aſſure que vous n'en
trouverez aucune, qui n'ait en ſoy des qualitez qui tendent à faire qu'elle ſe change, & en ſe changeant qu'elle
ſe reduiſe à quelqu'vne de celles des Elemens.

Comme par exemple, la flâme, dont la forme demande
d'avoir des parties qui ſe remuent tres-viſte, & qui avec
cela ayent quelque groſſeur, ainſi qu'il a eſté dit cy-deſſus, ne peut pas eſtre long-temps ſans ſe corrompre : Car,
ou la groſſeur de ſes parties leur donnant la force d'agir
contre les autres corps ſera cauſe de la diminution de leur
mouvement, ou la violence de leur agitation les faiſant
rompre en ſe heurtant contre les corps qu'elles rencontrent, ſera cauſe de la perte de leur groſſeur ; & ainſi elles
pourront peu à peu ſe reduire à la forme du troiſiéme
Element, ou à celle du ſecond, & meſme auſſi quelques-
vnes à celle du premier. Et par là vous pouvez connoiſtre
la difference qui eſt entre cette flâme, ou le feu commun
qui eſt parmy nous, & l'Element du Feu que j'ay décrit.
Et vous devez ſçavoir auſſi que les Elemens de l'Air & de
la Terre, c'eſt à dire le ſecond & troiſiéme Element, ne
ſont point ſemblables non plus à cét air groſſier que nous
reſpirons, ny à cette Terre ſur laquelle nous marchons ;
mais que generalement tous les corps qui paroiſſent autour de nous, ſont mélez ou compoſez, & ſujets à corruption.

Et toutesfois il ne faut pas pour cela penſer que les Elemens n'ayent aucuns lieux dans le monde qui leur ſoient
particulierement deſtinez, & où ils puiſſent perpetuellement ſe conſerver en leur pureté naturelle. Mais au contraire, puiſque chaque partie de la matiere tend toujours

the diverse motions, the diverse shapes and sizes, and the different arrangement of the parts of matter can lend to mixed bodies. I am sure you will find none that does not contain in itself qualities that tend to cause it to change and, in changing, to reduce to one of the forms of the elements.

Flame, for example, the form of which demands its having parts that move very fast and that in addition have some size (as has been said above), cannot last long without being corrupted. For either the size of its parts, in giving them the force to act against other bodies, will be the cause of the diminution of their motion, or the violence of their agitation, in causing them to break upon hurtling themselves against the bodies they encounter, will be the cause of their loss of size. Thus, little by little they will be able to reduce themselves to the form of the third element, or to that of the second, and even also some of them to that of the first.[21] Thereby you can see the difference between this flame, or the fire common among us, and the element of fire I have described. You should know also that the elements of air and of earth (i.e., the second and third elements) are not more similar to that grosser air we breathe nor to this earth on which we walk, but that generally all the bodies that appear about us are mixed or composite and subject to corruption.

And yet one need not think therefore that the elements have no places in the world that are particularly destined for them and where they can be perpetually conserved in their natural purity.[22] On the contrary, each part of matter always tends

à se reduire à quelques-vnes de leurs formes, & qu'y estant
vne fois reduite elle ne tend jamais à la quitter; quand
bien mesme Dieu n'auroit creé au commencement que
des corps mélez, neanmoins depuis le temps que le monde est, tous ces corps auroient eu le loisir de quitter leurs
formes, & de prendre celle des Elemens. De sorte que
maintenant il y a grande apparence, que tous les corps
qui sont assez grands pour estre contez entre les plus no-
tables parties de l'Vnivers, n'ont chacun la forme que de
l'vn des Elemens toute simple; & qu'il ne peut y avoir de
corps mélez ailleurs que sur les superficies de ces grands
corps : Mais là il faut de necessité qu'il y en ait. Car les
Elemens estant de nature fort contraire, il ne se peut faire que deux d'entr'eux s'entretouchent, sans qu'ils agis-
sent contre les superficies l'vn de l'autre, & donnent ainsi
à la matiere qui y est, les diverses formes de ces corps
mélez.

A propos dequoy, si nous considerons generalement
tous les corps dont l'Vnivers est composé, nous n'en
trouverons que de trois sortes qui puissent estre appellez
grands, & contez entre ses principales parties, c'est à sçavoir le Soleil & les Etoiles fixes pour la premiere, les Cieux
pour la seconde, & la Terre avecque les Planetes & les
Cometes pour la troisiéme. C'est pourquoy nous avons
grande raison de penser que le Soleil & les Etoilles fixes
n'ont point d'autre forme que celle du premier Element
toute pure; les Cieux celle du second; & la Terre, avec
les Planetes & les Cometes, celle du troisiéme.

Je joints les Planetes & les Cometes avec la Terre : Car
voyant qu'elles resistent comme elle à la Lumiere, &
qu'elles font reflechir ses rayons, je n'y trouve point de
difference. Je joints aussi le Soleil avec les Etoilles fixes, &

Hhh ij

44

to be reduced to one of their forms and, once having been reduced, tends never to leave that form. Hence, even if God at the beginning had created only mixed bodies, nevertheless since the world began all these bodies could have had the chance to leave their forms and to take on those of the elements. Thus, there is now much reason to think that all the bodies that are large enough to be counted among the most notable parts of the universe each have the form of only one of these elements alone and that there cannot be mixed bodies anywhere but on the surfaces of these large bodies. But there, of necessity, there must be some mixed bodies. For, the elements being of a very contrary nature, it cannot happen that two of them touch one another without acting against each other's surfaces and thus bestowing on the matter there the diverse forms of these mixed bodies.

Apropos of this, if we consider in general all the bodies of which the universe is composed, we will find among them only three sorts that can be called large and be counted among the principal parts, to wit, the sun and the fixed stars as the first sort, the heavens as the second, and the earth with the planets and the comets as the third. That is why we have good reason to think that the sun and the fixed stars have no other form than that of the wholly pure first element; the heavens that of the second; and the earth with the planets and comets that of the third.

I link the planets and the comets with the earth because, seeing that they, like her, resist light and reflect its rays, I find no difference between them. I also link the sun with the fixed stars and

428   LE MONDE DE RENE' DESCARTES,

leur attribuë vne nature toute contraire à celle de la Terre. Car la feule action de leur lumiere me fait affez connoiftre que leurs corps font d'vne matiere fort fubtile &
fort agitée.

Pour les Cieux, dautant qu'ils ne peuvent eftre apper-
ceus par nos fens, je penfe avoir raifon de leur attribuer
vne nature moyenne, entre celle des corps lumineux dont
nous fentons l'action , & celle des corps durs & pefans
dont nous fentons la refiftance.

Enfin nous n'appercevons point de corps mélez en aucun autre lieu que fur la fuperficie de la Terre ; & fi nous
confiderons que tout l'efpace qui les contient , fçavoir
tout celuy qui eft depuis les nuées les plus hautes , jufques
aux foffes les plus profondes que l'avarice des hommes ait
jamais creufées pour en tirer les métaux, eft extremément
petit à comparaifon de la Terre & des immenfes étenduës
du Ciel , nous pourrons facilement nous imaginer que
ces corps mélez ne font tous enfemble que comme vne
écorce qui eft engendrée au deffus de la Terre, par l'a-
gitation & le mélange de la matiere du Ciel qui l'environne.

Et ainfi nous aurons occafion de penfer que ce n'eft pas
feulement dans l'Air que nous refpirons, mais auffi dans
tous les autres corps compofez , jufques aux pierres les
plus dures & aux métaux les plus pefans , qu'il y a des parties de l'Element de l'Air mélées avec celles de la Terre,
& par confequent auffi des parties de l'Element du Feu,
parce qu'il s'en trouve toujours dans les pores de celuy
de l'Air.

Mais il faut remarquer , qu'encore qu'il y ait des parties
de ces trois Elemens mélées l'vne avec l'autre en tous ces
corps, il n'y a toutefois à proprement parler , que celles

46

attribute to them a nature totally contrary to that of the earth because the action of their light alone is enough to make me know that their bodies are of a very subtle and very agitated matter.

As for the heavens, inasmuch as they cannot be perceived by our senses, I think I am right in attributing to them a middle nature between that of the luminous bodies whose action we perceive and that of the solid and heavy bodies whose resistance we perceive.

Finally, we do not perceive mixed bodies in any place other than on the surface of the earth.[23] And, if we consider that the whole space that contains them (i.e., all that which stretches from the highest clouds to the deepest mines that the greed of man has ever dug out to draw metals from them) is extremely small in comparison with the earth and with the immense expanses of the heavens, we will easily be able to imagine to ourselves that these mixed bodies taken all together are but as a crust engendered on top of the earth by the agitation and mixing of the matter of the heavens surrounding it.

And thus we have reason to think that it is not only in the air we breathe, but also in all the other composite bodies right down to the hardest rocks and the heaviest metals, that there are parts of the element of air mixed with those of earth and, consequently, also parts of the element of fire, because they are always found in the pores of the element of air.

But one should note that, even though there are parts of these three elements mixed with one another in all bodies, nonetheless, properly speaking, only those

qui à caufe de leur groffeur ou de la difficulté qu'elles ont à fe mouvoir peuvent eftre rapportées au troifiéme, qui compofent tous ceux que nous voyons autour de nous : Car les parties des deux autres Elemens font fi fubtiles, qu'elles ne peuvent eftre apperceuës par nos fens. Et l'on peut fe reprefenter tous ces corps ainfi que des éponges, dans lefquelles encore qu'il y ait quantité de pores, ou petits trous, qui font toujours pleins d'air ou d'eau, ou de quelqu'autre femblable liqueur, on ne juge pas toutefois que ces liqueurs entrent en la compofition de l'éponge.

Il me refte icy encore beaucoup d'autres chofes à expliquer, & je ferois mefme bien aife d'y adjouter quelques raifons pour rendre mes opinions plus vray-femblables : Mais afin que la longueur de ce difcours vous foit moins ennuyeufe, j'en veux envelopper vne partie dans l'invention d'vne fable, au travers de laquelle j'efpere que la verité ne laiffera pas de paroiftre fuffifamment, & qu'elle ne fera pas moins agreable à voir, que fi je l'expofois toute nuë.

CHAPITRE VI.

Defcription d'vn nouveau Monde ; & des qualitez de la matiere dont il eft compofé.

PERMETTEZ donc pour vn peu de temps à voftre penfée de fortir hors de ce Monde, pour en venir voir vn autre tout nouveau, que je feray naiftre en fa prefence dans les efpaces imaginaires. Les Philofophes nous difent que ces'efpaces font infinis ; & ils doivent bien en eftre crûs, puifque ce font eux-mefmes qui les ont faits.

Hhh iij

which (because of their size or the difficulty they have in moving) can be ascribed to the third element compose all the bodies we see about us. For the parts of the two other elements are so subtle that they cannot be perceived by our senses. One may picture all these bodies as sponges; even though a sponge has a quantity of pores, or small holes, which are always full of air or water or some other liquid, one nonetheless does not think that these liquids enter into its composition.

Many other things remain for me to explain here, and I would myself be happy to add here several arguments to make my opinions more plausible. In order, however, to make the length of this discourse less boring for you, I want to wrap part of it in the cloak of a fable, in the course of which I hope that the truth will not fail to come out sufficiently and that it will be no less agreeable to see than if I were to set it forth wholly naked.

CHAPTER 6

Description of a New World, and on the Qualities of the Matter of Which it is Composed

For a short time, then, allow your thought to wander beyond this world to view another, wholly new one, which I shall cause to unfold before it in imaginary spaces. The philosophers tell us that these spaces are infinite, and they should very well be believed, since it is they themselves who have made the spaces so. [24]

430 LE MONDE DE RENE' DESCARTES,

Mais afin que cette infinité ne nous empefche & ne nous embaraffe point, ne tâchons pas d'aller jufques au bout; Entrons-y feulement fi avant, que nous puiffions perdre de veuë toutes les creatures que Dieu fift il y a cinq ou fix mille ans; Et aprés nous eftre arreftez là en quelque lieu déterminé, fuppofons que Dieu crée de nouveau tout autour de nous tant de matiere, que de quelque cofté que noftre imagination fe puiffe eftendre, elle n'y apperçoive plus aucun lieu qui foit vuide.

Bien que la mer ne foit pas infinie, ceux qui font au milieu fur quelque vaiffeau, peuvent eftendre leur veuë ce femble à l'infiny; & toutesfois il y a encore de l'eau au delà de ce qu'ils voyent; Ainfi encore que noftre imagination femble fe pouvoir eftendre à l'infiny, & que cette nouvelle matiere ne foit pas fuppofée eftre infinie, nous pouvons bien toutesfois fuppofer, qu'elle remplit des efpaces beaucoup plus grands que tous ceux que nous aurons imaginé. Et mefme, afin qu'il n'y ait rien en tout cecy où vous puiffiez trouver à redire, ne permettons pas à noftre imagination de s'eftendre fi loin qu'elle pourroit; mais retenons-la tout à deffein dans vn efpace déterminé, qui ne foit pas plus grand, par exemple, que la diftance qui eft depuis la Terre jufques aux principales étoiles du Firmament; Et fuppofons que la matiere que Dieu aura creée s'eftend bien loin au delà de tous coftez, jufques à vne diftance indéfinie. Car il y a bien plus d'apparence, & nous avons bien mieux le pouvoir, de prefcrire des bornes à l'action de noftre penfée, que non pas aux œuvres de Dieu.

Or puifque nous prenons la liberté de feindre cette matiere à noftre fantaifie, attribuons luy, s'il vous plaift, vne nature en laquelle il n'y ait rien du tout que chacun

Yet, in order that this infinity not impede us and not embarrass us, let us not try to go all the way to the end; let us enter only so far in that we can lose from view all the creatures that God made five or six thousand years ago and, after having stopped there in some fixed place, let us suppose that God creates from anew so much matter all about us that, in whatever direction our imagination can extend itself, it no longer perceives any place that is empty.

Although the sea is not infinite, those who are on some vessel in the middle of it can extend their view seemingly to infinity, and nevertheless there is still water beyond what they see.[25] Thus, even though our imagination seems to be able to extend itself to infinity, and this new matter is not assumed to be infinite, we can nonetheless well suppose that it fills spaces much greater than all those we shall have imagined. Indeed, in order that there be nothing in all this that you could find to blame, let us not permit our imagination to extend itself as far as it could, but let us purposely restrict it to a determinate space that is no greater, say, than the distance between the earth and the principal stars of the firmament, and let us suppose that the matter that God shall have created extends quite far beyond in all directions, out to an indefinite distance. For there is more reason, and we have much better power, to prescribe limits to the action of our thought than to the works of God.

Now, since we are taking the liberty of imagining this matter to our fancy, let us attribute to it, if you will, a nature in which there is absolutely nothing that anyone

OU TRAITE' DE LA LUMIERE. 431

ne puiffe connoiftre auffi parfaitement qu'il eft poffible.
Et pour cét effet, fuppofons expreffémét qu'elle n'a point
la forme de la Terre, ny du Feu, ny de l'Air, ny aucune
autre plus particuliere, comme du bois, d'vne pierre, ou
d'vn métal, non plus que les qualitez d'eftre chaude ou
froide, féche ou humide, legere ou pefante, ou d'avoir
quelque goût, ou odeur, ou fon, ou couleur, ou lumiere,
ou autre femblable, en la nature de laquelle on puiffe dire qu'il y ait quelque chofe qui ne foit pas évidemment
connu de tout le monde.

Et ne penfons pas auffi d'autre cofté qu'elle foit cette
matiere premiere des Philofophes, qu'on a fi bien dé-
poüillée de toutes fes formes & qualitez, qu'il n'y eft rien
demeuré de refte qui puiffe eftre clairement entendu:
Mais concevons-la comme vn vray corps parfaitement
folide, qui remplit également toutes les longueurs, lar-
geurs, & profondeurs de ce grand efpace au milieu duquel nous avons arrefté noftre penfée; en forte que chacune de fes parties occupe toujours vne partie de cet efpace tellement proportionnée à fa grandeur, qu'elle n'en
fçauroit remplir vne plus grande, ny fe refferrer en vne
moindre, ny fouffrir que pendant qu'elle y demeure, quelqu'autre y trouve place.

Adjoûtons à cela que cette matiere peut eftre divifée
en toutes les parties & felon toutes les figures que nous
pouvons imaginer; & que chacune de fes parties eft capable de recevoir en foy tous les mouvemens que nous
pouvons auffi concevoir. Et fuppofons deplus que Dieu
la divife veritablement en plufieurs telles parties, les vnes
plus groffes, les autres plus petites; les vnes d'vne figure,
les autres d'vne autre, telles qu'il nous plaira de les feindre; non pas qu'il les fepare pour cela l'vne de l'autre en

cannot know as perfectly as possible. To that end, let us expessly assume that it does not have the form of earth, nor of fire, nor of air, nor any more particular form (such as of wood, or stone, or metal); nor does it have the qualities of being hot or cold, dry or moist, light or heavy, or of having some taste, or smell, or sound, or color, or light, or suchlike, in the nature of which one could say that there is something that is not clearly known by everyone.[26]

Let us not also think, on the other hand, that our matter is that prime matter of the philosophers that has been so well stripped of all its forms and qualities that nothing more remains that can be clearly understood.[27] Let us rather conceive of it as a real, perfectly solid body, which uniformly fills the entire length, breadth, and depth of the great space at the center of which we have halted our thought. Thus, each of its parts always occupies a part of that space and is so proportioned to its size that it could not fill a larger one nor squeeze itself into a smaller one, nor (while it remains there) suffer another to find a place there.

Let us add further that this matter can be divided into any parts and according to any shapes that we can imagine, and that each of its parts is capable of receiving in itself any motions that we can also conceive. Let us suppose in addition that God truly divides it into many such parts, some larger and some smaller, some of one shape and some of another, as it pleases us to imagine them. It is not that He thereby separates them from one another,

432   LE MONDE DE RENE' DESCARTES,

ſorte qu'il y ait quelque vuide entre deux ; mais penſons
que toute la diſtinction qu'il y met,conſiſte dans la diver-
ſité des mouvemens qu'il leur donne, faiſant que dés le
premier inſtant qu'elles ſont creées, les vnes commencent à ſe mouvoir d'vn coſté,les autres d'vn autre;les vnes
plus viſte, les autres plus lentement (ou meſme ſi vous
voulez point du tout) & qu'elles continüent par aprés
leur mouvement ſuivant les loix ordinaires de la Nature.
Car Dieu a ſi merveilleuſement eſtably ces Loix, qu'encore que nous ſuppoſions qu'il ne crée rien de plus que ce
que j'ay dit, & meſme qu'il ne mette en cecy aucun ordre
ny proportion, mais qu'il en compoſe vn cahos le plus
confus & le plus embroüillé que les Poëtes puiſſent décrire, elles ſont ſuffiſantes pour faire que les parties de ce cahos ſe démélent d'elles-meſmes, & ſe diſpoſent en ſi bon
ordre, qu'elles auront la forme d'vn Monde tres-parfait,
& dans lequel on pourra voir non ſeulement de la Lumiere, mais auſſi toutes les autres choſes, tant generales que
particulieres, qui paroiſſent dans ce vray Monde.

Mais avant que j'explique cecy plus au long, arreſtez-
vous encore vn peu à conſiderer ce cahos, & remarquez
qu'il ne contient aucune choſe qui ne vous ſoit ſi parfaitement connuë, que vous ne ſçauriez pas meſme feindre
de l'ignorer. Car pour les qualitez que j'y ay miſes,ſi vous
y avez pris garde, je les ay ſeulement ſuppoſées telles que
vous les pouviez imaginer. Et pour la matiere dont je l'ay
compoſé,il n'y a rien de plus ſimple, ny de plus facile à
connoiſtre dans les creatures inanimées ; Et ſon idée eſt
tellement compriſe en toutes celles que noſtre imagination peut former, qu'il faut neceſſairement que vous la
conceviez, ou que vous n'imaginiez jamais aucune choſe.

Toutesfois parce que les Philoſophes ſont ſi ſubtils,
qu'ils

so that there is some void in between them; rather, let us think that the entire distinction that He makes there consists in the diversity of the motions He gives to them. From the first instant that they are created, He makes some begin to move in one direction and others in another, some faster and others slower (or indeed, if you wish, not at all); thereafter, He makes them continue their motions according to the ordinary laws of nature. For God has so wondrously established these laws that, even if we suppose that He creates nothing more than what I have said, and even if He does not impose any order or proportion on it but makes of it the most confused and most disordered chaos that the poets could describe, the laws are sufficient to make the parts of that chaos untangle themselves and arrange themselves in such right order [28] that they will have the form of a most perfect world, in which one will be able to see not only light, but also all the other things, both general and particular, that appear in this true world.

But, before I explain this at greater length, stop again for a bit to consider that chaos, and note that it contains nothing that is not so perfectly known to you that you could not even pretend not to know it. For, as regards the qualities that I have posited there, I have, if you have noticed, supposed them to be only such as you can imagine. And, as regards the matter from which I have composed the chaos, there is nothing simpler nor easier to know among inanimate creatures. The idea of that matter is so included in all those that our imagination can form that you must necessarily conceive of it or you can never imagine anything.

Nonetheless, because the philosophers are so subtle

qu'ils fçavent trouver des difficultez dans les chofes qui
femblét extremement claires aux autres hommes ; & que
le fouvenir de leur matiere premiere, qu'ils fçavent eftre
affez mal-aifée à concevoir, les pourroit divertir de la
connoiffance de celle dont je parle, il faut que je leur dife
en cét endroit, que fi je ne me trompe, toute la difficulté
qu'ils éprouvent en la leur, ne vient que de ce qu'ils la
veulent diftinguer de fa propre quantité, & de fon eftenduë exterieure, c'eft à dire de la proprieté qu'elle a d'occuper de l'efpace. En quoy toutesfois je veux bien qu'ils
croyent avoir raifon, car je n'ay pas deffein de m'arrefter
à les contredire : Mais ils ne doivent pas auffi trouver
eftrange, fi je fupofe que la quantité de la matiere que
j'ay décrite, ne differe non plus de fa fubftance, que le
nombre fait des chofes nombrées ; & fi je conçois fon
eftenduë, ou la proprieté qu'elle a d'occuper de l'efpace,
non point comme vn accident, mais comme fa vraye forme & fon effence : car ils ne fçauroient nier qu'elle ne foit
tres-facile à concevoir en cette forte. Et mon deffein
n'eft pas d'expliquer comme eux les chofes qui font
en effet dans le vray monde ; mais feulement d'en feindre vn à plaifir, dans lequel il n'y ait rien que les plus
groffiers Efprits ne foient capables de concevoir, & qui
puiffe toutesfois eftre creé tout de mefme que je l'auray
feint.

   Si j'y mettois la moindre chofe qui fût obfcure, il fe
pourroit faire que parmy cette obfcurité il y auroit quelque repugnance cachée dont je ne me ferois pas apperceu, & ainfi que fans y penfer je fuppoferois vne chofe
impoffible ; au lieu que pouvant diftinctement imaginer
tout ce que j'y mets, il eft certain qu'encore qu'il n'y euft
rien de tel dans l'ancien monde, Dieu le peut toutesfois

                                               Iii

that they can find difficulties in things that appear extremely clear to other men, and because the memory of their prime matter (which they know to be rather difficult to conceive of) could divert them from knowledge of the matter of which I speak, I should say to them at this point that, unless I am mistaken, the whole problem they face with their matter derives only from their wanting to distinguish it from its own proper quantity and from its outward extension, i.e., from the property it has of occupying space. In this, however, I am willing that they think themselves correct, for I have no intention of stopping to contradict them. But they should also not find it strange if I suppose that the quantity of the matter I have described does not differ from its substance any more than number differs from the things numbered. Nor should they find it strange if I conceive of its extension, or the property it has of occupying space, not as an accident, but as its true form and its essence. For they cannot deny that it is quite easy to conceive of it in that way. And my plan is not to set out (as they do) the things that are in fact in the true world, but only to make up as I please from [this matter] a [world] in which there is nothing that the densest minds are not capable of conceiving, and which nevertheless could be created exactly the way I have made it up.

Were I to posit in this new world the least thing that is obscure, it could happen that, within that obscurity, there might be some hidden contradiction I had not perceived, and thus that, without thinking, I might suppose something impossible. Instead, being able to imagine distinctly everything I am positing there, it is certain that, even if there be no such thing in the old world, God can nevertheless

434   LE MONDE DE RENE'DESCARTES,
créer dans vn nouveau : Car il eſt certain qu'il peut créer
toutes les choſes que nous pouvons imaginer.

CHAPITRE VII.

Des loix de la Nature de ce nouveau Monde.

MAIS je ne veux pas differer plus long-temps à
vous dire par quel moyen la Nature ſeule pourra
déméler la confuſion du Cahos dont j'ay parlé, & quelles
ſont les Loix que Dieu luy a impoſées.

Sçachez donc premierement, que par la Nature je
n'entens point icy quelque Déeſſe, ou quelque autre ſorte de puiſſance imaginaire; Mais que je me ſers de ce mot,
pour ſignifier la Matiere meſme, entant que je la conſidere avec toutes les qualitez que je luy ay attribuées, compriſes toutes enſemble, & ſous cette condition que Dieu
continuë de la conſerver en la meſme façon qu'il l'a creée:
Car de cela ſeul qu'il continuë ainſi de la conſerver, il ſuit
de neceſſité qu'il doit y avoir pluſieurs changemens en
ſes parties, leſquels ne pouvant ce me ſemble eſtre proprement attribuez à l'action de Dieu, parce qu'elle ne
change point, je les attribuë à la Nature ; & les regles ſuivant leſquelles ſe font ces changemens, je les nomme les
Loix de la Nature.

Pour mieux entendre cecy, ſouvenez-vous qu'entre les
qualitez de la matiere, nous avons ſuppoſé que ſes parties
avoient eu divers mouvemens dés le commencement
qu'elles ont eſté creées ; & outre cela qu'elles s'entre-
touchoient toutes de tous coſtez, ſans qu'il y eût aucun
vuide entre-deux; D'où il ſuit de neceſſité, que dés-lors,
en commençant à ſe mouvoir, elles ont commencé auſſi

create it in a new one; for it is certain that He can create everything we can imagine.[29]

CHAPTER 7

On the Laws of Nature of this New World

But I do not want to delay any longer telling you by what means nature alone could untangle the confusion of the chaos of which I have been speaking, and what the laws of nature are that God has imposed on her.

Know, then, first that by "nature" I do not here mean some deity or other sort of imaginary power. Rather, I use that word to signify matter itself, insofar as I consider it taken together with all the qualities that I have attributed to it, and under the condition that God continues to preserve it in the same way that He created it. For from that alone (i.e., that He continues thus to preserve it) it follows of necessity that there may be many changes in its parts that cannot, it seems to me, be properly attributed to the action of God (because that action does not change) and hence are to be attributed to nature. The rules according to which these changes take place I call the "laws of nature."

To understand this better, recall that, among the qualities of matter, we have supposed that its parts have had diverse motions since the beginning when they were created, and furthermore that they all touch one another on all sides, without there being any void in between. Whence it follows of necessity that from then on, in beginning to move, they also began

OU TRAITÉ DE LA LUMIERE. 435

à changer & diverſifier leurs mouvemens par la rencontre l'vne de l'autre : Et ainſi que ſi Dieu les conſerve par
aprés en la meſme façon qu'il les a creées, il ne les conſerve pas au meſme eſtat ; C'eſt à dire, que Dieu agiſſant
toujours de meſme, & par conſequent produiſant toujours le meſme effet en ſubſtance, il ſe trouve comme par
accident pluſieurs diverſitez en cét effet. Et il eſt facile à
croire, que Dieu, qui comme chacun doit ſçavoir eſt immuable, agit toujours de meſme façon. Mais ſans m'en-
gager plus avant dans ces conſiderations Metaphyſiques,
je mettray icy deux ou trois des principales regles ſuivant
leſquelles il faut penſer que Dieu fait agir la Nature de ce
nouveau Monde, & qui ſuffiront comme je croy pour
vous faire connoiſtre toutes les autres.

La premiere eſt, Que chaque partie de la matiere en
particulier, continuë toujours d'eſtre en vn meſme eſtat,
pendant que la rencontre des autres ne la contraint point
de le changer. C'eſt à dire, que ſi elle a quelque groſſeur,
elle ne deviendra jamais plus petite, ſinon que les autres
la diviſent : Si elle eſt ronde ou quarrée, elle ne changera
jamais cette figure, ſans que les autres l'y contraignent :
Si elle eſt arreſtée en quelque lieu, elle n'en partira jamais,
que les autres ne l'en chaſſent : Et ſi elle a vne fois commencé à ſe mouvoir, elle continuëra toujours avec vne
égale force, juſques à ce que les autres l'arreſtent ou la
retardent.

Il n'y a perſonne qui ne croye que cette meſme Regle
s'obſerve dans l'ancien Monde, touchant la groſſeur, la
figure, le repos, & mille autres choſes ſemblables ; mais
les Philoſophes en ont excepté le Mouvement, qui eſt
pourtant la choſe que je deſire le plus expreſſément y
comprendre. Et ne penſez pas pour cela que j'aye deſſein

Iii ij

to change and diversify their motions by colliding
with one another. Thus, if God preserves them
thereafter in the same way that He created them,
He does not preserve them in the same state. That is
to say, with God always acting in the same way and
consequently always producing the same effect in
substance, there occur, as by accident, many
diversities in that effect. And it is easy to believe
that God, who, as everyone must know, is
immutable, always acts in the same way. Without,
however, involving myself any further in these
metaphysical considerations, I will set out here two
or three of the principal rules according to which
one must think God causes the nature of this new
world to act, and which will suffice, I believe, for
you to know all the others.[30]

The first is that each individual part of matter
always continues to remain in the same state unless
collision with others forces it to change that state.
That is to say, if the part has some size, it will never
become smaller unless others divide it; if it is round
or square, it will never change that shape without
others forcing it to do so; if it is stopped in some
place it will never depart from that place unless
others chase it away; and if it has once begun to
move, it will always continue with an equal force
until others stop or retard it.

There is no one who does not believe that this
same rule is observed in the old world with respect
to size, shape, rest, and a thousand other like
things. But from it the philosophers have exempted
motion, which is, however, the thing I most
expressly desire to include in it. Do not think thereby that I intend

436   LE MONDE DE RENE' DESCARTES,
de les contredire, le mouvement dont iis parlent eſt ſi fort different de celuy que j'y conçoy, qu'il ſe peut aiſé-ment faire, que ce qui eſt vray de l'vn, ne le ſoit pas de l'autre.

Ils avoüent eux-meſmes que la Nature du leur eſt fort peu connuë; Et pour la rendre en quelque façon intelligible, ils ne l'ont encore ſceu expliquer plus clairement qu'en ces termes, *Motus eſt actus entis in potentia, prout in potentia eſt*, leſquels ſont pour moy ſi obſcurs, que je ſuis contraint de les laiſſer icy en leur langue, parce que je ne les ſçaurois interpreter. (Et en effet ces mots, le mouve-ment eſt l'acte d'vn Eſtre en puiſſance, entant qu'il eſt en puiſſance, ne ſont pas plus clairs, pour eſtre François.) Mais au contraire, la Nature du Mouvement duquel j'en-tens icy parler eſt ſi facile à connoiſtre, que les Geome-tres meſmes, qui entre tous les hommes le ſont le plus eſtudié à concevoir bien diſtinctement les choſes qu'ils ont conſiderées, l'ont jugée plus ſimple & plus intelligi-ble que celle de leurs ſuperficies, & de leurs lignes; ainſi qu'il paroiſt, en ce qu'ils ont expliqué la ligne par le mou-vement d'vn point, & la ſuperficie par celuy d'vne ligne.

Les Philoſophes ſuppoſent auſſi pluſieurs mouvemens qu'ils penſent pouvoir eſtre faits ſans qu'aucun corps change de place, comme ceux qu'ils appellent, *Motus ad formam, motus ad calorem, motus ad quantitatem*, (Mou-vement à la forme, mouvement à la chaleur, mouvement à la quantité,) & mille autres; Et moy je n'en connois aucun que celuy qui eſt plus aiſé à concevoir que les li-gnes des Geometres, qui fait que les corps paſſent d'vn lieu en vn autre, & occupent ſucceſſivement tous les eſpa-ces qui ſont entre-deux.

Outre cela, ils attribüent au moindre de ces mouve-

62

to contradict them. The motion of which they speak is so very different from that which I conceive that it can easily happen that what is true of the one is not true of the other.

They themselves avow that the nature of their motion is very little known.[31] To render it in some way intelligible, they have still not been able to explain it more clearly than in these terms: *motus est actus entis in potentia, prout in potentia est,*[32] which terms are for me so obscure that I am constrained to leave them here in their language, because I cannot interpret them. (And, in fact, the words, "motion is the act of a being in potency, insofar as it is in potency," are not clearer for being in [English].) On the contrary, the nature of the motion of which I mean to speak here is so easy to know that mathematicians themselves, who among all men studied most to conceive very distinctly the things they were considering, judged it simpler and more intelligible than their surfaces and their lines. So it appears from the fact that they explained the line by the motion of a point, and the surface by that of a line.

The philosophers also suppose several motions that they think can be accomplished without any body's changing place, such as those they call *motus ad formam, motus ad calorem, motus ad quantitatem* ("motion with respect to form," "motion with respect to heat," "motion with respect to quantity"), and myriad others. As for me, I conceive of none except that which is easier to conceive of than the lines of mathematicians: the motion by which bodies pass from one place to another and successively occupy all the spaces in between.

Beyond that, the philosophers attribute to the least of these

OU TRAITE' DE LA LUMIERE. 437

mens vn Eſtre beaucoup plus ſolide & plus veritable qu'ils
ne font au repos, lequel ils diſent n'en eſtre que la privation; Et moy je conçois que le repos eſt auſſi bien vne
qualité qui doit eſtre attribuée à la matiere, pendant
qu'elle demeure en vne place, comme le mouvement en
eſt vne qui luy eſt attribuée, pendant qu'elle en change.

Enfin le mouvement dont ils parlent eſt d'vne Nature
ſi eſtrange, qu'au lieu que toutes les autres choſes ont
pour fin leur perfection, & ne tâchent qu'à ſe conſerver,
il n'a point d'autre fin ny d'autre but que le repos; & contre toutes les Loix de la Nature il tâche ſoy-meſme à ſe
détruire. Mais au contraire, celuy que je ſuppoſe ſuit les
meſmes Loix de la Nature que font generalement toutes
les diſpoſitions & toutes les qualitez qui ſe trouvent en la
matiere; auſſi bien celles que les Doctes appellent, *Modos*
& entia rationis cum fundamento in re, (Des modes & des
eſtres de raiſon avec fondement dans la choſe,) comme
qualitates reales, (leurs qualitez réelles) dans leſquelles je
confeſſe ingenûment ne trouver pas plus de realité que
dans les autres.

Je ſuppoſe pour ſeconde Regle, Que quand vn corps
en pouſſe vn autre, il ne ſçauroit luy donner aucun mouvement qu'il n'en perde en meſme temps autant du ſien,
ny luy en oſter que le ſien ne s'augmente d'autant. Cette
Regle jointe avec la precedente ſe rapporte fort bien à
toutes les experiences dans leſquelles nous voyons qu'vn
corps commence ou ceſſe de ſe mouvoir, parce qu'il eſt
pouſſé ou arreſté par quelque autre. Car ayant ſuppoſé la
precedente, nous ſommes exempts de la peine où ſe trouvent les Doctes, quand ils veulent rendre raiſon de ce
qu'vne pierre continuë de ſe mouvoir quelque temps
aprés eſtre hors de la main de celuy qui l'a jettée : car on

I ii iij

motions a being much more solid and real than they do to rest, which they say is nothing but the privation of motion. As for me, I conceive of rest as being a quality also, which should be attributed to matter while it remains in one place, just as motion is a quality attributed to it while it is changing place.[33]

Finally, the motion of which they speak is of such a strange nature that, whereas all other things have as a goal their perfection and strive only to preserve themselves, it has no other end and no other goal than rest. Contrary to all the laws of nature, it strives on its own to destroy itself. By contrast, the motion I suppose follows the same laws of nature as do generally all the dispositions and all the qualities found in matter, as well those which the scholars call *modos et entia rationis cum fundamento in re* (modes and beings of thought with foundation in the thing) as *qualitates reales* (their real qualities), in which I frankly confess I can find no more reality than in the others.

I suppose as a second rule that, when one of these bodies pushes another, it cannot give the other any motion except by losing as much of its own at the same time; nor can it take away from the other body's motion unless its own is increased by as much. This rule, joined to the preceding, agrees quite well with all experiences in which we see one body begin or cease to move because it is pushed or stopped by some other. For, having supposed the preceding rule, we are free from the difficulty in which the scholars find themselves when they want to explain why a stone continues to move for some time after being out of the hand of him who threw it. For one

438   LE MONDE DE RENE' DESCARTES,

nous doit plutoſt demander pourquoy elle ne continuë
pas toujours de ſe mouvoir? Mais la raiſon eſt facile à rendre : Car qui eſt-ce qui peut nier que l'air dans lequel elle
ſe remuë, ne luy faſſe quelque reſiſtance ? On l'entend
ſiffler lors qu'elle le diviſe , & ſi l'on remuë dedans vn
évantail, ou quelque autre corps fort leger & fort eſten-
du, on pourra meſme ſentir au pois de la main qu'il en
empeſche le mouvement, bien loin de le continüer, ainſi
que quelques-vns ont voulu dire. Mais ſi l'on manque
d'expliquer l'effet de ſa reſiſtance ſuivant noſtre ſeconde
Regle, & que l'on penſe que plus vn corps peut reſiſter,
plus il ſoit capable d'arreſter le mouvement des autres,
ainſi que peut-eſtre d'abord on ſe pourroit perſuader, on
aura derechef bien de la peine à rendre raiſon, pourquoy
le mouvement de cette pierre s'amortit plutoſt en rencontrant vn corps mol, & dont la reſiſtance eſt mediocre,
qu'il ne fait lors qu'elle en rencontre vn plus dur , & qui
luy reſiſte davátage? comme auſſi pourquoy ſi-toſt qu'elle a fait vn peu d'effort contre ce dernier, elle retourne
incontinent comme ſur ſes pas, plutoſt que de s'arreſter
ny d'interrompre ſon mouvement pour ſon ſujet? Au lieu
que ſuppoſant cette Regle, il n'y a point du tout en cecy
de difficulté: Car elle nous apprend que le mouvement
d'vn corps n'eſt pas retardé par la rencontre d'vn autre à
proportion de ce que celuy-cy luy reſiſte, mais ſeulement
à proportion de ce que ſa reſiſtance en eſt ſurmontée, &
qu'en luy obeïſſant, il reçoit en ſoy la force de ſe mouvoir
que l'autre quitte.

Or encore qu'en la pluſpart des mouvemens que nous
voyons dans le vray Monde, nous ne puiſſions pas appercevoir que les corps qui commencent ou ceſſent de ſe
mouvoir ſoient pouſſez ou arreſtez par quelques autres,

should ask instead, why does it not continue to
move always? Yet the reason is easy to give. For
who is there who can deny that the air in which it is
moving offers it some resistance? One hears it
whistle when it divides the air; and, if one moves in
the air a fan or some other very light and very
extended body, one will even be able to feel by the
weight of one's hand that the air is impeding its
motion, far from continuing it, as some have
wanted to say. If, however, one fails to explain the
effect of the air's resistance according to our
second rule, and if one thinks that the more a body
can resist the more it is capable of stopping the
motion of others (as one can perhaps be persuaded
at first), one will in turn have a great deal of trouble
explaining why the motion of this stone is
weakened more in colliding with a soft body of
middling resistance than it is when it collides with a
harder one that resists it more. Or also why, as
soon as it has made a little effort against the latter,
it spontaneously turns on its heels rather than
stopping or interrupting the motion it has.
Whereas, supposing this rule, there is no difficulty
at all in this. For it teaches us that the motion of a
body is not retarded by collision with another in
proportion to how much the latter resists it, but
only in proportion to how much the latter's resistance is surmounted, and to the extent that, in
obeying the law, it receives into itself the force of
motion that the former surrenders.[34]

Now, even though in most of the motions we see
in the true world we cannot perceive that the bodies
that begin or cease to move are pushed or stopped
by some others,

nous n'avons pas pour cela occafion de juger que ces deux Regles n'y foient pas exactement obfervées : Car il eft certain que ces corps peuvent fouvent recevoir leur agitation des deux Elemens de l'Air & du Feu, qui fe trouvent toujours parmy eux, fans y pouvoir eftre fentis, ainfi qu'il a tantoft efté dit, ou mefme de l'Air plus groffier, qui ne peut non plus eftre fenty; & qu'ils peuvent la transferer, tantoft à cét Air plus groffier, & tantoft à toute la maffe de la Terre, en laquelle eftant difperfée, elle ne peut auffi eftre apperceuë.

Mais encore que tout ce que nos fens ont jamais experimenté dans le vray Monde, femblât manifeftemét eftre contraire à ce qui eft contenu dans ces deux Regles, la raifon qui me les a enfeignées me femble fi forte, que je ne laifferois pas de croire eftre obligé de les fuppofer dans le nouveau que je vous décris : Car quel fondement plus ferme & plus folide pourroit-on trouver pour eftablir vne verité, encore qu'on le voulût choifir à fouhait, que de prendre la fermeté mefme, & l'immutabilité qui eft en Dieu.

Or eft-il que ces deux Regles fuivent manifeftement de cela feul que Dieu eft immuable, & qu'agiffant toujours en mefme forte il produit toujours le mefme effet. Car fuppofant qu'il a mis certaine quantité de mouvemens dans toute la matiere en general dés le premier inftant qu'il l'a creée, il faut avoüer qu'il y en conferve toujours autant, ou ne pas croire qu'il agiffe toujours en mefme forte; Et fuppofant avec cela que dés ce premier inftant les diverfes parties de la matiere en qui ces mouvemens fe font trouvez inégalement difperfez, ont commencé à les retenir, ou à les transferer de l'vne à l'autre, felon qu'elles en ont pû avoir la force, il faut neceffaire-

we do not thereby have reason to judge that these two rules are not being observed exactly. For it is certain that those bodies can often receive their agitation from the two elements of air and fire, which are always found among them without being perceptible (as has just been said), or even from the grosser air, which also cannot be perceived. And they can transfer the agitation, sometimes to that grosser air and sometimes to the whole mass of the earth; dispersed therein, it also cannot be perceived.

But, even if all that our senses have ever experienced in the true world seemed manifestly contrary to what is contained in these two rules, the reasoning that has taught them to me seems to me so strong that I would not cease to believe myself obliged to suppose them in the new world I am describing to you. For what more firm and solid foundation could one find to establish a truth (even if one wanted to choose it at will) than to take the very firmness and immutability that is in God? [35]

Now it is the case that these two rules manifestly follow from this alone: that God is immutable and that, acting always in the same way, He always produces the same effect. For, supposing that He placed a certain quantity of motion in all matter in general at the first instant He created it, one must either avow that He always conserves the same amount of it there or not believe that He always acts in the same way. Supposing in addition that, from that first instant, the diverse parts of matter, in which these motions are found unequally dispersed, began to retain them or to transfer them from one to another according as they had the force to do, one must of necessity

440   LE MONDE DE RENE' DESCARTES,

ment penſer qu'il leur fait toujours continuer la meſme choſe. Et c'eſt ce que contiennent ces deux Regles.

J'ajouteray pour la Troiſiéme, Que lors qu'vn corps meut, encore que ſon mouvement ſe faſſe le plus ſouvent en ligne courbe, & qu'il ne s'en puiſſe jamais faire aucun qui ne ſoit en quelque façon circulaire, ainſi qu'il a eſté dit cy-deſſus, toutesfois chacune de ſes parties en particulier tend toujours à continuer le ſien en ligne droite; Et ainſi leur action, c'eſt à dire l'inclination qu'elles ont à ſe mouvoir, eſt differente de leur mouvement.

Par exemple, ſi l'on fait tourner vne rouë ſur ſon eſſieu, encore que toutes ſes parties aillent en rond, parce qu'eſtant jointes l'vne à l'autre elles ne ſçauroient aller autrement, toutesfois leur inclination eſt d'aller droit; ainſi qu'il paroiſt clairement ſi par hazard quelqu'vne ſe détache des autres; car auſſi-toſt qu'elle eſt en liberté ſon mouvement ceſſe d'eſtre circulaire, & ſe continuë en ligne droite.

De meſme, quand on fait tourner vne pierre dans vne fronde, non ſeulement elle va tout droit auſſi-toſt qu'elle en eſt ſortie; mais deplus, pendant tout le temps qu'elle y eſt, elle preſſe le milieu de la fronde, & fait tendre la corde; montrant évidemment par là qu'elle a toujours inclination d'aller en droite ligne, & qu'elle ne va en rond que par contrainte.

Cette Regle eſt appuyée ſur le meſme fondement que les deux autres, & ne dépend que de ce que Dieu conſerve chaque choſe par vne action continuë, & par conſequent qu'il ne la conſerve point telle qu'elle peut avoir eſté quelque temps auparavant, mais préciſément telle qu'elle eſt au meſme inſtant qu'il l'a conſerve. Or eſt-il que de tous les mouvemens il n'y a que le droit qui ſoit

entierement

think that He causes them always to continue the same thing. And that is what those two rules contain.

I will add as a third rule that, when a body is moving, even if its motion most often takes place along a curved line and (as has been said above) can never take place along any line that is not in some way circular, nevertheless each of its individual parts tends always to continue its motion along a straight line. And thus their action, i.e., the inclination they have to move, is different from their motion.

For example, if a wheel is made to turn on its axle, even though its parts go around (because, being linked to one another, they cannot do otherwise), nevertheless their inclination is to go straight ahead, as appears clearly if perchance one of them is detached from the others. For, as soon as it is free, its motion ceases to be circular and continues in a straight line.

By the same token, when one whirls a stone in a sling, not only does it go straight out as soon as it leaves the sling, but in addition, throughout the time it is in the sling, it presses against the middle of the sling and causes the cord to stretch. It clearly shows thereby that it always has an inclination to go in a straight line and that it goes around only under constraint.

This rule rests on the same foundation as the two others and depends only on God's conserving everything by a continuous action and, consequently, on His conserving it not as it may have been some time earlier but precisely as it is at the same instant that He conserves it. Now it is the case that, of all motions, only the straight is

71

OU TRAITE' DE LA LUMIÈRE. 441

entierement simple, & dont toute la Nature soit comprise en vn instant: Car pour le concevoir, il suffit de penser qu'vn corps est en action pour se mouvoir vers vn certain costé, ce qui se trouve en chacun des instans qui peuvent estre déterminez pendant le temps qu'il se meut: Au lieu que pour concevoir le mouvement circulaire, ou quelqu'autre que ce puisse estre, il faut au moins considerer deux de ses instans, ou plutost deux de ses parties, & le rapport qui est entr'elles. Mais afin que les Philosophes, ou plutost les Sophistes, ne prennent pas icy occasion d'exercer leurs subtilitez superfluës, remarquez que je ne dis pas pour cela que le mouvement droit se puisse faire en vn instant; mais seulement que tout ce qui est requis pour le produire, se trouve dans les corps en chaque instant qui puisse estre déterminé pendant qu'ils se meuvent, & non pas tout ce qui est requis pour produire le circulaire.

Comme, par exemple, si vne pierre se meut dans vne

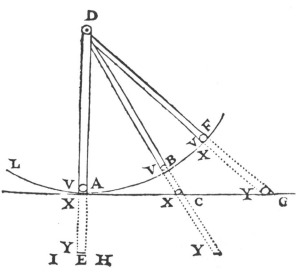

fronde, suivant le cercle marqué **A B**, & que vous la consideriez précisément telle qu'elle est à l'instât qu'elle arrive au point A, vous trouvez bien qu'elle est en action pour se

Kkk

entirely simple; its whole nature is understood in an instant. For, to conceive of it, it suffices to think that a body is in the act of moving in a certain direction, and that this is the case in each instant that might be determined during the time it is moving. By contrast, to conceive of circular motion, or of any other possible motion, one must consider at least two of its instants, or rather two of its parts, and the relation between them.[36] But, so that the philosophers (or rather the sophists) do not find occasion here to exercise their superfluous subtleties, note that I do not say that rectilinear motion can take place in an instant; but only that all that is required to produce it is found in bodies in each instant that might be determined while they are moving, and not all that is required to produce circular motion.

For example, suppose a stone is moving in a sling along the cir- cle marked AB and you consider it precisely as it is at the instant it arrives at point A: you will readily find that it is in the act of

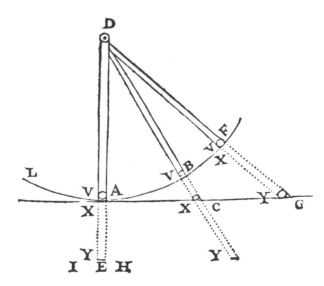

442 LE MONDE DE RENE' DESCARTES;

mouvoir, car elle ne s'y arreſte pas, & pour ſe mouvoir vers vn certain coſté, à ſçavoir vers C, car c'eſt vers là que ſon action eſt déterminée en cét inſtant ; mais vous n'y ſçauriez rien trouver qui faſſe que ſon mouvement ſoit circulaire. Si bien que ſuppoſant qu'elle commence pour lors à ſortir de la fronde, & que Dieu continuë de la conſerver telle qu'elle eſt en ce moment, il eſt certain qu'il ne la conſervera point avec l'inclination d'aller circulairement ſuivant la ligne A B, mais avec celle d'aller tout droit vers le point C.

Donc ſuivant cette Regle, il faut dire que Dieu ſeul eſt l'Autheur de tous les mouvemens qui ſont au monde, entant qu'ils ſont, & entant qu'ils ſont droits ; mais que ce ſont les diverſes diſpoſitions de la matiere qui les rendent irreguliers & courbez ; Ainſi que les Theologiens nous apprennent que Dieu eſt auſſi l'Autheur de toutes nos actions, entant qu'elles ſont, & entant qu'elles ont quelque bonté ; mais que ce ſont les diverſes diſpoſitions de nos volontez qui les peuvent rendre vicieuſes.

Je pourrois mettre encore icy pluſieurs regles, pour déterminer en particulier quand & comment & de combien le mouvement de chaque corps peut-eſtre détourné, & augmenté ou diminué, par la rencontre des autres; ce qui comprend ſommairement tous les effets de la Nature. Mais je me contenteray de vous avertir, qu'outre les trois loix que j'ay expliquées, je n'en veux point ſuppoſer d'autres, que celles qui ſuivent infailliblement de ces veritez eternelles ſur qui les Mathematiciens ont accoûtumé d'appuyer leurs plus certaines & plus évidentes demonſtrations ; Ces veritez, dis-je, ſuivant leſquelles Dieu meſme nous a enſeigné qu'il avoit diſpoſé toutes choſes en nombre, en pois, & en meſure ; & dont la con-

moving[37] (for it does not stop there) and of moving in a certain direction (that is, toward C), for it is in that direction that its action is directed in that instant. But you can find nothing there that makes its motion circular. Thus, supposing that the stone then begins to leave the sling and that God continues to preserve it as it is at that moment, it is certain that He will not preserve it with the inclination to go circularly along the line AB, but with the inclination to go straight ahead toward point C.

According to this rule, then, one must say that God alone is the author of all the motions in the world, insofar as they exist and insofar as they are straight, but that it is the diverse dispositions of matter that render the motions irregular and curved. So the theologians teach us that God is also the author of all our actions, insofar as they exist and insofar as they have some goodness, but that it is the diverse dispositions of our wills that can render those actions evil.

I could set out here many additional rules for determining in detail when and how and by how much the motion of each body can be diverted and increased or decreased by colliding with others, something that comprises summarily all the effects of nature.[38] But I shall be content with showing you that, besides the three laws that I have explained, I wish to suppose no others but those that most certainly follow from the eternal truths on which the mathematicians are wont to support their most certain and most evident demonstrations; the truths, I say, according to which God Himself has taught us He disposed all things in number, weight, and measure.[39] The knowl-

OU TRAITE' DE LA LUMIERE. 443

noiſſance eſt ſi naturelle à nos Ames, que nous ne ſçau-rions ne les pas juger infaillibles, lors que nous les con-cevons diſtinctement ; ny douter que ſi Dieu avoit creé pluſieurs Mondes, elles ne fuſſent en tous auſſi veritables qu'en celuy-cy. De ſorte que ceux qui ſçauront ſuffiſam-ment examiner les conſequences de ces veritez & de nos regles, pourront connoiſtre les effets par leurs cauſes ; & pour m'expliquer en termes de l'Ecole, pourront avoir des demonſtrations *a Priori*, de tout ce qui peut eſtre produit en ce nouveau Monde.

Et afin qu'il n'y ait point d'exception qui en empeſche, nous adjouterons, s'il vous plaiſt, à nos ſuppoſitions, que Dieu n'y fera jamais aucun miracle, & que les Intelligen-ces, ou les Ames raiſonnables que nous y pourrons ſup-poſer cy-aprés, n'y troubleront en aucune façon le cours ordinaire de la Nature. Enſuite dequoy neantmoins je ne vous promets pas de mettre icy des demonſtrations exa-ctes de toutes les choſes que je diray ; ce ſera aſſez que je vous ouvre le chemin par lequel vous les pourrez trouver de vous-meſme, quand vous prendrez la peine de les chercher. La pluſpart des Eſprits ſe dégoutent lors qu'on leur rend les choſes trop faciles. Et pour faire icy vn Ta-bleau qui vous agrée, il eſt beſoin que j'y employe de l'ombre auſſi bien que des couleurs claires. Si bien que je me contenteray de pourſuivre la deſcription que j'ay commencée, comme n'ayant autre deſſein que de vous raconter vne fable.

K к к ij

edge of those laws is so natural to our souls that we cannot but judge them infallible when we conceive them distinctly, nor doubt that, if God had created many worlds, the laws would be as true in all of them as in this one. Thus, those who can examine sufficiently the consequences of these truths and of our rules will be able to know effects by their causes and (to explain myself in the language of the School) will be able to have demonstrations *a priori* of everything that can be produced in that new world.

And so that there will be no exception that impedes this, we will, if you wish, suppose in addition that God will never make any miracle in the new world and that the intelligences, or the rational souls, which we might hereafter suppose to be there, will in no way disturb the ordinary course of nature. Nonetheless, in consequence of this, I do not promise you to set out here exact demonstrations of all the things I will say. It will be enough for me to open to you the path by which you will be able to find them yourselves, whenever you take the trouble to look for them. Most minds lose interest when one makes things too easy for them. And to compose here a setting that pleases you, I must employ shadow as well as bright colors. Thus I will be content to pursue the description I have begun, as if having no other design than to tell you a fable.

CHAPITRE VIII.

De la formation du Soleil & des Etoiles de ce nouveau Monde.

QUELQUE inégalité & confufion que nous puif-fions fuppofer que Dieu ait mife au commence-ment entre les parties de la Matiere, il faut fuivant les loix qu'il a impofées à la Nature, que par aprés elles fe foient reduites prefque toutes à vne groffeur & à vn mou-vement mediocre, & ainfi qu'elles ayent pris la forme du fecond Element, telle que je l'ay cy-deffus expliquée. Car pour confiderer cette Matiere en l'eftat qu'elle auroit pû eftre avant que Dieu eût commencé de la mouvoir, on la doit imaginer comme le corps le plus dur & le plus folide qui foit au monde. Et comme on ne fçauroit pouffer au-cune partie d'vn tel corps, fans pouffer auffi ou tirer par mefme moyen toutes les autres ; ainfi faut-il penfer que l'action ou la force de fe mouvoir & de fe divifer qui aura efté mife d'abord en quelques-vnes de fes parties, s'eft épanduë & diftribuée en toutes les autres au mefme in-ftant, auffi également qu'il fe pouvoit.

Il eft vray que cette égalité n'a pû totalement eftre par-faite. Car premierement, à caufe qu'il n'y a point du tout de vuide en ce nouveau Monde, il a efté impoffible que toutes les parties de la Matiere fe foient muës en ligne droite : Mais eftant égales à peu prés, & pouvant prefque auffi facilement eftre détournées les vnes que les autres, elles ont dû s'accorder toutes enfemble à quelques mou-vemens circulaires. Et toutesfois, à caufe que nous fup-pofons que Dieu les a muës d'abord diverfement, nous

CHAPTER 8

On the Formation of the Sun and the Stars of the New World

Whatever inequality and confusion we might suppose God put among the parts of matter at the beginning, afterwards the parts must, according to the laws He imposed on nature, almost all have been reduced to one size and to one middling motion and thus have taken the form of the second element as I described it above. For to consider this matter in the state in which it could have been before God began to move it, one should imagine it as the hardest and most solid body in the world. And, since one could not push any part of such a body without pushing or pulling all the other parts by the same means, so one must imagine that the action or the force of moving or dividing, which had first been placed in some of the parts of matter, spread out and distributed itself in all the others in the same instant, as equally as it could.

It is true that this equality could not be totally perfect. First, because there is no void at all in the new world, it was impossible for all the parts of matter to move in a straight line. Rather, all of them being just about equal and as easily divertible, they all had to unite in some circular motions. And yet, because we suppose that God first moved them diversely, we

OU TRAITE' DE LA LUMIERE. 445

ne devons pas penſer qu'elles ſe ſoient toutes accordées à tourner autour d'vn ſeul centre, mais au tour de pluſieurs differens, & que nous pouvons imaginer diverſement ſituez les vns à l'égard des autres.

Enſuite dequoy l'on peut conclure qu'elles ont dû naturellement eſtre moins agitées, ou plus petites, ou l'vn & l'autre enſemble, vers les lieux les plus proches de ces centres, que vers les plus éloignez : Car ayant toutes inclination à continuer leur mouvement en ligne droite, il eſt certain que ce ſont les plus fortes, c'eſt à dire les plus groſſes entre celles qui eſtoient également agitées, & les plus agitées entre celles qui eſtoient également groſſes, qui ont dû décrire les plus grands cercles, comme eſtant les plus approchans de la ligne droite. Et pour la matiere contenuë entre trois ou pluſieurs de ces cercles, elle a pû d'abord ſe trouver beaucoup moins diviſée & moins agitée que toute l'autre. Et qui plus eſt, dautant que nous ſuppoſons que Dieu a mis au commencement toute ſorte d'inégalité entre les parties de cette Matiere, nous devons penſer qu'il y en a eu pour lors de toutes ſortes de groſſeurs & figures, & de diſpoſées à ſe mouvoir, ou ne ſe mouvoir pas, en toutes façons & en tous ſens.

Mais cela n'empeſche pas que par aprés elles ne ſe ſoient renduës preſque toutes aſſez égales, principalement celles qui ſont demeurées à pareille diſtance des centres autour deſquels elles tournoyoient : Car ne ſe pouvant mouvoir les vnes ſans les autres, il a falu que les plus agitées communicaſſent de leur mouvement à celles qui l'eſtoient moins, & que les plus groſſes ſe rompiſſent & diviſaſſent, afin de pouvoir paſſer par les meſmes lieux que celles qui les precedoient, ou bien qu'elles montaſſent plus haut : Et ainſi elles ſe ſont arrangées en peu de

K κ κ iij

should not imagine that they all came together to turn around a single center, but around many different ones, which we may imagine to be diversely situated with respect to one another.

Consequently, one can conclude that they had to be naturally less agitated or smaller, or both, toward the places nearest to these centers than toward those farthest away. For, all of them having an inclination to continue their motion in a straight line, it is certain that the strongest (i.e., the largest among those equally agitated and the most agitated among those equally large) had to describe the greatest circles, i.e., the circles most approaching a straight line. As for the matter contained in between three or more of these circles, it could have been at first much less divided and less agitated than all the other. What is more, especially since we suppose that at the beginning God placed every sort of inequality among the parts of this matter, we must imagine that there were then all sorts of sizes and shapes, and dispositions to move or not to move, in all ways and in all directions.

But that does not prevent them from having afterwards been rendered almost all fairly equal, principally those that remained an equal distance from the centers around which they were turning. For, since some could not move without the others' moving, the more agitated had to communicate some of their motion to those that were less so, and the larger had to break and divide in order to be able to pass through the same places as those that preceded them, or in order to rise higher. Thus, in a short time all the parts were

446　　LE MONDE DE RENE' DESCARTES,

temps toutes par ordre ; en telle forte que chacune s'eſt trouvée plus ou moins éloignée du centre au tour duquel elle a pris ſon cours , ſelon qu'elle a eſté plus ou moins groſſe & agitée à comparaiſon des autres. Et meſmes, dautant que la groſſeur repugne toujours à la vitcſſe du mouvement, on doit penſer que les plus éloignées de cha-que centre ont eſté celles qui eſtant vn peu plus petites que les plus proches ont eſté avec cela de beaucoup plus agitées.

Tout de meſme , pour leurs figures, encore que nous ſuppoſions qu'il y en ait eu au commencement de toutes ſortes , & qu'elles ayent eu pour la pluſpart pluſieurs an-gles & pluſieurs coſtez , ainſi que les pieces qui s'éclatent d'vne pierre quand on la rompt , il eſt certain que par aprés en ſe remuant & ſe heurtant les vnes contre les au-tres , elles ont dû rompre peu à peu les petites pointes de leurs angles, & émouſſer les quarres de leurs coſtez , juſ-ques à ce qu'elles ſe ſoient renduës à peu prés toutes ron-des ; ainſi que font les grains de ſable & les cailloux, lors qu'ils roulent avec l'eau d'vne riviere. Si bien qu'il ne peut y avoir maintenant aucune notable difference entre celles qui ſont aſſez voiſines, ny meſme auſſi entre celles qui ſont fort éloignées, ſinon en ce qu'elles peuvent ſe mouvoir vn peu plus vîte , & eſtre vn peu plus petites ou plus groſſes l'vne que l'autre ; & cecy n'empeſche pas qu'on ne leur puiſſe attribuer à toutes la meſme forme.

Seulement en faut-il excepter quelques-vnes, qui ayant eſté dés le commencement beaucoup plus groſſes que les autres n'ont pû ſi facilement ſe diviſer, ou qui ayant eu des figures fort irregulieres & empeſchantes, ſe ſont plu-toſt jointes pluſieurs enſemble, que de ſe rompre pour s'arrondir ; & ainſi elles ont retenu la forme du troiſiéme

arranged in order, so that each was more or less distant from the center about which it had taken its course, according as it was more or less large and agitated in comparison with the others. Indeed, inasmuch as size always resists speed of motion, one must imagine that the parts more distant from each center were those which, being a bit smaller than the ones closer to the center, were thereby much more agitated.[40]

Exactly the same holds for their shapes. Even if we were to suppose that there were at the beginning all sorts of shapes and that they had for the most part many angles and many sides, like the pieces that fly off from a stone when it is broken, it is certain that afterward, in moving and hurtling themselves against one another, they little by little had to break the small points of their angles and dull the square edges of their sides, until they had almost all been rendered round, just as grains of sand and pebbles do when they roll with the water of a river. Thus there cannot now be any notable difference among those parts that are rather close, nor indeed even among those that are quite distant, except that one can move a bit more quickly than another and be a bit larger or a bit smaller, and that does not prevent one's attributing the same form to all of them.

Only one must except some which, having been from the beginning much larger than the others, could not be so easily divided, or which, having had very irregular and impeding shapes, joined together severally rather than breaking up and rounding off. Thus, they have retained the form of the third

OU TRAITE' DE LA LUMIERE.

Element , & ont fervy à compofer les Planetes & les Cometes , comme je vous diray cy-aprés.

Deplus , il eft befoin de remarquer que la Matiere qui eft fortie d'autour des parties du fecond Element, à mefure qu'elles ont rompu & émouffé les petites pointes de leurs angles pour s'arrondir, a dû neceffairement acquerir vn mouvement beaucoup plus vîte que le leur, & enfemble vne facilité à fe divifer & à changer à tous momens de figure, pour s'accommoder à celle des lieux où elle fe trouvoit ; & ainfi qu'elle a pris la forme du premier Element.

Je dis qu'elle a dû acquerir vn mouvement beaucoup plus vîte que le leur ; & la raifon en eft évidente : Car devant fortir de cofté, & par des paffages fort étroits, hors des petits efpaces qui eftoient entr'elles, à mefure qu'elles s'alloient rencontrer de front l'vne l'autre , elle avoit beaucoup plus de chemin qu'elles à faire en mefme temps.

Il eft auffi befoin de remarquer, que ce qui fe trouve de ce premier Element de plus qu'il n'en faut pour remplir les petits intervalles que les parties du fecond, qui font rondes, laiffent neceffairement autour d'elles, fe doit retirer vers les centres autour defquels elles tournent , à caufe qu'elles occupent tous les autres lieux plus éloignez ; Et que là il doit compofer des corps ronds, parfaitement liquides & fubtils , lefquels tournant fans ceffe beaucoup plus vîte, & en mefme fens que les parties du fecond Element qui les environne , ont la force d'augmenter l'agitation de celle dont ils font les plus proches ; & mefmes de les pouffer toutes de tous coftez, en tirant du centre vers la circonference ; ainfi qu'elles fe pouffent auffi les vnes les autres ; & ce par vne action qu'il

element and have served to compose the planets and the comets, as I shall tell you below.

It is necessary to note in addition that, to the extent that the parts of the second element broke and dulled the small points of their angles in rounding off, the matter that came out from around them necessarily had to acquire a much faster motion than theirs and along with it a facility for dividing and changing shape at every moment to accommodate itself to the shape of the places where it is. Thus, it took the form of the first element.

I say that it had to acquire a much faster motion than theirs, and the reason is clear. For, having to go off to the side through very narrow passages and out of the small spaces left between the parts of the second element as they proceeded to collide head-on with one another, it had much more of a path than they to traverse in the same time.

It is also necessary to note that what there is of that first element beyond what is needed to fill the small intervals that the parts of the second (which are round) necessarily leave around them must draw back toward the centers about which those parts turn, because [the parts of the second] occupy all the other, more distant places. At those centers, the remaining first element must compose perfectly liquid and subtle round bodies which, incessantly turning much faster than, and in the same direction as, the parts of the second element surrounding them, have the force to increase the agitation of those parts to which they are closest and even (in moving from the center toward the circumference) to push the parts in all directions, just as they push one another. This takes place by an action that I

448 LE MONDE DE RENE' DESCARTES,

faudra tantoſt que j'explique le plus exactement que je
pourray. Car je vous advertis icy par avance , que c'eſt
cette action que nous prendrons pour la Lumiere ; comme auſſi que nous prendrons ces corps ronds compoſez
de la Matiere du premier Element toute pure, l'vn pour le
Soleil, & les autres pour les Eſtoiles fixes du nouveau
Monde que je vous décris ; & la Matiere du ſecond Element qui tourne autour d'eux , pour les Cieux.

Imaginez-vous, par exemple, que les points, S. E. ɛ. A.
ſont les centres dont je vous parle ; & que toute la Matiere compriſe en l'eſpace F. G. G. F. eſt vn Ciel qui tourne
autour du Soleil marqué S ; & que toute celle de l'eſpace
H. G. G. H. en eſt vn autre qui tourne autour de l'Etoille
marquée ɛ. & ainſi des autres ; En ſorte qu'il y a autant
de divers Cieux , comme il y a d'Etoiles , & comme leur
nombre eſt indéfiny , celuy des Cieux l'eſt de meſme ; &
que le Firmament n'eſt autre choſe que la ſuperficie ſans
épaiſſeur qui ſepare tous ces Cieux les vns des autres.

Penſez auſſi que les parties du ſecond Element qui ſont
vers F. ou vers G. ſont plus agitées que celles qui ſont
vers K , ou vers L ; en ſorte que leur viteſſe diminuë peu
à peu , depuis la circonference exterieure de chaque Ciel,
juſques à vn certain endroit, comme par exemple juſques à la Sphere K , K , autour du Soleil , ɛ ; iſques à la
Sphere L , L , autour de l'Etoile, ɛ : puis qu'elle augmente
de là peu à peu juſques aux centres de ces Cieux , à cauſe
de l'agitation des Aſtres qui s'y trouvent. Enſorte que
pendant que les parties du ſecond Element qui ſont vers
K , ont le loiſir d'y décrire vn cercle entier autour du Soleil , celles qui ſont vers T , que je ſuppoſe en eſtre dix fois
plus proches , n'ont pas ſeulement le loiſir d'y en décrire
dix , ainſi qu'elles feroient ſi elles ne ſe mouvoient qu'é-
galement

86

must soon explain as exactly as I can. For I tell you here in advance that it is this action that we shall take to be light, as also we shall take one of those round bodies composed purely of the matter of the first element to be the sun, and the others to be the fixed stars, of the new world I am describing to you; and we shall take the matter of the second element turning about them to be the heavens.

Imagine, for example, that the points S, E, ε, and A are the centers of which I speak, that all the matter contained in the space FGGF is a heaven turning about the sun marked S, that all the matter of the space HGGH is another heaven turning about the star marked ε, and so on for the others. Thus, there are as many different heavens as there are stars, and, since the number of stars is indefinite, so too is the number of heavens. Thus also the firmament is nothing other than a surface without thickness, separating all the heavens from one another.

Imagine also that the parts of the second element toward F, or toward G, are more agitated than those toward K, or toward L, so that their speed decreases little by little from the outside circumference of each heaven to a certain place (such as, for example, to the sphere KK about the sun, and to the sphere LL about the star ε) and then increases little by little from there to the centers of the heavens because of the agitation of the stars that are found there. Thus, while the parts of the second element toward K have the chance to describe there a complete circle about the sun, those toward T, which I suppose to be ten times closer, have not only the chance to describe ten circles (as they would do if they moved only

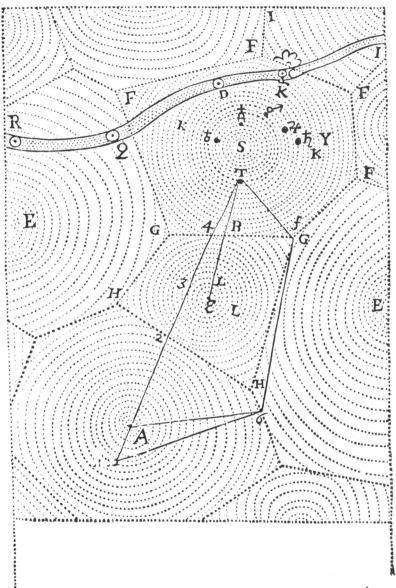

galement vîte, mais peut-eſtre plus de trente. Et derechef, celles qui ſont vers F, ou vers G, que je ſuppoſe en

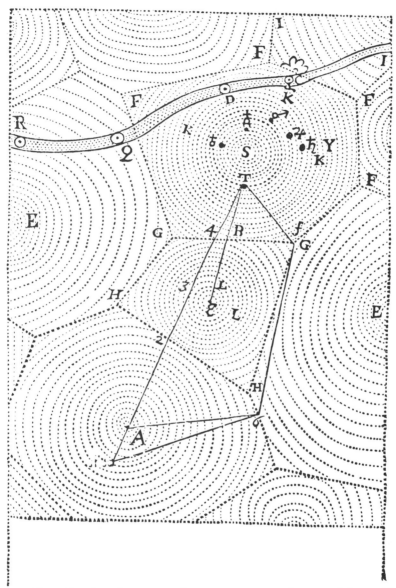

equally fast), but perhaps more than thirty.[41] Again, those parts toward F, or toward G, which I suppose

450 LE MONDE DE RENE' DESCARTES;

eftre deux ou trois mille fois plus éloignées, en peuvent peut-eftre décrire plus de foixante. D'où vous pourrez entendre tantoft, que les Planetes qui font les plus hautes, fe doivent mouvoir plus lentement que celles qui font plus baffes, ou plus proches du Soleil ; & tout enfemble plus lentement que les Cometes, qui en font toutesfois plus éloignées.

Pour la groffeur de chacune des parties du fecond Element, on peut penfer qu'elle eft égale en toutes celles qui font depuis la circonference exterieure du Ciel F G G F, jufques au cercle K K ; ou mefmes que les plus hautes d'entr'elles font quelque peu plus petites que les plus baffes, pourveu qu'on ne fuppofe point la difference de leur groffeur, plus grande à proportion que celle de leur viteffe. Mais il faut penfer au contraire, que depuis le cercle K jufques au Soleil, ce font les plus baffes qui font les plus petites, & mefmes que la difference de leur groffeur eft plus grande, ou du moins auffi grande à proportion, que celle de leur viteffe : Car autrement ces plus baffes eftant les plus fortes, à caufe de leur agitation, elles iroient occuper la place des plus hautes.

Enfin remarquez, que vû la façon dont j'ay dit que le Soleil & les autres Etoiles fixes fe formoient, leurs corps peuvent eftre fi petits à l'égard des Cieux qui les contiennent, que mefme tous les cercles K K, L L, & femblables, qui marquent jufques où leur agitation fait avancer le cours de la matiere du fecond Element, ne feront confiderables, à comparaifon de ces Cieux, que comme des points qui marquent leur centre ; Ainfi que les nouveaux Aftronomes ne confiderent quafi que comme vn point toute la Sphere de Saturne, à comparaifon du Firmament.

to be two or three thousand times more distant, can perhaps describe more than sixty circles. Whence you will be able to understand immediately that the highest planets must move more slowly than the lowest (i.e., those closest to the sun), and that all the planets together move more slowly than the comets, which are nonetheless more distant.

As for the size of each of the parts of the second element, one can imagine that it is equal among all those between the outside circumference FGGF of the heaven and the circle KK, or even that the highest among them are a bit smaller than the lowest (provided that one does not suppose the difference of their sizes to be proportionately greater than that of their speeds). By contrast, however, one must imagine that, from circle K to the sun, it is the lowest parts that are the smallest, and even that the difference of their sizes is proportionately greater than (or at least proportionately as great as) that of their speeds. Otherwise, since those lowest parts are the strongest (due to their agitation), they would go out to occupy the place of the highest.

Note finally that, given the manner in which I have said the sun and the other fixed stars were formed, their bodies can be so small with respect to the heavens containing them that even all the circles KK, LL, etc., which mark the point to which the agitation of those bodies advances the course of the matter of the second element, can be considered merely as the points that mark the heavens' center. In the same way, the new astronomers consider the whole sphere of Saturn as but a point in comparison with the firmament.

CHAPITRE IX.

De l'Origine, & du cours des Planetes & des Cometes
en general; & en particulier des Cometes.

OR afin que je commence à vous parler des Planetes & des Cometes, considerez que vû la di-
verſité des parties de la Matiere que j'ay ſuppoſée, bien
que la pluſpart d'entr'elles, en ſe froiſſant & diviſant
par la rencontre l'vne de l'autre, ayent pris la forme
du premier ou du ſecond Element, il ne laiſſe pas neantmoins de s'en eſtre encore trouvé de deux ſortes, qui
ont dû retenir la forme du troiſiéme ; Sçavoir celles
dont les figures ont eſté ſi étenduës & ſi empeſchantes, que lors qu'elles ſe ſont rencontrées l'vne l'autre,
il leur a eſté plus aiſé de ſe joindre pluſieurs enſemble,
& par ce moyen de devenir groſſes, que de ſe rompre & s'amoindrir ; Et celles qui ayant eſté dés le commencement les plus groſſes & les plus maſſives de toutes, ont bien pû rompre & froiſſer les autres en les heurtant, mais non pas reciproquement en eſtre briſées &
froiſſées.

Or ſoit que vous vous imaginiez que ces deux ſortes
de parties ayent eſté d'abord fort agitées, ou meſme
fort peu, ou point du tout, il eſt certain que par aprés
elles ont dû ſe mouvoir de meſme branſle que la Matiere
du Ciel qui les contenoit : Car ſi d'abord elles ſe ſont
muës plus vîte que cette Matiere, n'ayant pû manquer
de la pouſſer en la rencontrant en leur chemin, elles
ont dû en peu de temps luy transferer vne partie de leur

CHAPTER 9

On the Origin and the Course of the Planets and Comets in General; and of Comets in Particular

Now, for me to begin to tell you about the planets and comets, consider that, given the diversity of the parts of the matter I have supposed, even though most of them in breaking and dividing by collision with one another have taken the form of the first or second element, there nevertheless does not cease still to be found among them two sorts that had to retain the form of the third element, to wit, those of which the shapes were so extended and so impeding that, when they collided with one another, it was easier for several to join together, and by this means to become larger than to break up and become smaller; and those which, having been from the beginning the largest and most massive of all, could well break and shatter the others in striking them but not in turn be broken or shattered themselves.

Now, whether you imagine that these two sorts of parts were at first very agitated or very little agitated, or not at all, it is certain that afterward they had to move with the same agitation as the matter of the heaven that contained them. For, if at first they were moving more quickly than that matter, then, not having been able to avoid pushing it upon colliding with it in their path, in a short time they had to transfer to it a part of their

agitation ; Et si au contraire elles n'ont eu en elles-
mesmes aucune inclination à se mouvoir , neantmoins
estant environnées de toutes parts de cette matiere du
Ciel , elles ont dû necessairement suivre son cours;
Ainsi que nous voyons tous les jours que les batteaux,
& les autres divers corps qui flotent dans l'eau , aussi
bien les plus grands & les plus massifs que ceux qui
le sont moins , suivent le cours de l'eau dans laquelle
ils sont , quand il n'y a rien d'ailleurs qui les en empesche.

Et remarquez qu'entre les divers corps qui flotent
ainsi dans l'eau , ceux qui sont assez durs & assez massifs , comme sont ordinairement les batteaux , principalement les plus grands & les plus chargez , ont toujours beaucoup plus de force qu'elle à continuer leur
mouvement , encore mesme que ce soit d'elle seule qu'ils
l'ayent receuë ; Et qu'au contraire ceux qui sont fort legers , tels que peuvent estre ces amas d'écume blan-
che qu'on voit floter le long des rivages en temps de
tempeste , en ont moins. En sorte que si vous imaginez deux Rivieres qui se joignent en quelque endroit
l'vne à l'autre , & qui se separent derechef vn peu aprés,
avant que leurs eaux , qu'il faut supposer fort calmes &
d'vne force assez égale , mais avec cela fort rapides,
ayent le loisir de se mêler , les Batteaux ou autres corps
assez massifs & pesans qui seront emportez par le cours
de l'vne , pourront facilement passer en l'autre : au lieu
que les plus legers s'en éloigneront , & seront rejettez
par la force de cette eau vers les lieux où elle est le moins
rapide.

agitation. And if, on the contrary, they had in themselves no inclination to move, nevertheless, being surrounded on all sides by that matter of the heaven, they necessarily had to follow its course, just as we see all the time that boats and diverse other bodies floating on water (both the largest and most massive and those that are less so) follow the course of the water they are in when there is nothing else to impede them from doing so.[42]

And note that, among the diverse bodies that thus float on water, those that are rather solid and rather massive (as boats ordinarily are, principally the largest and most heavily laden boats) always have much more force than the water to continue their motion, even though it is from the water alone that they have received their motion. By contrast, those floating bodies that are very light, like those lumps of white scum that one sees floating along the shores during storms, have less force to continue moving. Thus, if you imagine two rivers that join with one another at some point and then separate again shortly thereafter before their waters (which one must suppose to be very calm and to have a rather equal force, but also to be very rapid) have a chance to mix, then boats or other rather massive and heavy bodies that are borne by the course of the one river will be easily able to pass into the other river, while the lightest bodies will turn away from it and will be thrown back by the force of the water toward the places where it is the least rapid.

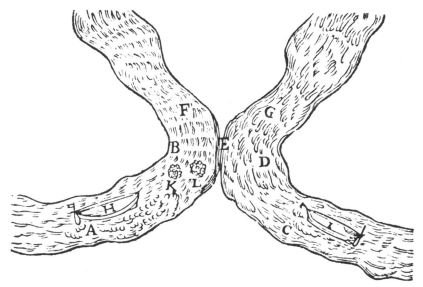

[Par exemple, fi ces deux Rivieres font A B F, & C D G, qui venant de deux coftez differens, fe rencontrent vers E, puis de là fe détournent, A B vers F, & C D vers G ; Il eft certain que le bateau H, fuivant le cours de la Riviere A B, doit paffer par E, vers G, & reciproquement le bateau I, vers F, fi ce n'eft qu'ils fe rencontrent tous deux au paffage en mefme temps, auquel cas le plus grand & le plus fort brifera l'autre : Et qu'au contraire l'écume, les feüilles d'arbres & les plumes, les fêtus & autres tels corps fort legers, qui peuvent floter vers A, doivent eftre pouffez par le cours de l'eau qui les contient, non pas vers E & vers G, mais vers B ; où il faut penfer que l'eau eft moins forte & moins rapide que vers E, puifqu'elle y prend fon cours fuivant vne ligne qui eft moins approchante de la droite.

Et deplus, il faut confiderer que non feulement

L l l iiij

96

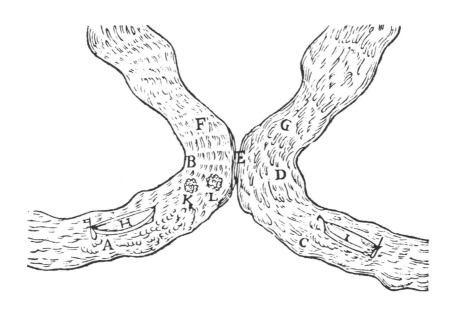

For example, if ABF and CDG are two rivers which, coming from two different directions, meet at E and then turn away from there, AB going toward F and CD toward G, it is certain that boat H following the course of river AB must pass through E toward G, and reciprocally boat I toward F, unless both meet at the passage at the same time, in which case the larger and stronger will break the other. By contrast, scum, leaves of trees, feathers, straw, and other such light bodies that can be floating at A must be pushed by the course of the water containing them, not toward E and toward G, but toward B, where one must imagine that the water is less strong and less rapid than at E, since at B it takes its course along a line that less approaches a straight line.

Moreover, one must consider that not only

454   LE MONDE DE RENE' DESCARTES,

ces corps legers , mais aussi que d'autres plus pesans
& plus massifs , se peuvent joindre en se rencontrant,
& que tournoyant alors avec l'eau qui les entraîne,
ils peuvent plusieurs ensemble composer de grosses
boules , telles que vous voyez K , & L , dont les vnes
comme L , vont vers E , & les autres comme K , vont
vers B , selon que chacune est plus ou moins solide , & composée de parties plus ou moins grosses &
massives.

A l'exemple dequoy il est aisé de comprendre, qu'en
quelque endroit que se soient trouvées au commencement les parties de la Matiere qui ne pouvoient prendre la forme du second Element ny du premier , toutes les plus grosses & plus massives d'entr'elles , ont dû
en peu de temps prendre leur cours vers la circonference exterieure des Cieux qui les contenoient , & passer aprés continuellement des vns de ces Cieux dans
les autres, sans s'arrester jamais beaucoup de temps de
suite dans le mesme Ciel : Et qu'au contraire toutes les
moins massives ont dû estre poussées , chacunes vers le
centre du Ciel qui les contenoit , par le cours de la matiere de ce Ciel. Et que vû les figures que je leur ay attribuées, elles ont dû en se rencontrant l'vne l'autre , se
joindre plusieurs ensemble, & composer de grosses boules , qui tournoyant dans les Cieux , y ont vn mouvement temperé de tous ceux que pourroient avoir leurs
parties estant separées ; en sorte que les vnes se vont rendre vers les circonferences de ces Cieux , & les autres vers
leurs centres.

Et sçachez que ce sont celles qui se vont ainsi ranger
vers le centre de quelque Ciel , que nous devons prendre
icy pour les Planettes , & celles qui passent au travers de

these light bodies, but also others heavier and more massive, can join upon meeting and that, turning then with the water that bears them, several together can compose large balls such as you see at K and L, of which some, such as L, go toward E and others, such as K, go toward B, according as each is more or less solid and composed of more or less large and massive parts.

By this example, it is easy to understand that, wherever the parts of matter that could not take the form of the second or of the first element may have been at the beginning, all the larger and more massive among them shortly had to take their course toward the outside circumference of the heavens that contained them and thereafter pass continually from one of these heavens into another without ever stopping for a very long period of time in the same heaven. By contrast, all the less massive had to be pushed, each toward the center of the heaven containing it, by the course of the matter of that heaven. And (given the shapes that I have attributed to them) upon colliding with one another, they had to join together severally and compose large balls which, turning in the heavens, have there a motion tempered by all the motions their separate parts could have if they were in fact separate. Thus, some tend to move toward the circumference of those heavens, and others toward their centers.

Know also that we should take those that thus tend to range toward the center of any heaven to be the planets, and we should take those that pass across

divers Cieux , que nous devons prendre pour des Cometes.

Or premierement touchant ces Cometes, il faut remarquer qu'il y en doit avoir peu en ce nouveau Monde , à comparaison du nombre des Cieux : Car quand
bien mesme il y en auroit eu beaucoup au commencement , elles auroient dû par succession de temps, en
passant au travers de divers Cieux , se heurter & se bri-
ser presque toutes les vnes les autres , ainsi que j'ay
dit que font deux bateaux quand ils se rencontrent; en
sorte qu'il n'y pourroit maintenant rester que les plus
grosses.

Il faut aussi remarquer que lors qu'elles passent ainsi
d'vn Ciel dans vn autre , elles poussent toujours devant soy quelque peu de la matiere de celuy d'où elles sortent , & en demeurent quelque temps envelop-
pées , jusques à ce qu'elles soient entrées assez avant
dans les limites de l'autre Ciel ; où estant , elles s'en
dégagent enfin comme tout d'vn coup , & sans y em-
ployer peut-estre plus de temps que fait le Soleil à se
lever le matin sur nostre horison : En sorte qu'elles se
meuvent beaucoup plus lentement lors qu'elles tendent
ainsi à sortir de quelque Ciel , qu'elles ne font vn peu
aprés y estre entrées.

Comme vous voyez icy que la Comete qui prend son
cours suivant la ligne C D Q R , estant déja entrée assez
avant dans les limites du Ciel F G , lors qu'elle est au
point C , demeure neantmoins encore envelopée de la
matiere du Ciel F I , d'où elle vient , & n'en peut estre
entierement délivrée, avant qu'elle soit environ le point
D. Mais si-tost qu'elle y est parvenuë , elle commence à suivre le cours du Ciel F G, & ainsi à se mouvoir

different heavens to be comets.

Now, concerning these comets, one must note first that there must be few of them in this new world in comparison to the number of heavens. For, even if there were many at the beginning, over the course of time in passing across different heavens almost all of them would have to have collided with one another and broken one another up (just as I have said two boats do when they meet), so that now only the largest could remain.

One must also note that, when they pass thus from one heaven into another, they always push before them some small bit of the matter of the heaven they are leaving and remain enveloped by it for some time until they have entered far enough within the limits of the other heaven. Once there, they finally loose themselves from it almost all at once and without taking perhaps more time to do so than does the sun in rising at morning on our horizon. In this way, they move much more slowly when they thus tend to leave some heaven than they do shortly after having entered it.

For example, you see here that the comet that takes its course along the line CDQR, having already entered rather far within the limits of the heaven FG, nevertheless when it is at point C still remains enveloped by matter from the heaven FI, from which it comes, and cannot be entirely freed of that matter before it is around point D. But, as soon as it has arrived there, it begins to follow the course of heaven FG and thus to move

beaucoup plus vîte qu'elle ne faisoit auparavant. Puis
continuant son cours de là vers R , son mouvement
doit se retarder derechef peu à peu , à mesure qu'elle
approche du point Q; tant à cause de la resistance du
Ciel F G H , dans les limites duquel elle commence à
entrer , qu'à cause qu'y ayant moins de distance entre
S & D, qu'entre S & Q, toute la matiere du Ciel qui est
entre S & D, où la distance est moindre, s'y meut plus
vîte ; ainsi que nous voyons que les rivieres coulent
toujours plus promptement aux lieux où leur lict est
plus estroit & resserré, qu'en ceux où il est plus large &
estendu.

Deplus, il faut remarquer que cette Comete ne doit
paroistre à ceux qui habitent vers le centre du Ciel F G,
que pendant le temps qu'elle employe à passer depuis D
jusques à Q, ainsi que vous entendrez tantost plus clairement, lors que je vous auray dit ce que c'est que la Lumiere ; Et par mesme moyen vous connoistrez que son
mouvement leur doit paroistre beaucoup plus viste , &
son corps beaucoup plus grand, & sa lumiere beaucoup
plus claire, au commencement du temps qu'ils la voyent,
que vers la fin.

Et outre cela , si vous considerez vn peu curieusement
en quelle sorte la lumiere qui peut venir d'elle se doit ré-
pandre & distribuer de tous costez dans le Ciel , vous
pourrez bien aussi entendre , qu'estant fort grosse, comme nous la devons supposer , il peut paroistre certains
rayons autour d'elle , qui s'y estendent quelquesfois en
forme de chevelure de tous costez , & quelquesfois se
ramassent en forme de queuë d'vn seul costé , selon les
divers endroits où se trouvent les yeux qui la regardent:
En sorte qu'il ne manque à cette Comete pas vne de
toutes

much faster than it did before. Then, continuing its course from there toward R, its motion must again slow down little by little in proportion as it approaches point Q, both because of the resistance of the heaven FGH, within the limits of which it is beginning to enter, and because, there being less distance between S and D than between S and Q, all the matter of the heaven between S and D (where the distance is smaller) moves faster there, just as we see that rivers always flow more swiftly in the places where their bed is narrower and more confined than in those where it is wider and more extended.[43]

Moreover, one should note that this comet should be visible to those who live at the center of the heaven FG only during the time it takes to pass from D to Q, as you will soon understand more clearly when I have told you what light is. In the same way, you will see that its motion should appear to viewers to be much faster, its body much greater, and its light much brighter, at the beginning of the time they see it than at the end.

Beyond that, if you consider with some care the way in which the light that can come from the comet must spread out and be distributed in all directions in the heaven, you will also be well able to understand that, being very large (as we must suppose it to be), there can appear around it certain rays that sometimes extend in the form of a halo on all sides and sometimes gather together in the form of a tail on one side only, according to the different places from which it is viewed. Thus, this comet lacks none of

OU TRAITE' DE LA LUMIERE.

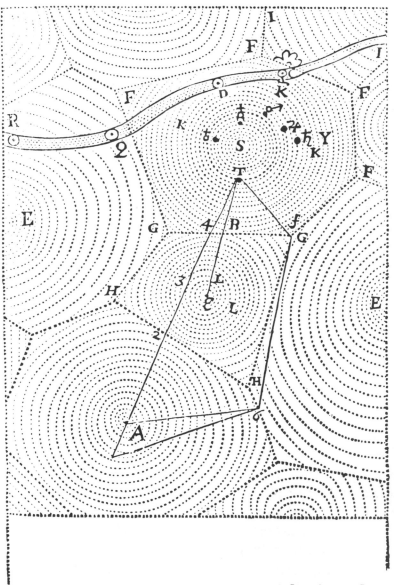

toutes les particularitez qui ont esté observées jusques
icy en celles qu'on a veuës dans le vray monde, du moins

Mmm

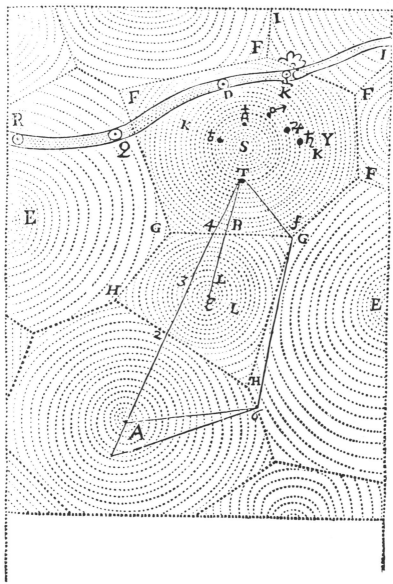

all the properties that have been observed up to
now in those that have been seen in the real world,
at least

458   LE MONDE DE RENE' DESCARTES;

de celles qui doivent eſtre tenuës pour veritables. Car ſi quelques Hiſtoriens, pour faire vn prodige qui menace le croiſſant des Turcs, nous racontent qu'en l'an 1450. la Lune a eſté éclipſée par vne Comete qui paſſoit au deſ-ſous, ou choſe ſemblable; Et ſi les Aſtronomes calculant mal la quantité des refractions des Cieux, laquelle ils ignorent, & la viteſſe du mouvement des Cometes, qui eſt incertaine, leur attribuent aſſez de paralaxe pour eſtre placées auprés des Planetes, ou meſme au deſſous, où quel-ques-vns les veulent tirer comme par force, nous ne ſom-mes pas obligez de les croire.

CHAPITRE X.

Des Planetes en general ; & en particulier de la Terre, & de la Lune.

IL y a tout de meſme touchant les Planetes pluſieurs choſes à remarquer; dont la premiere eſt, qu'encore qu'elles tendent toutes vers les centres des Cieux qui les contiennent, ce n'eſt pas à dire pour cela qu'elles puiſ-ſent jamais parvenir juſques au dedans de ces centres:car comme j'ay déja dit cy-devant, c'eſt le Soleil & les autres Eſtoilles fixes qui les occupent. Mais afin que je vous faſſe entendre diſtinctement en quels endroits elles doivent s'arreſter, voyez par exemple celle qui eſt marquée ♄, que je ſuppoſe ſuivre le cours de la matiere du Ciel qui eſt vers le cercle K ; & conſiderez que ſi cette Planete avoit tant ſoit peu plus de force à continuer ſon mouvement en ligne droite que n'ont les parties du ſecond Element qui l'environnent, au lieu de ſuivre toujours ce cercle K, elle iroit vers Y, & ainſi elle s'éloigneroit plus qu'elle n'eſt du

none of those properties that should be taken as true. Some historians, in order to concoct a miracle that warns of the Turkish crescent, tell us that in the year 1450 the moon was eclipsed by a comet that passed below it, or something similar, and astronomers calculated badly the amount of refraction (which they do not know) of the heavens and the speed of motion of comets (which is uncertain), attribute to them enough parallax to be placed among the planets, or even below them (where some wish to pull them as by force). But we are not obliged to believe them.[44]

CHAPTER 10

On the Planets in General, and in Particular on the Earth and Moon

Similarly, there are several things to note concerning the planets. First, even though they all tend toward the centers of the heavens containing them, that is not to say thereby that they could ever arrive at those centers. For, as I have already said above, the sun and the other fixed stars occupy them. But, in order to make you understand distinctly in what places the planets should stop, look for example at the one marked ♄, [45] which I suppose to follow the course of the matter of the heaven toward the circle K, and consider that, if this planet had the slightest bit more force to continue its motion in a straight line than do the parts of the second element surrounding it, then, instead of always following that circle K, it would go toward Y, and thus it would be more distant than it is from

107

OU TRAITE' DE LA LUMIERE.

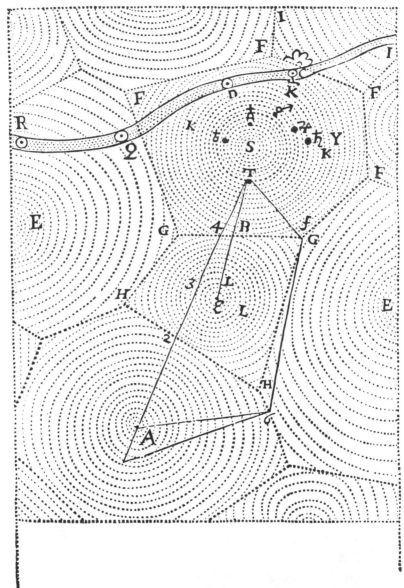

centre S. Puis dautant que les parties du fecond Element
qui l'environneroient vers Y, fe meuvent plus vîte, &

Mmm ij

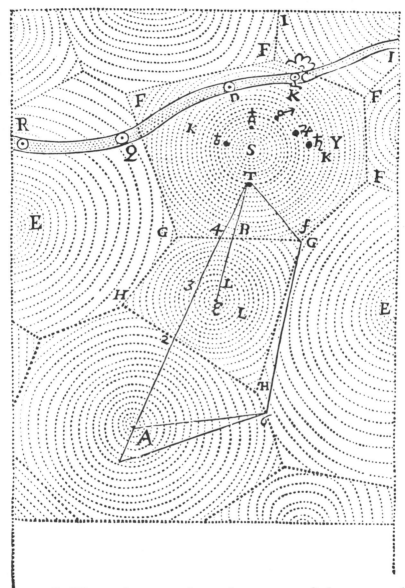

center S. Then, inasmuch as the parts of the second element that would surround it at Y move faster and

460   LE MONDE DE RENE' DESCARTES ;

mefme font vn peu plus petites,ou du moins ne font point
plus groffes que celles qui font vers K , elles luy donne-
roient encore plus de force pour paffer outre vers F; en
forte qu'elle iroit jufques à la circonference de ce Ciel,
fans fe pouvoir arrefter en aucune place qui foit entre-
deux ; puis de là elle pafferoit facilement dans vn autre
Ciel ; & ainfi au lieu d'eftre vne Planette,elle deviendroit
vne Comete.

D'où vous voyez qu'il ne fe peut arrefter aucun Aftre
en tout ce vafte efpace qui eft depuis le cercle K, jufques
à la circonference du Ciel F G G F, par où les Cometes
prennent leur cours ; & outre cela qu'il faut de neceffité
que les Planetes n'ayent point plus de force à continuer
leur mouvement en ligne droite, que les parties du fecond Element qui font vers K, lors qu'elles fe meuvent
de mefme branle avec elles, & que tous les corps qui en
ont plus font des Cometes.

Penfons donc maintenant que cette Planete ♄ a moins
de force que les parties du fecond Element qui l'environnent ; En forte que celles qui la fuivent, & qui font placées vn peu plus bas qu'elle, puiffent la détourner, & faire
qu'au lieu de fuivre le cercle K , elle defcende vers la Planete marquée ♃, où eftant , il fe peut faire qu'elle fe trouvera juftement auffi forte que les parties du fecond Element qui pour lors l'environneront : Dont la raifon eft,
que ces parties du fecond Element eftant plus agitées que
celles qui font vers K, elles l'agiteront auffi davantage, &
qu'eftant avec cela plus petites, elles ne luy pourront pas
tant refifter ; auquel cas elle demeurera juftement balan-
cée au milieu d'elles, & y prendra fon cours en mefme
fens qu'elles font autour du Soleil , fans s'éloigner de luy
plus ou moins vne fois que l'autre , qu'autant qu'elles

110

even are a bit smaller (or at least are not larger) than those at K, they would give it still more force to pass beyond toward F, so that it would go out to the circumference of that heaven, without being able to stop anywhere in between. Then from there it would easily pass into another heaven and thus, instead of being a planet, would become a comet.

Whence you see that no star can stop anywhere in all that vast space between the circle K and the circumference of the heaven FGGF, through which the comets take their course. In addition, the planets of necessity cannot have more force to continue their motion in a straight line than have the parts of the second element at K, when those planets move with the same agitation along with these parts; and all bodies that have more are comets.

Therefore, let us now imagine that this planet ♄ has less force than the parts of the second element surrounding it, so that those parts that follow it and that are placed a bit lower than it can divert it with the result that, instead of following circle K, it descends toward the planet marked ♃.[46] The planet ♄ being there, it can happen that it is exactly as strong as the parts of the second element that will then surround it. The reason for this is that, these parts of the second element being more agitated than those at K, they will also agitate the planet more; being in addition smaller, they will not be able to resist it as much. In this case, the planet will remain perfectly balanced in the middle of them and will there take its course in the same direction as they about the sun, without being at one time or another more or less·distant from the sun, except insofar as they

111

OU TRAITE' DE LA LUMIERE. 461

pourront auffi s'en éloigner.

Mais fi cette Planete eftant vers ♃, a encore moins de force à continuer fon mouvement en ligne droite, que la matiere du Ciel qu'elle y trouvera, elle fera pouffée par elle encore plus bas, vers la Planete marquée ♂. & ainfi de fuite, jufques à ce qu'enfin elle fe trouve environnée d'vne matiere qui n'ait ny plus ny moins de force qu'elle.

Et ainfi vous voyez qu'il peut y avoir diverfes Planetes, les vnes plus & les autres moins éloignées du Soleil, telles que font icy ♄. ♃. ♂. ♁. ♀. ☿ ; dont les plus baffes & moins maffives peuvent atteindre jufques à fa fuperficie, mais dont les plus hautes ne paffent jamais au delà du cercle K ; qui bien que tres-grand à comparaifon de chaque Planete en particulier, eft neantmoins fi extrememeint petit à comparaifon de tout le Ciel F G G F, que comme j'ay déja dit cy-devant, il peut eftre confideré comme fon centre.

Que fi je ne vous ay pas encore affez fait entendre la caufe qui peut faire que les parties du Ciel qui font au delà du cercle K, eftant incomparablement plus petites que les Planetes, ne laiffent pas d'avoir plus de force qu'elles à continuer leur mouvement en ligne droite, confiderez que cette force ne dépend pas feulement de la quantité de la matiere qui eft en chaque corps, mais auffi de l'éten-duë de fa fuperficie. Car encore que lors que deux corps fe meuvent également vîte, il foit vray de dire que fi l'vn contient deux fois autant de matiere que l'autre, il a auffi deux fois autant d'agitation, ce n'eft pas à dire pour cela qu'il ait deux fois autant de force à continuer de fe mou-voir en ligne droite ; mais il en aura juftement deux fois autant, fi avec cela fa fuperficie eft juftement deux fois auffi étenduë, à caufe qu'il rencontrera toujours deux

Mmm iij

can also be more or less distant from it.

But, if this planet ♄, being at ♃, still has less force to continue its motion in a straight line than has the matter of the heaven found there, it will again be pushed lower by the matter, toward the planet marked ♂,[47] and so on, until finally it is surrounded by a matter that has neither more nor less force than it.

Thus you see that there can be diverse planets, some more or others less distant from the sun, such as here ♄, ♃, ♂, T, ♀, ☿.[48] Of these the lowest and least massive can reach to the sun's surface, but the highest never pass beyond circle K which, although very large in comparison with each planet in particular, is nevertheless so extremely small in comparison with the whole of heaven FGGF that, as I have already said above, it can be considered as its center.

But, if I still have not made you understand well enough why it can happen that the parts of the heaven beyond circle K, being incomparably smaller than the planets, do not cease to have more force than they to continue their motion in a straight line, consider that this force does not depend solely on the quantity of the matter that is in each body, but also on the extent of its surface. For, even though when two bodies move equally fast it is correct to say that, if one contains twice as much matter as the other, it also has twice as much agitation, that is not to say thereby that it has twice as much force to continue to move in a straight line; rather, it will have exactly twice as much if, in addition, its surface is exactly twice as extended, because it will always meet twice

113

462　LE MONDE DE RENE' DESCARTES,
fois autant d'autres corps qui luy feront refiftance ; & il
en aura beaucoup moins , fi fa fuperficie eft eftenduë
beaucoup plus de deux fois.

Or vous fçavez que les parties du Ciel font à peu prés
toutes rondes , & ainfi qu'elles ont celle de toutes les figures qui comprend le plus de matiere fous vne moindre
fuperficie : Et qu'au contraire les Planetes eftant compofées de petites parties qui ont des figures fort irregulieres
& eftenduës , ont beaucoup de fuperficie à raifon de la
quantité de leur matiere ; en forte qu'elles peuvent en
avoir plus que la plufpart de ces parties du Ciel; & toutesfois auffi en avoir moins que quelques-vnes des plus petites , & qui font les plus proches des centres : Car il faut
fçavoir qu'entre deux boules toutes maffives , telles que
font ces parties du Ciel , la plus petite a toujours plus de
fuperficie à raifon de fa quantité, que la plus groffe.

Et l'on peut aifément confirmer tout cecy par l'experience. Car pouffant vne groffe boule compofée de plufieurs branches d'arbres confufément jointes & entaffées
l'vne fur l'autre, ainfi qu'il faut imaginer que font les parties de la matiere dont les Planetes font compofées , il eft
certain qu'elle ne pourra pas continuer fi loin fon mouvement , quand bien mefme elle feroit pouffée par vne
force entierement proportionnée à fa groffeur , comme
feroit vne autre boule beaucoup plus petite & compofée
du mefme bois , mais qui feroit toute maffive ; Il eft certain auffi tout au contraire qu'on pourroit faire vne autre boule du mefme bois & toute maffive , mais qui feroit
fi extremement petite , qu'elle auroit beaucoup moins de
force à continuer fon mouvement que la premiere; Enfin
il eft certain que cette premiere peut avoir plus ou moins
de force à continuer fon mouvement , felon que les bran-

as many other bodies resisting it, and it will have much less force to continue if its surface is extended much more than twice.[49]

Now, you know that the parts of the heaven are just about all round and thus that, of all shapes, they have the one that includes the most matter within the least surface, whereas the planets, being composed of small parts having very irregular and extended shapes, have large surfaces in proportion to the quantity of their matter. Thus, the planets can have [a greater ratio of surface to volume] than most of those parts of the heaven and nevertheless also have a smaller one than some of the smallest parts that are closest to the centers. For one must know that, among two wholly massive balls such as are those parts of the heavens, the smaller always has more surface in proportion to its quantity than has the larger.[50]

One can easily confirm all this by experience. For, if one pushes a large ball composed of many tree branches confusedly joined and piled on top of one another (as one must imagine are the parts of matter of which the planets are composed), it is certain that, even if it be pushed by a force entirely proportional to its size, it will not be able to continue its motion as far as would another ball, very much smaller and composed of the same wood, but wholly massive. By contrast, it is also certain that one could make another ball of the same wood and wholly massive, but so extremely small that it would have much less force to continue its motion than had the first. Finally it is certain that this first ball can have more or less force to continue its motion according as the branches

115

OU TRAITE' DE LA LUMIERE. 46;

ches qui la compofent font plus ou moins groffes & preffées.

D'où vous voyez comment diverfes Planetes peuvent eftre fufpenduës au dedans du cercle K, à diverfes diftances du Soleil ; & comment ce ne font pas fimplement celles qui paroiffent à l'exterieur les plus groffes, mais celles qui en leur interieur font les plus folides & les plus maffives, qui en doivent eftre les plus éloignées.

Il faut remarquer aprés cela, que comme nous experimentons que les batteaux qui fuivent le cours d'vne riviere, ne fe meuvent jamais fi vîte que l'eau qui les entraîne, ny mefme les plus grands d'entre-eux fi vîte que les moindres ; ainfi encore que les Planetes fuivent le cours de la matiere du Ciel fans refiftance, & fe meuvent de mefme branle avec elle, ce n'eft pas à dire pour cela qu'elles fe meuvent jamais du tout fi vîte : Et mefme l'inégalité de leur mouvement doit avoir quelque raport à celle qui fe trouve entre la groffeur de leur maffe & la petiteffe des parties du Ciel qui les environnent. Dont la raifon eft, que generalement parlant, plus vn corps eft gros, plus il luy eft facile de communiquer vne partie de fon mouvement aux autres corps, & plus il eft difficile aux autres de luy communiquer quelque chofe du leur : Car encore que plufieurs petits corps, en s'accordant tous enfemble pour agir contre vn plus gros, puiffent avoir autant de force que luy, toutesfois ils ne le peuvent jamais faire mouvoir fi vîte en tous fens comme ils fe meuvent; à caufe que s'ils s'accordent en quelques-vns de leurs mouvemens, lefquels ils luy communiquent, ils different infailliblement en d'autres en mefme temps, lefquels ils ne luy peuvent communiquer.

Or il fuit de cecy deux chofes, qui me femblent fort

composing it are more or less large and compressed.

Whence you see how diverse planets can be suspended within circle K at diverse distances from the sun, and how it is not simply those that outwardly appear the largest, but those that are the most solid and the most massive in their interior, that should be the most distant.

Thereafter, one must note that, just as we experience that boats following the course of a river never move as fast as the water that bears them, nor indeed the larger among them as fast as the smaller, so too, even though the planets follow the course of the matter of the heaven without resistance and move with the same agitation as it, that is not to say thereby that the planets ever move entirely as fast as the matter. Indeed, the inequality of their motion must bear some relation to the inequality between the size of their mass and the smallness of the parts of the heaven that surround them. The reason for this is that, generally speaking, the larger a body is, the easier it is for it to communicate a part of its motion to other bodies, and the more difficult it is for the others to communicate to it something of their own motion. For, even though many small bodies all working together to act upon a larger one may have as much force as it, nevertheless they can never make it move as fast as they in all directions because, if they agree in some of their motions which they communicate to it, at the same time they most certainly differ in others which they cannot communicate to it.

Now, from this follow two things that seem to me very

464   LE MONDE DE RENE' DESCARTES,

confiderables ; La premiere eft , que la matiere du Ciel
ne doit pas feulement faire tourner les Planetes autour
du Soleil , mais auffi autour de leur propre centre (ex:
cepté lors qu'il y a quelque caufe particuliere qui les en
empefche) & enfuite qu'elle doit compofer de petits
Cieux autour d'elles, qui fe meuvent en mefme fens que
le plus grand. Et la feconde eft,que s'il fe rencontre deux
Planetes inégales en groffeur, mais difpofées à prendre
leur cours dans le Ciel à vne mefme diftance du Soleil,
en forte que l'vne foit juftement d'autant plus maffive,
que l'autre fera plus groffe,la plus petite de ces deux ayant
vn mouvement plus vîte que la plus groffe , devra fe joindre au petit Ciel qui fera autour de cette plus groffe, &
tournoyer continuellement avec luy.

Car puifque les
parties du Ciel qui
font par exemple
vers A , fe meuvent
plus vîte que la Pla-
nete marquée T.
qu'elles pouffét vers
Z , il eft évident
qu'elles doivét eftre
détournées par elle,
& contraintes de
prendre leur cours
vers B ; Je dis vers
B , plutoft que vers

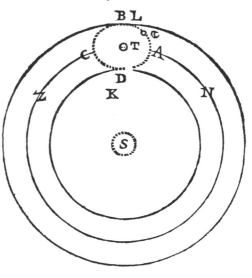

D : Car ayant inclination à continuer leur mouvement
en ligne droite , elles doivent plutoft aller vers le dehors
du cercle A C Z N qu'elles décrivent, que vers le centre S. Or paffant ainfi d'A vers B , elles obligent la Pla:
                                                    nete

worth considering. The first is that the matter of
the heaven must make the planets turn not only
about the sun, but also about their own center
(except when there is some particular cause that
hinders them from doing so), and consequently
that the matter must compose around the planets
small heavens that move in the same direction as
the greater heaven. The second is that, if there
should meet two planets unequal in size but
disposed to take their course in the heaven at the
same distance from the sun, and the planets are
such that one is exactly as much more massive as
the other is larger, then the smaller of the two,
having a faster motion than that of the larger, will
have to link itself to the small heaven around that
larger planet and turn continually about it.

For, since the
parts of the heaven
that are, say, at A
move faster than
the planet marked
T, which they push
toward Z, it is
evident that they
must be diverted
by it and con-
strained to take
their course
toward B. I say
toward B rather

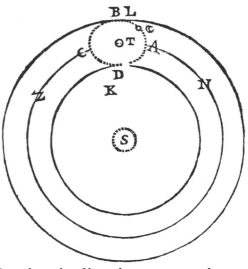

than toward D, for, having inclination to continue
their motion in a straight line, they must go toward
the outside of the circle ACZN they are describing,
rather than toward the center S. Now, passing thus
from A to B, they force the planet

OU TRAITE' DE LA LUMIERE.   465

ñete T de tourner avec elles autour de fon centre, & reciproquement cette Planete en tournant ainfi, leur donne
occafion de prendre leur cours de B vers C, puis vers D,
& vers A ; & ainfi de former vn Ciel particulier autour
d'elle, avec lequel elle doit toujours aprés continuer à fe
mouvoir de la partie qu'on nomme l'Occident, vers celle
qu'on nomme l'Orient, non feulement autour du Soleil,
mais aufli autour de fon propre centre.

Deplus, fçachant que la Planete marquée ℭ eft difpofée à prendre fon cours fuivant le cercle N A C Z, aufli
bien que celle qui eft marquée T, & qu'elle doit fe mouvoir plus vîte, à caufe qu'elle eft plus petite, il eft aifé à
entendre, qu'en quelque endroit du Ciel qu'elle puiffe
s'eftre trouvée au commencement, elle a dû en peu de
temps s'aller rendre contre la fuperficie exterieure du petit Ciel A B C D, & que s'y eftant vne fois jointe, elle doit
toujours aprés fuivre fon cours autour de T, avec les parties du fecond Element qui font vers cette fuperficie.

Car puifque nous fuppofons qu'elle auroit juftement
autant de force que la matiere de ce Ciel a tourner fuivant le cercle N A C Z, fi l'autre Planete n'y eftoit point,
il faut penfer qu'elle en a quelque peu plus à tourner fuivant le cercle A B C D, à caufe qu'il eft plus petit, & par
confequent qu'elle s'éloigne toujours le plus qu'il eft poffible du centre T ; ainfi qu'vne pierre eftant agitée dans
vne fronde tend toujours à s'éloigner du centre du cercle
qu'elle décrit. Et toutesfois cette Planete eftant vers A,
n'ira pas pour cela s'écarter vers L, dautant qu'elle entre-
roit en vn endroit du Ciel dont la matiere auroit la force
de la repouffer vers le cercle N A C Z; Et tout de mefme
eftant vers C, elle n'ira pas defcendre vers K, dautant
qu'elle s'y trouveroit environnée d'vne matiere, qui luy

Nnn

120

T to turn with them about its center. In turn, this planet in so turning gives them occasion to take their course from B to C, then to D and to A, and thus to form about the planet a particular heaven, with which it must thereafter continue to move from the direction one calls the "occident" toward that which one calls the "orient", not only about the sun but also about its own center.

Moreover, knowing that the planet marked ☾ [51] is disposed to take its course along the circle NACZ (just as is the planet marked T) and that it must move faster because it is smaller, it is easy to understand that, wherever it might have been in the heavens at the beginning, it shortly had to tend toward the exterior surface of the small heaven ABCD, and that, once having joined that heaven, it must thereafter always follow its course about T along with the parts of the second element that are at the surface.

For, since we suppose that it would have exactly as much force as the matter of that heaven to turn along circle NACZ, if the other planet were not there, then we must imagine that it has a bit more force to turn along circle ABCD, because it is smaller and consequently always moves as far away as possible from the center T. In the same way, a stone being-moved in a sling always tends to move away from the center of the circle it is describing. This planet, however, being at A, will not thereby act to move off toward L, inasmuch as it would then enter a place in the heaven of which the matter had the force to push it back toward circle NACZ. By the same token, being at C, it will not act to descend toward K, inasmuch as it would there be surrounded by a matter that would

121

466　LE MONDE DE RENE' DESCARTES;

donneroit la force de remonter vers ce mefme cerclé
N A C Z; Elle n'ira pas non plus de B vers Z, ny beaucoup moins de D vers N, dautant qu'elle n'y pourroit aller fi facilement ny fi vîte que vers C & vers A ; fi bien
qu'elle doit demeurer comme attachée à la fuperficie du
petit Ciel A B C D, & tourner continuellement avec elle
autour de T ; ce qui empefche qu'il ne fe forme vn autre
petit Ciel autour d'elle, qui la faffe tourner derechef autour de fon centre.

Je n'adjoute point icy comment il fe peut rencontrer
vn plus grand nombre de Planetes jointes enfemble, &
qui prennent leur cours l'vne autour de l'autre, comme
celles que les nouveaux Aftronomes ont obfervées autour
de Jupiter & de Saturne, car je n'ay pas entrepris de dire
tout ; & je n'ay parlé en particulier de ces deux, qu'afin
de vous reprefenter la Terre que nous habitons, par celle
qui eft marquée T, & la Lune qui tourne autour d'elle,
par celle qui eft marquée ☾.

CHAPITRE XI.

De la Pefanteur.

MAIs je defire maintenant que vous confideriez
quelle eft la pefanteur de cette Terre, c'eft à dire
la force qui vnit toutes fes parties, & qui fait qu'elles tendent toutes vers fon centre, chacunes plus ou moins felon qu'elles font plus ou moins groffes & folides ; laquelle
n'eft autre, & ne confifte qu'en ce que les parties du petit
Ciel qui l'environne, tournant beaucoup plus vîte que
les fiennes autour de fon centre, tendent auffi avec plus
de force à s'en éloigner, & par confequent les y repouf-

give it the force to ascend again toward that same circle NACZ. Nor will it go from B toward Z— much less from D toward N—in as much as it could not go as easily nor as fast as it could toward C and toward A.[52] Thus, it must remain as if attached to the surface of the small heaven ABCD and turn continually with it about T. That is what impedes its forming another small heaven about it, which would make it turn again about its own center.

I shall not add here how one can find a greater number of planets joined together and taking their course about one another, such as those that the new astronomers have observed about Jupiter and Saturn.[53] For I have not undertaken to say everything, and I have spoken in particular about the two planets discussed above only in order to represent to you (by the planet marked T) the earth we inhabit and (by that marked ℂ) the moon that turns about it.

CHAPTER 11

On Weight

Now, however, I would like you to consider what the weight of this earth is; that is to say, what the force is that unites all its parts and that makes them all tend toward its center, each more or less according as it is more or less large and solid. That force is nothing other than, and consists in nothing other than, the fact that, since the parts of the small heaven surrounding it turn much faster than its parts about its center, they also tend to move away with more force from its center and consequently to push the parts of the earth back towards its center.

ſent. En quoy ſi vous trouvez quelque difficulté ſur ce que j'ay tantoſt dit que les corps les plus maſſifs & les plus ſolides , tels que j'ay ſuppoſé ceux des Cometes , s'alloient rendre vers les circonferences des Cieux, & qu'il n'y avoit que ceux qui l'eſtoient moins qui fuſſent repouſſez vers leurs centres ; comme s'il devoit ſuivre de là , que ce fuſſent ſeulement les parties de la Terre les moins ſolides qui pûſſent eſtre pouſſées vers ſon centre, & que les autres dûſſent s'en éloigner ; remarquez que lors que j'ay dit que les corps les plus ſolides & les plus maſſifs tendoient à s'éloigner du centre de quelque Ciel, j'ay ſuppoſé qu'ils ſe mouvoient déja auparavant de meſme branle que la matiere de ce Ciel. Car il eſt certain que s'ils n'ont point encore commencé à ſe mouvoir , ou s'ils ſe meuvent, pourveu que ce ſoit moins vîte qu'il n'eſt requis pour ſuivre le cours de cette matiere , ils doivent d'abord eſtre chaſſez par elle vers le centre autour duquel elle tourne : Et meſme il eſt certain que dautant qu'ils ſeront plus gros & plus ſolides , ils y ſeront pouſſez avec plus de force & de viteſſe. Et toutesfois cela n'empeſche pas que s'ils le ſont aſſez pour compoſer des Cometes, ils ne s'aillent rendre peu aprés vers les circonferences exterieures des Cieux : Dautant que l'agitation qu'ils auront acquiſe en deſcendant vers quelqu'vn de leurs centres , leur donnera infailliblement la force de paſſer outre , & de remonter vers ſa circonference.

You may find some difficulty in this, in light of my just saying that the most massive and most solid bodies—such as I have supposed those of the comets to be—tend to move outward toward the circumferences of the heavens and that only those that are less massive and solid are pushed back toward their centers. For it should follow therefrom that only the less solid parts of the earth could be pushed back toward its center and that the others should move away from it. But note that, when I said that the most solid and most massive bodies tended to move away from the center of any heaven, I supposed that they were already previously moving with the same agitation as the matter of that heaven. For it is certain that, if they have not yet begun to move, or if they are moving less fast than is required to follow the course of this matter, they must at first be pushed by it toward the center about which it is turning. Indeed, it is certain that, to the extent that they are larger and more solid, they will be pushed with more force and speed. Nevertheless, if they are solid and massive enough to compose comets, this does not hinder them from tending to move shortly thereafter toward the exterior circumferences of the heavens, inasmuch as the agitation they have acquired in descending toward any one of the heavens' centers will most certainly give them the force to pass beyond and to ascend again toward its circumference.

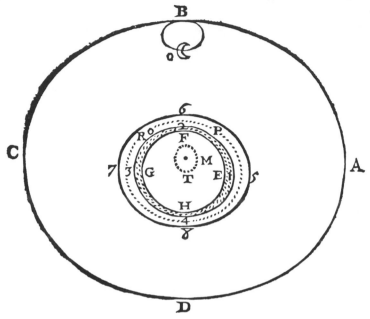

Mais afin que vous entendiez cecy plus clairement, confiderez la Terre E F G H, avec l'eau 1. 2. 3. 4, & l'air 5. 6. 7. 8. qui comme je vous diray cy-aprés, ne font compofez que de quelques-vnes des moins folides de fes parties, & font vne mefme maffe avec elle. Puis confiderez auffi la matiere du Ciel, qui remplit non feulement tout l'efpace qui eft entre les cercles A. B. C. D. & 5. 6. 7. 8. mais encore tous les petits intervalles qui font au deffous entre les parties de l'Air, de l'Eau, & de la Terre. Et penfez que ce Ciel & cette Terre tournant enfemble autour du centre T, toutes leurs parties tendent à s'en éloigner, mais beaucoup plus fort celles du Ciel que celles de la Terre, à caufe qu'elles font beaucoup plus agitées ; Et mefme auffi entre celles de la Terre, les plus agitées vers le mefme cofté que celles du Ciel, tendent plus à s'en éloigner que les autres. En forte que fi tout l'efpace qui

126

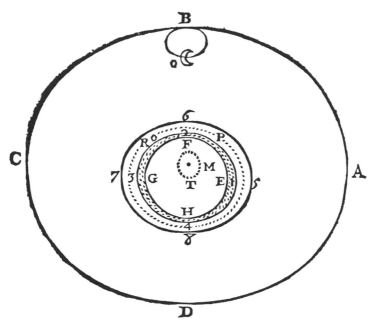

But, in order to understand this more clearly, consider the earth EFGH with water 1234 and air 5678, which (as I shall tell you below) are composed simply of some of the less solid of the earth's parts and constitute a single mass with it. Then consider also the matter of the heaven, which fills not only all the space between the circles ABCD and 5678 but also all the small intervals below it among the parts of the air, the water, and the earth. And imagine that, as that heaven and this earth turn together about center T, all their parts tend to move away from it, but those of the heaven much more quickly than those of the earth, because the former are much more agitated. Or, indeed, imagine that, among the parts of the earth, those more agitated in the same direction as those of the heaven tend to move away from the center more than do the others. Thus, if the whole space

127

OU TRAITE' DE LA LUMIERE. 469

eſt au delà du cercle A. B. C. D. eſtoit vuide, c'eſt à dire, n'eſtoit remply que d'vne matiere qui ne pût reſiſter aux actions des autres corps, ny produire aucun effet conſiderable (car c'eſt ainſi qu'il faut prendre le nom de vuide) toutes les parties du Ciel qui ſont dans le cercle A. B. C. D. en ſortiroient les premieres, puis celles de l'Air & de l'Eau les ſuivroient, & enfin auſſi celles de la Terre, chacune d'autant plus promptement qu'elle ſe trouveroit moins attachée au reſte de ſa maſſe ; En meſme façon qu'vne pierre ſort hors de la fronde en laquelle elle eſt agitée, ſi-toſt qu'on luy laſche la corde ; & que la pouſſiere que l'on jette ſur vne piroüete pendant qu'elle tourne, s'en écarte tout auſſi-toſt de tous coſtez.

Puis conſiderez que n'y ayant point ainſi aucun eſpace au delà du cercle A. B. C. D. qui ſoit vuide, ny où les parties du Ciel contenuës au dedans de ce cercle puiſſent aller, ſi ce n'eſt qu'au meſme inſtant il en rentre d'autres en leur place, qui leur ſoient toutes ſemblables, les parties de la Terre ne peuvent auſſi s'éloigner plus qu'elles ne ſont du centre T, ſi ce n'eſt qu'il en deſcende en leur place de celles du Ciel, ou d'autres terreſtres, tout autant qu'il en faut pour la remplir ; ny reciproquement s'en approcher, qu'il n'en monte tout autant d'autres en leur place. En ſorte qu'elles ſont toutes oppoſées les vnes aux autres, chacunes à celles qui doivent entrer en leur place, en cas qu'elles montent, & de meſme à celles qui doivent y entrer en cas qu'elles deſcendent, ainſi que les deux coſtez d'vne balance le ſont l'vn à l'autre ; C'eſt à dire que comme l'vn des coſtez de la balance ne peut ſe hauſſer ny ſe baiſſer, que l'autre ne faſſe au meſme inſtant tout le contraire, & que toujours le plus peſant emporte l'autre ; ainſi la pierre R, par exemple, eſt tellement op-

Nnn iij

beyond circle ABCD were void, i.e., were filled only with a matter that could not resist the actions of other bodies nor produce any considerable effect (for it is thus that we must construe the name "void"), then all the parts of the heaven in the circle ABCD would be the first to leave it; then those of the air and of the water would follow them, and finally also those of the earth, each that much sooner as it were less attached to the rest of its mass.[54] In the same way, a stone leaves the sling in which it is being moved as soon as one releases the cord, and the dust one throws on a top while it is turning immediately flys off from it in all directions.

Then consider that, since there is no such space beyond circle ABCD that is void and where the parts of the heaven contained within that circle can go, unless at the same instant others completely like them enter in their place, the parts of the earth also cannot move away any farther than they do from center T, unless there descend in their place just as many parts of the heaven or other terrestrial parts as are needed to fill it. Nor, in turn, can they move closer to the center unless just as many others rise in their stead. Thus they are all opposed to one another, each to those that must enter in its place in the case that it should rise, and similarly to those that must enter therein in the case that it should descend, just as the two sides of a balance are opposed to one another. That is to say, just as one side of a balance can be raised or lowered only if the other side does exactly the contrary at the same instant and just as the heavier always raises the lighter, so too the stone R, for example, is so op-

470 LE MONDE DE RENE' DESCARTES,

poſée à la quantité d'air (juſtement égale à ſa groſſeur) qui eſt au deſſus d'elle, & dont elle devroit occuper la place en cas qu'elle s'éloignât davantage du centre T, qu'il faudroit neceſſairement que cet air deſcendit à meſure qu'elle monteroit ; Et de meſme auſſi elle eſt tellement oppoſée à vne autre pareille quantité d'air qui eſt au deſſous d'elle, & dont elle doit occuper la place en cas qu'elle s'approche de ce centre, qu'il eſt beſoin qu'elle deſcende lors que cet air monte.

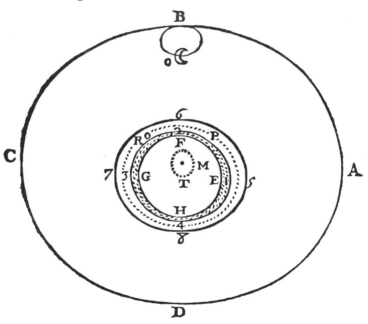

Or il eſt évident que cette pierre contenant en ſoy beaucoup plus de la matiere de la Terre, & en recompenſe en contenant d'autant moins de celle du Ciel qu'vne quantité d'air d'égale eſtenduë, & meſme ſes parties terreſtres eſtant moins agitées par la matiere du Ciel que celle de cét air, elle ne doit pas avoir la force de monter au deſſus de luy ; mais bien luy au contraire doit avoir

posed to the quantity (exactly equal in size) of air above it, whose place it should occupy in the case that it were to move farther away from center T, that the air would necessarily have to descend to the extent that the stone rose. And, in the same way, it is also so opposed to another like quantity of air below it, whose place it should occupy in the case that it were to move closer to that center, that the stone must descend when this air rises.

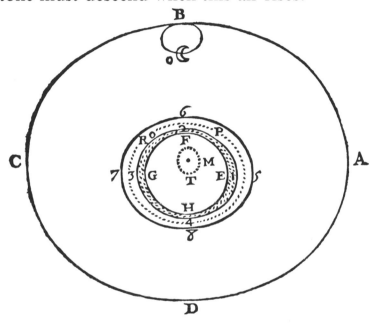

Now, it is evident that, since this stone contains in it much more of the matter of the earth than a quantity of air of equal extent—and in recompense contains that much less of the matter of the heaven —and since also its terrestrial parts are less agitated by the matter of the heaven than those of that air, the stone should not have the force to rise above that quantity of air, but on the contrary the quantity of air should have

OU TRAITÉ DE LA LUMIERE.

la force de la faire defcendre au deffous : En forte qu'il fe trouve leger eftant comparé avec elle ; au lieu qu'eftant comparé avec la matiere du Ciel toute pure, il eft pefant. Et ainfi vous voyez que chaque partie des corps terreftres eft preffée vers T ; non pas indifferemment par toute la matiere qui l'environne, mais feulement par vne quantité de cette matiere juftement égale à fa groffeur, qui eftant au deffous peut prendre fa place en cas qu'elle defcende. Ce qui eft caufe qu'entre les parties d'vn mefme corps, qu'on nomme Homogene, comme entre celles de l'air ou de l'eau, les plus baffes ne font point notablement plus preffées que les plus hautes ; & qu'vn homme eftant au deffous d'vne eau fort profonde, ne la fent point davantage pefer fur fon dos que s'il nageoit tout au deffus.

Mais s'il vous femble que la matiere du Ciel faifant ainfi defcendre la pierre R vers T, au deffous de l'air qui l'environne, la doive auffi faire aller vers 6, ou vers 7, c'eft à dire vers l'Occident ou vers l'Orient, plus vîte que cét air, en forte qu'elle ne defcende pas tout droit & à plomb, ainfi que font les corps pefans fur la vraye Terre ; Confiderez premierement, que toutes les parties terreftres comprifes dans le cercle 5. 6. 7. 8. eftant preffées vers T, par la matiere du Ciel, en la façon que je viens d'expliquer, & ayant avec cela des figures fort irregulieres & diverfes, fe doivent joindre & accrocher les vnes aux autres, & ainfi ne compofer qu'vne maffe, qui eft emportée toute entiere par le cours du Ciel A B C D ; en telle forte que pendant qu'elle tourne, celles de fes parties qui font par exemple vers 6, demeurent toujours vis à vis de celles qui font vers 2, & vers F, fans s'en écarter notablement ny çà ny là, qu'autant que les vents ou les autres caufes particulieres les y contraignent.

the force to make the stone fall downward. Thus, that quantity of air is light when compared with the stone but is heavy when instead it is compared with the wholly pure matter of the heaven. And so you see that each part of terrestrial bodies is pressed toward T, not indifferently by the whole matter surrounding it, but only by a quantity of this matter exactly equal to the size of the part; that quantity, being underneath the part, can take its place in the case that the part falls. That is the reason why, among the parts of any single body designated ''homogeneous'' (such as among those of air or water), the lowest are not notably more pressed than the highest, and why a man down below in very deep water does not feel it weigh on his back any more than if he were swimming right on top.[55]

But it may seem to you that the matter of the heaven, in thus causing the stone R to fall toward T and below the air surrounding it, should also cause it to go toward 6 or toward 7 (i.e., toward the occident or toward the orient) faster than this air, so that the stone does not fall in a straight plumb line as heavy bodies do on the real earth. If so, consider first that all the terrestrial parts contained in the circle 5678, in being pressed toward T by the matter of the heaven in the way I have just explained, and having in addition very irregular and diverse shapes, must join together and approach one another and thus compose only one mass, which is borne as a whole by the course of the heaven ABCD. Thus, while the mass turns, those of its parts that are, say, at 6 always remain opposite those that are at 2 and at F, without notably moving aside one way or the other except insofar as winds or other particular causes constrain them to do so.

472   LE MONDE DE RENE' DESCARTES,

Et de plus remarquez que ce petit Ciel A B C D, tourne beaucoup plus vîte que cette Terre ; mais que celles
de ses parties qui sont engagées dans les pores des corps
terrestres, ne peuvent pas tourner notablement plus vîte
que ces corps autour du centre T, encore qu'elles se meuvent beaucoup plus vîte en divers autres sens, selon la disposition de ces pores.

Puis afin que vous sçachiez qu'encore que la matiere
du Ciel fasse approcher la pierre R de ce centre, à cause
qu'elle tend avec plus de force qu'elle à s'en éloigner, elle
ne doit pas tout de mesme la contraindre de reculer vers
l'Occident, bien qu'elle tende aussi avec plus de force
qu'elle à aller vers l'Orient ; Considerez que cette matiere
du Ciel tend à s'éloigner du centre T, parce qu'elle tend
à continuer son mouvement en ligne droite, mais qu'elle
ne tend de l'Occident vers l'Orient, que simplement
parce qu'elle tend à le continuer de mesme vitesse, &
qu'il luy est d'ailleurs indifferent de se trouver vers 6, ou
vers 7.

Or il est évident qu'elle se meut quelque peu plus en
ligne droite, pendant qu'elle fait descendre la pierre R
vers T, qu'elle ne feroit en la laissant vers R ; mais elle ne
pourroit pas se mouvoir si vîte vers l'Orient, si elle la faisoit reculer vers l'Occident, que si elle la laisse en sa
place, ou mesme que si elle la pousse devant soy.

Et toutesfois, afin que vous sçachiez aussi qu'encore
que cette matiere du Ciel ait plus de force à faire descendre cette pierre R vers T, qu'à y faire descendre l'air qui
l'environne, elle ne doit pas tout de mesme en avoir plus
à la pousser devant soy de l'Occident vers l'Orient, ny par
consequent la faire mouvoir plus vîte que l'air en ce sens
là ; Considerez qu'il y a justement autant de cette matiere
du

Note moreover that the little heaven ABCD turns much faster than the earth, but that those of its parts caught in the pores of terrestrial bodies cannot turn notably faster than those bodies about the center T, even though those parts move much faster in diverse other directions, according to the disposition of these pores.

Then you should know that, even though the matter of the heaven makes the stone R move closer to that center (because the matter tends to move away from it with more force than the stone), the matter nevertheless cannot force the stone to back up toward the occident, even though the matter also tends with more force than the stone to go toward the orient. To see this, consider that this matter of the heaven tends to move away from the center T because it tends to continue its motion in a straight line; but it tends to move from the occident toward the orient only because it tends to continue its motion at the same speed and because it is moreover indifferent toward being at 6 or at 7.

Now it is evident that the matter moves a bit more in a straight line while causing the stone R to fall toward T than it does in leaving the stone at R; but it could not move as fast toward the orient if it caused the stone to move back toward the occident as it could if it left the stone in its place or even if it pushed the stone before it.

You should also know, however, that, even though this matter of the heaven has more force to cause this stone R to descend toward T than to cause the air surrounding the stone to descend there, it should nevertheless not have more force to push the stone before it from the occident toward the orient, nor consequently to cause the stone to move faster in that direction than the air. To see this, consider that there is exactly as much of this matter

OU TRAITÉ DE LA LUMIERE. 473

du Ciel qui agit contre elle pour la faire defcendre vers T, & qui y employe toute fa force, qu'il en entre de celle de la Terre en la compofition de fon corps; & que dautant qu'il y en entre beaucoup davantage qu'en vne quantité d'air de parcille eftenduë, elle doit eftre preffée beaucoup plus fort vers T, que n'eft cét air : Mais que pour la faire tourner vers l'Orient, c'eft toute la matiere du Ciel contenuë dans le cercle R, qui agit contre elle, & conjointement contre toutes les parties terreftres de l'air contenu en ce mefme cercle : En forte que n'y en ayant point davantage qui agiffe contre elle que contre cét air, elle ne doit point tourner plus vifte que luy en ce fens là.

Et vous pouvez entendre de cecy, que les raifons dont fe fervent plufieurs Philofophes pour refuter le mouvement de la vraye Terre, n'ont point de force contre celuy de la Terre que je vous décris. Comme lors qu'ils difent que fi la Terre fe mouvoit, les corps pefans ne devroient pas defcendre à plomb vers fon centre, mais plutoft s'en écarter çà & là vers le Ciel ; Et que les canons pointez vers l'Occident, devroient porter beaucoup plus loin qu'eftant pointez vers l'Orient ; Et que l'on devroit toujours fentir en l'air de grands vents, & oüir de grands bruits, & chofes femblables, qui n'ont lieu qu'en cas qu'on fuppofe qu'elle n'eft pas emportée par le cours du Ciel qui l'environne, mais qu'elle eft muë par quelqu'autre force, & en quelqu'autre fens que ce Ciel.

O oo

of the heaven acting on the stone to cause it to fall toward T (and using its full force to that end) as there is matter of the earth in the composition of the stone's body and that, inasmuch as there is much more matter of the earth in the stone than in a quantity of air of equal extent, the stone must be pressed much more strongly toward T than is that air. By contrast, to cause the stone to turn toward the orient, all the matter of the heaven contained in circle R acts on it and conjointly on all the terrestrial parts of the air contained in that same circle. Thus, there being no more acting on the stone than on this air, the stone should not turn faster than the air in that direction.

You can understand from this that the arguments that many philosophers use to refute the motion of the real earth have no force against the motion of the earth I am describing to you. For example, when they say that, if the earth moved, heavy bodies could not descend in a plumb line toward its center, but rather would have to depart from it every which way toward the heaven; and that cannons pointed toward the occident should carry much farther than if pointed toward the orient; and that one should always feel great winds in the air and hear great noises: these and like things do not take place except in the case that one supposes that the earth is not carried by the course of the heaven surrounding it, but that it is moved by some other force and in some other direction than that heaven.[56]

CHAPITRE XII.

Du flux & du reflux de la Mer.

OR aprés vous avoir ainfi expliqué la pefanteur des parties de cette Terre, qui eft caufée par l'action de la matiere du Ciel qui eft en fes pores, il faut maintenant que je vous parle d'vn certain mouvement de toute fa maffe, qui eft caufé par la prefence de la Lune, comme auffi de quelques particularitez qui en dépendent.

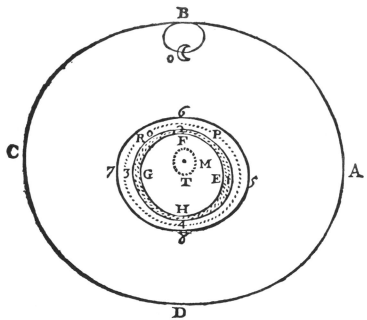

Pour cét effet confiderez la Lune par exemple vers B, où vous pouvez la fuppofer comme immobile, à comparaifon de la viteffe dont fe meut la matiere du Ciel qui eft fous elle ; & confiderez que cette matiere du Ciel ayant moins d'efpace entre o. & 6. pour y paffer, qu'elle n'en

CHAPTER 12

On the Ebb and Flow of the Sea

Now, after having thus explained the weight of the parts of this earth, which is caused by the action of the matter of the heaven in their pores, I must now speak to you about a certain motion of its whole mass, which is caused by the presence of the moon, and also about some particular things that depend on that motion.

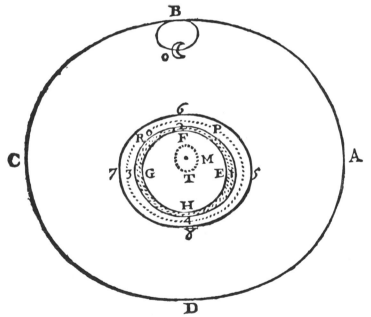

To that end, consider the moon at, say, B (where you can suppose it to be immobile in comparison with the speed at which the matter of the heaven below it moves), and consider that this matter of the heaven, having less space to pass through between 0 and 6 than

OU TRAITE' DE LA LUMIERE. 475

:uroit entre B. & 6, (fi la Lune n'occupoit point l'efpace
qui eft entre o. & B,) & par confequent s'y devant mouvoir vn peu plus vifte , elle ne peut manquer d'avoir la
force de pouffer quelque peu toute la Terre vers D , en
forte que fon centre T s'éloigne , comme vous voyez ,
quelque peu du point M, qui eft le centre du petit Ciel
A B C D : Car il n'y a rien que le feul cours de la matiere
de ce Ciel qui la fouftienne au lieu où elle eft. Et parce
que l'air 5. 6. 7. 8, & l'eau 1. 2. 3. 4. qui environnent cette
Terre, font des corps liquides, il eft évident que la mefme
force qui la preffe en cette façon, les doit auffi faire baif-
fer vers T, non feulement du cofté 6. 2 , mais auffi de fon
oppofé 8. 4 : & en recompenfe les faire hauffer aux endroits 5. 1. & 7.3 ; En forte que la fuperficie de la Terre
E F G H demeurant ronde , à caufe qu'elle eft dure, celle
de l'eau 1. 2. 3. 4. & celle de l'air 5. 6. 7.8, qui font liquides , fe doivent former en ovale.

Puis confiderez que la Terre tournant cependant autour de fon centre , & par ce moyen faifant les jours,
qu'on peut divifer en 24. heures , comme les noftres, celuy de fes coftez F , qui eft maintenant vis à vis de la Lune , & fur lequel pour cette raifon l'eau 2. eft moins haute , fe doit trouver dans fix heures vis-à-vis du Ciel marqué C , où cette eau fera plus haute , & dans 12. heures
vis-à-vis de l'endroit du Ciel marqué D, où l'eau derechef
fera plus baffe. En forte que la Mer qui eft reprefentée
par cette eau 1. 2. 3. 4. doit avoir fon flux & fon reflux autour de cette Terre de fix heures en fix heures , comme
elle a autour de celle que nous habitons.

Confiderez auffi que pendant que cette Terre tourne
d'E par F vers G , c'eft à dire de l'Occident par le Midy,
vers l'Orient, l'enflure de l'eau & de l'air qui demeure

O o o ij

between B and 6 (if the moon does not occupy the space between 0 and B), and consequently having to move a bit faster there, cannot fail to have the force to push the whole earth a little bit toward D, so that its center T moves away (as you can see) a little bit from the point M, which is the center of the small heaven ABCD. For nothing but the course alone of the matter of that heaven maintains the earth in the place where it is. And, because the air 5678 and the water 1234 surrounding this earth are liquid bodies, it is evident that the same force that presses the earth in this way must also make them sink toward T, not only from the side 6, 2 but also from its opposite 8, 4, and in recompense cause them to rise in the places 5, 1 and 7, 3. Thus, the surface EFGH of the earth remaining round (because it is hard), that of the water 1234 and that of the air 5678 (which are liquids) must form an oval.

Then consider that, since the earth is meanwhile turning about its center and by this means making the days that one divides up into 24 hours (like ours), the side F, which is now directly opposite the moon and on which the water is for that reason less high, must in six hours be directly opposite the heaven marked C, in which position this water will be higher; in twelve hours it should be directly opposite the place of the heaven marked D, where again the water will be lower. Thus the sea, which is represented by this water 1234, should have its ebb and flow about this earth once every six hours, just as it has about the earth we inhabit.

Consider also that, while this earth turns from E through F to G (i.e. from the occident through the meridian toward the orient), the flood of the water and the air that remains

141

476   LE MONDE DE RENE' DESCARTES;

vers 1. & 5. & vers 3. & 7. paſſe de ſa partie Orientale vers l'Occidentale, y faiſant vn flux ſans reflux, tout ſemblable à celuy qui ſelon le rapport de nos Pilotes rend la naviga-tion beaucoup plus facile dans nos mers de l'Orient vers l'Occident, que de l'Occident vers l'Orient. Et pour ne rien oublier en cét endroit, adjoutons que la Lune fait en chaque mois le meſme tour que la Terre fait en chaque Jour, & ainſi qu'elle fait avancer peu à peu vers l'Orient les points 1.2. 3. 4, qui marquent les plus hautes & les plus baſſes marées ; en ſorte que ces marées ne changent pas preciſément de ſix heures en ſix heures, mais qu'elles re-tardent d'environ la cinquiéme partie d'vne heure à cha-que fois, ainſi que font auſſi celles de nos mers.

Conſiderez outre cela que le petit Ciel A B C D n'eſt pas exactement rond, mais qu'il s'eſtend avec vn peu plus de liberté vers A & vers C, & s'y meut à proportion plus lentement que vers B, & vers D, où il ne peut pas ſi aiſé-ment rompre le cours de la matiere de l'autre Ciel qui le contient ; En ſorte que la Lune qui demeure toujours comme attachée à ſa ſuperficie exterieure, ſe doit mou-voir vn peu plus viſte, & s'écarter moins de ſa route, & enſuite eſtre cauſe que les flux & les reflux de la Mer ſoient beaucoup plus grands, lors qu'elle eſt vers B, où elle eſt pleine, & vers D, où elle eſt nouvelle, que lors qu'elle eſt vers A, & vers C, où elle n'eſt qu'à demy plei-ne ; qui ſont des particularitez que les Aſtronomes obſer-vent auſſi toutes ſemblables en la vraye Lune, bien qu'ils n'en puiſſent peut-eſtre pas ſi facilement rendre raiſon par les hypotheſes dont ils ſe ſervent.

at 1 and 5 and at 3 and 7 passes from its oriental side toward the occidental, there causing a flow without ebb very much like that which, according to the report of our pilots, makes navigation on our seas much easier going from the orient to the occident than from the occident to the orient.

In order to forget nothing at this point, let us add that the moon each month makes the same circuit as the earth does each day, and thus that it causes to advance little by little toward the orient the points 1, 2, 3, 4 that mark high and low water. Hence, these waters do not change precisely every six hours, but rather lag behind by approximately the fifth part of an hour each time as do those of our seas also.

Consider in addition that the small heaven ABCD is not exactly round, but that it extends a bit more freely at A and at C and there moves proportionately more slowly than at B and at D, where it cannot so easily break the course of the matter of the other heaven containing it. Thus the moon, which always remains as if attached to its exterior surface, must move a bit faster and remove itself less from its path, and consequently be the reason why the ebb and flow of the sea are much greater when the moon is at B (where it is full) and at D (where it is new) than when it is at A or at C (where it is only half full). These are peculiarities also wholly like those that the astronomers observe in the real moon, although they perhaps cannot explain them as easily by the hypotheses they use.

OU TRAITE' DE LA LUMIERE.

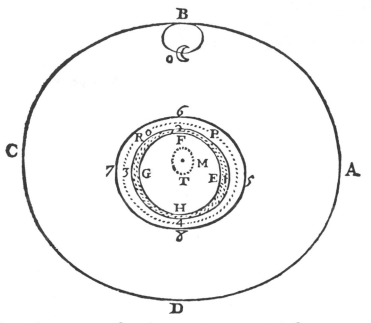

Pour les autres effets de cette Lune, qui different quand elle eft pleine de quand elle eft nouvelle, ils dépendent manifeftement de fa lumiere. Et pour les autres particularitez du flux & du reflux, elles dépendent en partie de la diverfe fituation des coftes de la Mer, & en partie des vents qui regnent aux temps & aux lieux qu'on les obferve. Enfin pour les autres mouvemens generaux, tant de la Terre & de la Lune, que des autres Aftres & des Cieux, où vous les pouvez affez entendre de ce que j'ay dit, ou bien ils ne fervent pas à mon fujet, & ne fe faifant pas en mefme plan que ceux dont j'ay parlé, je ferois trop long à les décrire : Si bien qu'il ne me refte plus icy qu'à expliquer cette action des Cieux & des Aftres que j'ay tantoft dit devoir eftre prife pour leur Lumiere.

O oo iij

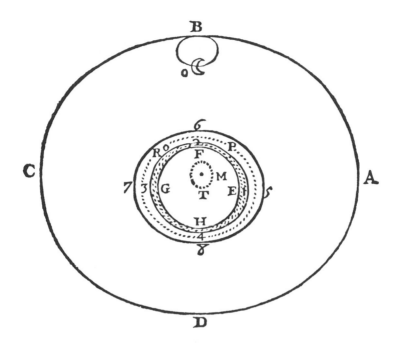

As for the other effects of this moon, which are different when it is full from when it is new, they manifestly depend on its light. And as for the other special properties of the ebb and flow of the sea, they depend in part on the diverse situation of the seacoasts and in part on the winds prevailing at the time and at the place they are observed. Finally, as for the other general motions, both of the earth and moon and of the other stars and heavens, either you can understand them well enough from what I have said, or they do not serve my purpose here; not falling under the same heading as those of which I have spoken, they would take me too long to describe. Thus, there remains for me here only to explain this action of the heavens and the stars that I have just said should be taken to be their light.

CHAPITRE XIII.

De la Lumiere.

J'A y déja dit plusieurs fois, que les corps qui tournent en rond tendent toujours à s'éloigner des centres des cercles qu'ils décrivent ; Mais il faut icy que je détermine plus particulieremét vers quels costez tendent les parties de la matiere dont les Cieux & les Astres sont composez.

Et pour cela il faut sçavoir que lors que je dis qu'vn corps tend vers quelque costé, je ne veux pas pour cela qu'on s'imagine qu'il ait en soy vne pensée ou vne volonté qui l'y porte, mais seulement qu'il est disposé à se mouvoir vers là ; soit que veritablement il s'y meuve, soit plustost que quelqu'autre corps l'en empesche ; & c'est principalement en ce dernier sens que je me sers du mot de tendre, à cause qu'il semble signifier quelque effort, & que tout effort présupose de la resistance. Or dautant qu'il se trouve souvent diverses causes qui agissant ensemble contre vn mesme corps empeschent l'effet l'vne de l'autre, on peut selon diverses considerations dire qu'vn mesme corps tend vers divers costez en mesme temps; Ainsi qu'il a tantost esté dit que les parties de la Terre tendent à s'éloigner de son centre, entant qu'elles sont considerées toutes seules ; & qu'elles tendent au contraire à s'en approcher, entant que l'on considere la force des parties du Ciel qui les y pousse ; & derechef qu'elles tendent à s'en éloigner, si on les considere comme opposées à d'autres parties terrestres qui composent des corps plus massifs qu'elles ne sont.

Ainsi par exemple, la pierre qui tourne dans vne fronde

146

CHAPTER 13

On Light

I have already said several times that bodies that revolve always tend to move away from the centers of the circles they describe. Here, however, I must determine more specifically in what directions the parts of the matter of which the heavens and the stars are composed do tend.[57]

To that end, one must know that, when I say that a body tends in some direction, I do not thereby want anyone to imagine that there is in the body a thought or a desire carrying it there, but only that it is disposed to move there, whether it truly moves or, rather, some other body prevents it from doing so. It is principally in this last sense that I use the word *tend,* because it seems to signify some effort and because every effort presupposes some resistance. Now, inasmuch as there are often diverse causes which, acting together on the same body, impede one another's effect, one can, according to various points of view, say that the same body tends in different directions at the same time. Thus it has just been said that the parts of the earth tend to move away from its center insofar as they are considered all alone, and that they tend on the contrary to move closer to it insofar as one considers the force of the parts of the heaven pushing them there, and again that they tend to move away from it if one considers them as opposed to other terrestrial parts that compose bodies more massive than they.

Thus, for example, the stone turning in a sling

147

suivant le cercle A B, tend vers C, lors qu'elle est au point
A, si on ne considere autre chose que son agitation toute
seule; & elle tend circulairemét d'A vers B, si on considere son mouvement comme reglé & déterminé par la longueur de la corde.qui la retient ; & enfin la mesme pierre
tend vers E, si sans considerer la partie de son agitation
dót l'effet n'est point empesché, on en oppose l'autre partie à la resistáce que luy fait continuellemét cette fronde.

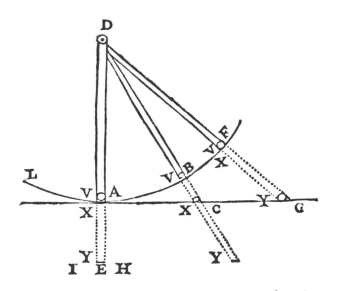

Mais pour entendre distinctement ce dernier point,
imaginez-vous l'inclination qu'a cette pierre à se mouvoir d'A vers C, comme si elle estoit composée de deux
autres, qui fussent, l'vne de tourner suivant le cercle A B,
& l'autre de monter tout droit suivant la ligne V X Y; &
ce en telle proportion , que se trouvant à l'endroit de la
fronde marquée V, lors que la fronde est à l'endroit du
cercle marqué A, elle se deust trouver par aprés à l'endroit marqué X, lors que la fronde seroit vers B, & à l'en-

along circle AB tends toward C when it is at point A, if one considers nothing other than its agitation all alone; and it tends circularly from A to B, if one considers its motion as regulated and determined by the length of the cord retaining it; and finally the same stone tends toward E if, without considering the part of its agitation of which the effect is not impeded, one opposes the other part of it to the resistance that this sling continually makes to it.

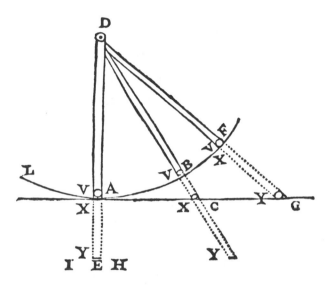

But, to understand this last point distinctly, imagine the inclination this stone has to move from A toward C as if it were composed of two other inclinations, of which one were to turn along the circle AB and the other to rise straight up along the line VXY; and imagine the inclinations were in such a proportion that, if the stone were at the place of the sling marked V when the sling was at the place of the circle marked A, it should thereafter be at the place marked X when the sling is at B, and at the place

480   LE MONDE DE RENE' DESCARTES,

droit marqué Y, lors qu'elle feroit vers F, & ainfi demeurer toujours en la ligne droite A C G. Puis fçachant que
l'vne des parties de fon inclination, à fçavoir celle qui la
porte fuivant le cercle A B, n'eft nullement empefchée
par cette fronde, vous verrez bien qu'elle ne trouve de
refiftance que pour l'autre partie, à fçavoir pour celle qui
la feroit mouvoir fuivant la ligne D V X Y, fi elle n'eftoit
point empefchée; & par confequent qu'elle ne tend, c'eft
à dire qu'elle ne fait effort que pour s'éloigner directement du centre D. Et remarquez que felon cette confi-
deration eftant au point A elle tend fi veritablement vers
E, qu'elle n'eft point du tout plus difpofée à fe mouvoir
vers H que vers I, bien qu'on pourroit aifément fe perfua-
der le contraire, fi on manquoit à confiderer la difference qui eft entre le mouvement qu'elle a déja, & l'inclination à fe mouvoir qui luy refte.

Or vous devez penfer de chacune des parties du fecond Element qui compofent les Cieux, tout le mefme
que de cette pierre; c'eft à fçavoir que celles qui font par
exemple vers E, ne tendent de leur propre inclination
que vers P; mais que la refiftance des autres parties du
Ciel qui font au deffus d'elles, les fait tendre, c'eft à dire
les difpofe à fe mouvoir fuivát le cercle E R. Et derechef,
que cette refiftance, oppofée à l'inclination qu'elles ont
de continuer leur mouvement en ligne droite, les fait
tendre, c'eft à dire, eft caufe qu'elles font effort pour fe
mouvoir vers M; Et ainfi, jugeant de toutes les autres en
mefme forte, vous voyez en quel fens on peut dire qu'elles
tendent vers les lieux qui font directement oppofez au
centre du Ciel qu'elles compofent.

Mais ce qu'il y a encore en elles à confiderer de plus
qu'en vne pierre qui tourne dans vne fronde, c'eft qu'elles
                                                        font

marked Y when the sling is at F, and thus should always remain in the straight line ACG. Then, knowing that one of the parts of its inclination (to wit, that which carries it along the circle AB) is in no way impeded by the sling, you will easily see that the stone meets resistance only for the other part (to wit, for that which would cause it to move along the line DVXY if it were not impeded). Consequently, it tends (that is, it makes an effort) only to move directly away from the center D. And note that, from this point of view, when the stone is at point A, it tends so truly toward E that it is not at all more disposed to move toward H than toward I, although one could easily persuade oneself of the contrary if one failed to consider the differences between the motion it already has and the inclination to move that remains with it.

Now, you should think of each of the parts of the second element that compose the heavens in the same way that you think of this stone, to wit, that those which are, say, at E tend of their own inclination only toward P, but that the resistance of the other parts of the heaven which are above them cause them to tend (i.e., dispose them to move) along the circle ER. In turn, this resistance, opposed to the inclination they have to continue their motion in a straight line, causes them to tend (i.e., is the reason why they make an effort to move) toward M. And thus, judging all the others in the same way, you see in what sense one can say that they tend toward the places that are directly opposite the center of the heaven they compose.

But there is still more to consider in the parts of the heaven than in a stone turning in a sling: the parts

OU TRAITE' DE LA LUMIERE. 481

font continuellement pouſſées, tant par toutes celles de
leurs ſemblables qui ſont entre-elles & l'Aſtre qui occupe
le centre de leur Ciel, que meſme par la matiere de cét
Aſtre, & qu'elles ne le ſont aucunement par les autres. Par
exemple, que celles qui ſont vers E, ne ſont point pouſſées

par celles qui ſont
vers M, ou vers T,
ou vers R , ou vers
K, ou vers H, mais
ſeulemét par tou-
tes celles qui ſont
entre les deux li-
gnes A F, D G, &
enſemble par la
matiere du Soleil;
Ce qui eſt cauſe
qu'elles tendent
non ſeulemét vers
M , mais auſſi vers
L, & vers N, & ge-
neralement vers
tous les points où
peuvent parvenir
les rayons, ou li-
gnes droites , qui

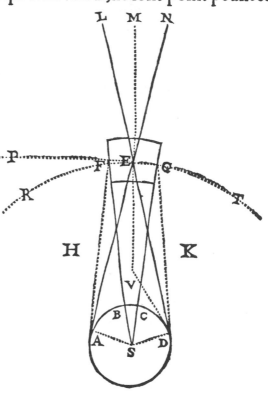

venant de quelque partie du Soleil paſſent par le lieu où
elles ſont.

Mais afin que l'explication de tout cecy ſoit plus facile, je deſire que vous conſideriez les parties du ſecond
Element toutes ſeules, & comme ſi tous les eſpaces qui
ſont occupez par la matiere du premier, tant celuy où eſt
le Soleil, que les autres, eſtoient vuides. Meſmes, à cauſe

Ppp

are continually pushed, both by all those like them between them and the star that occupies the center of their heaven and by the matter of that star; and they are not pushed at all by the others. For example, those at E are not pushed by those at M, at T, or at R, or at K, or at H, but only by all those that are between the two lines AF and DG together with the matter of the sun. That is why they tend, not only toward M, but also toward L and toward N, and generally toward all the points which the rays or straight lines, coming from

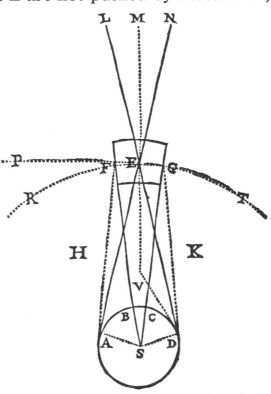

some part of the sun and passing through the place where the parts are, can reach. [58]

But, in order that the explanation of all this be easier, I want you to consider the parts of the second element all alone, as if all the spaces occupied by the matter of the first element, both [the space] where the sun is and the other [spaces], were void. Indeed, because

482   LE MONDE DE RENE' DESCARTES;

qu'il n'y a point de meilleur moyen pour fçavoir ſi vn corps eſt pouſſé par quelques autres, que de voir ſi ces au-tres s'avanceroient actuellement vers le lieu où il eſt pour le remplir en cas qu'il fuſt vuide, je deſire auſſi que vous imaginiez que les parties du ſecond Element qui ſont vers E en ſoient oſtées ; Et cela poſé, que vous regardiez en premier lieu, qu'aucunes de celles qui ſont au deſſus du cercle T E R , comme vers M, ne ſont point diſpoſées à remplir leur place , dautant qu'elles tendent tout au contraire à s'en éloigner ; Puis auſſi que celles qui ſont en ce cercle , à ſçavoir vers T , n'y ſont point non plus diſpo-ſées : car encore bien qu'elles ſe meuvent veritablement de T vers G , ſuivant le cours de tout le Ciel , toutesfois pource que celles qui ſont vers F, ſe meuvent auſſi avec pareille viteſſe vers R, l'eſpace E, qu'il faut imaginer mo-bile comme elles , ne laiſſeroit pas de demeurer vuide en-tre G & F , s'il n'en venoit d'autres d'ailleurs pour le remplir. Et en troiſiéme lieu, que celles qui ſont au deſ-ſous de ce cercle , mais qui ne ſont pas compriſes entre les lignes A F, D G, comme celles qui ſont vers H, & vers K, ne tendent auſſi aucunement à s'avancer vers cét eſpace E pour le remplir, encore que l'inclination qu'elles ont à s'éloigner du point S les y diſpoſe en quelque ſorte;ainſi que la peſanteur d'vne pierre la diſpoſe , non ſeulement à deſcendre tout droit en l'air libre , mais auſſi à rouler de travers ſur le penchant d'vne montagne, en cas qu'elle ne puiſſe deſcendre d'autre façon.

Or la raiſon qui les empeſche de tendre vers cet eſpa-ce,eſt que tous les mouvemens ſe continuënt autant qu'il eſt poſſible en ligne droite ; & par conſequent que lors que la Nature a pluſieurs voyes pour parvenir à vn meſme effect,elle ſuit toujours infailliblement la plus courte. Car

154

there is no better means of knowing if a body is being pushed by some others than to see if these others actually advance toward the place where it is in order to fill the place in the case that it is void,[59] I also want you to imagine that the parts of the second element at E are removed from it and, having posited that, to note in the first place that none of those above the circle TER, say at M, are disposed to fill their place, inasmuch as each tends on the contrary to move away from it. Then note in the second place also that those in that circle, to wit, at T, are no more disposed to do so; for, even though they really move from T toward G along the course of the whole heaven, nevertheless, because those at F also move with the same speed toward R, the space E (which one must imagine to be mobile like them) will not fail to remain void between G and F, provided others do not come from elsewhere to fill it. In the third place, those that are below that circle but that are not contained between the lines AF and DG (such as those at H and at K) also do not tend in any way to advance toward that space E to fill it, even though the inclination they have to move away from point S disposes them in some way to do so (as the weight of a stone disposes it, not only to descend along a straight line in the free air, but also to roll sideways on the slope of a mountain in the case that it cannot descend any other way).

Now the reason that impedes them from tending toward that space is that all motions continue, so far as is possible, in a straight line, and consequently, when nature has many ways of arriving at the same effect, she most certainly always follows the shortest.[60] For,

fi les parties du fecond Element qui font par exemple vers K, s'avançoient vers E, toutes celles qui font plus proches qu'elles du Soleil, s'avanceroient auffi au mefme inftant vers le lieu qu'elles quiteroient, & ainfi l'effet de leur mouvement ne feroit autre, finon que l'efpace E fe rempliroit, & qu'il y en auroit vn autre d'égale grandeur en la circonference A B C D, qui deviendroit vuide en mefme temps. Mais il eft manifefte que ce mefme effet peut fuivre beaucoup mieux, fi celles qui font entre les lignes A F, D G, s'avancent tout droit vers E ; & par confequent que lors qu'il n'y a rien qui en empefche cellescy, les autres n'y tendent point du tout: Non plus qu'vne

pierre ne tend jamais à defcendre obliquement vers le centre de la terre, lors qu'elle y peut defcendre en ligne droite.

Enfin confiderez que toutes les parties du fecód Element qui font entre les lignes A F, D G, doivent s'avancer enfemble vers cét efpace E, pour le remplir au mefme inftant qu'il eft vuide. Car encore qu'il n'y ait que l'inclina-

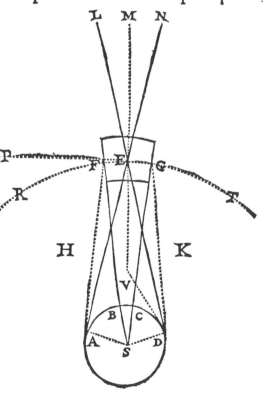

if the parts of the second element which are, say, at K advanced toward E, all those closer to the sun than they would also advance at the same instant toward the place they were leaving; hence, the effect of their motion would be only that space E would be filled and there would be another of equal size in the circumference ABCD that would become void at the same time. But it is manifest that that same effect can follow much better if those parts that are between the lines AF and DG advance straightaway toward E; and consequently, when there is nothing to impede the latter from doing so, the others do not tend at all toward E, no

more than a stone ever tends to fall obliquely toward the center of the earth when it can fall in a straight line.

Finally, consider that all the parts of the second element that are between the lines AF and DG must advance together toward that space E in order to fill it at the same instant it is void. For, even though it is only the inclina-

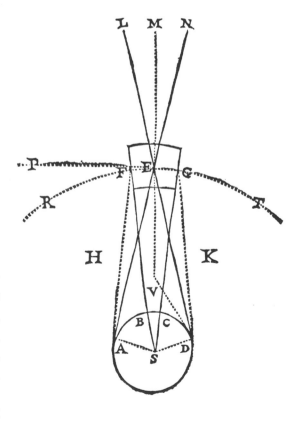

484 LE MONDE DE RENE' DESCARTES,

tion qu'elles ont à s'éloigner du point S qui les y porte,
& que cette inclination fasse que celles qui sont entre les
lignes B F, C G, tendent plus directement vers là, que celles qui restent entre les lignes A F, B F, & D G, C G, vous
verrez neantmoins que ces dernieres ne laissent pas
d'estre aussi disposées que les autres à y aller, si vous pre-
nez garde à l'effet qui doit suivre de leur mouvement, qui
n'est autre sinon, comme j'ay dit tout maintenant, que
l'espace E se remplisse, & qu'il y en ait vn autre d'égale
grandeur en la circonference A B C D, qui devienne vuide en mesme temps. Car pour le changement de situation
qui leur arrive dans les autres lieux qu'elles remplissoient
auparavant, & qui en demeurent aprés encore pleins, il
n'est aucunement considerable, dautant qu'elles doivent
estre supposées si égales & si pareilles en tout les vnes aux
autres, qu'il n'importe de quelles parties chacun de ces
lieux soit remply. Remarquez neantmoins qu'on ne doit
pas conclure de cecy qu'elles soient toutes égales, mais
seulement que les mouvemens dont leur inégalité peut
estre cause, n'appartiennent point à l'action dont nous
parlons.

Or il n'y a point de plus court moyen pour faire qu'vne
partie de l'espace E se remplissant, celuy par exemple qui
est vers D devienne vuide, que si toutes les parties de la
matiere qui se trouvent en la ligne droite D G, ou D E,
s'avancent ensemble vers E : Car s'il n'y avoit que celles
qui sont entre les lignes B F, C G, qui s'avançassent les
premieres vers cét espace E, elles en laisseroient vn autre
au dessous d'elles vers V, dans lequel devroient venir celles qui sont vers D ; en sorte que le mesme effet qui peut
estre produit par le mouvement de la matiere qui est en la
ligne droite D G, ou D E, le seroit par le mouvement de

tion they have to move away from point S that carries them toward E, and this inclination causes those between the lines BF and CG to tend more directly toward E than those that remain between the lines AF and BF and DG and CG, you will nevertheless see that these latter parts do not fail to be as disposed as the others to go there, if you take note of the effect that should follow from their motion. That effect is none other than, as I have just now said, that space E is filled and that there is another of equal size in the circumference ABCD that becomes void at the same time. For, as regards the change of position they undergo in the other places that they were previously filling and that still remain full of them afterwards, it is not at all considerable, inasmuch as they must be supposed to be so equal and so completely like one another that it does not matter by which parts each of these places is filled. Note, nevertheless, that one should not conclude from this that they are all equal, but merely that the motions of which their inequality can be the cause are not pertinent to the action of which we are speaking.

Now there is no shorter way of causing one part E of space to be filled while another, for example at D, becomes void than if all the parts of matter on the straight line DG, or DE, advance together toward E. For, if it were only those between the lines BF and CG that were to advance first toward that space E, they would leave another space below them at V, into which those which are at D had to come. Thus, the same effect that can be produced by the motion of the matter in the straight line DG, or DE, would be made by the motion of

OU TRAITE' DE LA LUMIERE.
celle qui eft en la ligne courbe D V E ; ce qui eft contraire aux loix de la Nature.

Mais fi vous trouvez icy quelque difficulté à comprendre comment les parties du fecond Element qui font entre les lignes A F, D G, peuvent s'avancer toutes enfemble vers E , fur ce qu'y ayant plus de diftance entre A &
D , qu'entre F & G, l'efpace où elles doivent entrer pour
s'avancer ainfi eft plus eftroit que celuy d'où elles doivent
fortir ; Confiderez que l'action par laquelle elles tendent
à s'éloigner du centre de leur Ciel , ne les oblige point à
toucher celles de leurs voifines qui font à pareille diftance qu'elles de ce centre, mais feulement à toucher celles
qui en font d'vn degré plus éloignées. Ainfi que la pefanteur des petites boules 1. 2. 3. 4. 5. n'oblige point celles

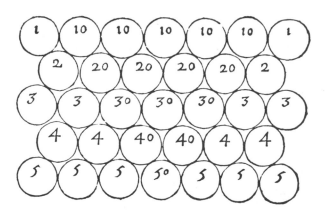

qui font marquées d'vn mefme chiffre à s'entretoucher,
mais feulement oblige celles qui font marquées 1. ou 10.
à s'appuyer fur celles qui font marquées 2. ou 20. & celles-
cy fur celles qui font marquées 3. ou 30. & ainfi de fuite :
En forte que ces petites boules peuvent bien n'eftre pas
feulement arrangées comme vous les voyez en cette
feptiéme figure , mais auffi comme elles font en la huict

Ppp iij

that in the curved line DVE, and that is contrary to the laws of motion.

But you may find here some difficulty in understanding how the parts of the second element between the lines AF and DG can advance all together toward E, considering that, since the distance between A and D is greater than that between F and G, the space they must enter to advance thus is narrower than that they must leave. If so, consider that the action by which they tend to move away from the center of their heaven does not force them to touch those of their neighbors that are at the same distance as they from that center, but only to touch those that are to a degree more distant from it.[61] Thus the weight of the small balls 1, 2, 3, 4, 5 does not force those marked by the

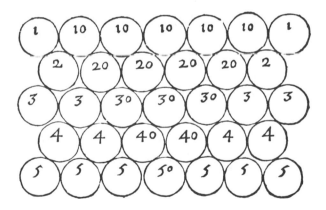

same numerals to touch one another, but only forces those marked 1 or 10 to rest on those marked 2 or 20, and the latter to rest on those marked 3 or 30, and so on. Thus, these small balls can well be arranged not only as you see them in Figure 7, but also as they are in Figures 8

486   LE MONDE DE RENE' DESCARTES;
& neufiéme, & en mille autres diverſes façons.

Puis conſiderez que ces parties du ſecond Element ſe

8. F.

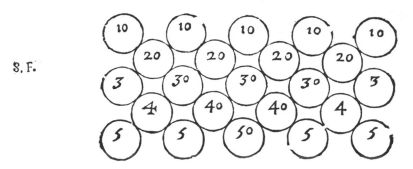

remuant ſeparément les vnes des autres, ainſi qu'il a eſté
dit cy-deſſus qu'elles doivent faire, ne peuvent jamais
eſtre arrangées comme les boules de la ſeptiéme figure;
& toutesfois qu'il n'y a que cette ſeule façon en laquelle
la difficulté propoſée puiſſe avoir quelque lieu: Car on ne
ſçauroit ſuppoſer ſi peu d'intervalle entre celles de ſes
parties qui ſont à pareille diſtance du centre de leur Ciel,
que cela ne ſuffiſe pour concevoir que l'inclination qu'elles ont à s'éloigner de ce centre, doit faire avancer celles
qui ſont entre les lignes A F, D G, toutes enſemble vers
l'eſpace E, lors qu'il eſt vuide; Ainſi que vous voyez en la
neufiéme figure, rapportée à la dixiéme, que la peſanteur

9. F.

and 9 and in myriad other diverse ways.

Then consider that those parts of the second

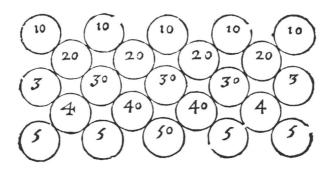

element, moving separately from one another (as has been said above that they must do), cannot ever be arranged like the balls in Figure 7. Nonetheless, it is only in that way [of arrangement] that the proposed difficulty can occur. For one could not suppose between those of its parts that are the same distance from the center of their heaven an interval so small that it would not suffice to conceive that the inclination they have to move away from that center must cause those between the lines AF and DG to advance all together toward the space E when it is void. Thus you see in Figure 9, compared with Figure 10, that the weight

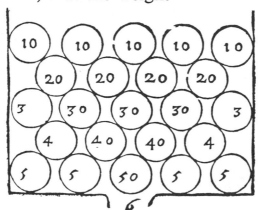

OU TRAITE' DE LA LUMIERE.

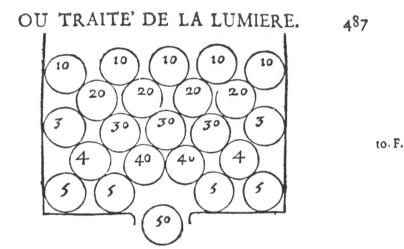

10. F.

des petites boules 40. 30. &c. les doit faire defcendre toutes enfemble vers l'efpace qu'occupe celle qui eft marquée 50, fi-toft que celle-cy en peut fortir.

Et l'on peut icy clairement appercevoir, comment celles de ces boules qui font marquées d'vn mefme chiffre,
fe rangent en vn efpace plus eftroit que n'eft celuy d'où
elles fortent, à fçavoir en s'approchant l'vne de l'autre.
On peut auffi appercevoir que les deux boules marquées
40. doivent defcendre vn peu plus vîte, & s'approcher à
proportion vn peu plus l'vne de l'autre, que les trois marquées 30. & ces trois, que les quatre marquées 20. & ainfi
des autres.

En fuite dequoy vous me direz peut-eftre, que comme
il paroift en la dixiéme figure, que les deux boules 40. 40.
aprés eftre tant foit peu defcenduës viennent à s'entretoucher (ce qui eft caufe qu'elles s'arreftent fans pouvoir
defcendre plus bas) tout de mefme les parties du fecond
Element qui doivent s'avancer vers E s'arrefteront, avant
que d'avoir achevé de remplir tout l'efpace que nous y
avons fuppofé.

Mais je répons à cela, qu'elles ne peuvent fi peu s'avan-

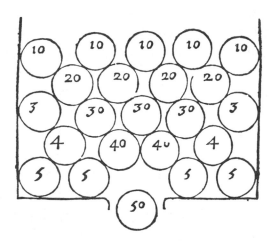

of the small balls 40, 30, etc. must cause them to fall all together toward the space occupied by that marked 50 as soon as the latter can leave it.

And one can clearly perceive here how those of the balls that are marked with the same numeral are arranged in a space narrower than that which they leave, that is, by moving closer to one another. One can also perceive that the two balls marked 40 must fall a bit faster, and move proportionately a bit closer to one another, than the three marked 30, and these three must move faster and closer to one another than the four marked 20, and so on.

Hereupon you will perhaps say to me that, as it appears in Figure 10, the two balls 40, 40, after having fallen the slightest bit, come to touch one another (which is why they stop without being able to fall lower). In the very same way, the parts of the second element that should advance toward E will stop before having succeeded in filling the whole space we have supposed there.

But I respond thereto that they cannot advance

cer vers là, que ce ne ſoit aſſez pour prouver parfaitement
ce que j'ay dit ; c'eſt à ſçavoir que tout l'eſpace qui y eſt,
eſtant déja plein de quelque corps, quel qu'il puiſſe eſtre,
elles preſſent continuellement ce corps , & font effort
contre luy comme pour le chaſſer hors de ſa place.

Puis outre cela je répons que leurs autres mouvemés qui
continuent en elles pendant qu'elles s'avancent ainſi vers
E , ne leur permettant pas de demeurer vn ſeul moment
arrangées en meſme ſorte , les empeſchent de s'entretoucher , ou bien font qu'aprés s'eſtre touchées elles ſe ſeparent incontinent derechef, & ainſi ne laiſſent pas pour
cela de s'avancer ſans interruption vers l'eſpace E , juſques à ce qu'il ſoit tout remply. De ſorte qu'on ne peut
conclure de cecy autre choſe, ſinon que la force dont elles tendent vers E , eſt peut-eſtre comme tremblante , &
ſe redouble & ſe relâche à diverſes petites ſecouſſes, ſelon
qu'elles changent de ſituation , ce qui ſemble eſtre vne
proprieté fort convenable à la lumiere.

Or ſi vous avez entendu tout cecy ſuffiſamment, en
ſuppoſant les eſpaces E , & S , & tous les petits angles qui
ſont entre les parties du Ciel, comme vuides , vous l'en-
tendrez encore mieux, en les ſuppoſant eſtre remplis de
la matiere du premier Element. Car les parties de ce premier Element qui ſe trouvent en l'eſpace E , ne peuvent
empeſcher que celles du ſecond, qui ſont entre les lignes
A F, D G, ne s'avancent pour le remplir, tout de meſme
que s'il eſtoit vuide ; à cauſe qu'eſtant extremement ſubtiles , & extremement agitées , elles ſont toujours auſſi
preſtes à ſortir des lieux où elles ſe trouvent, que puiſſe
eſtre aucun autre corps à y entrer. Et pour cette meſme
raiſon , celles qui occupent les petits angles qui ſont entre les parties du Ciel, cedent leur place ſans reſiſtance à
celles

toward E the slightest bit without it being enough to prove perfectly what I have said, to wit, that since the whole space that is there is already filled by some body (whatever it might be), the parts press continually on that body and make an effort against it as if to chase it out of its place.[62]

Then, beyond that, I reply that, since their other motions, which continue in them while they are thus advancing toward E, do not permit them for a moment to remain arranged in the same way, those motions impede them from touching one another, or rather cause them, upon touching, immediately to separate again and thus not to cease for that reason to advance uninterruptedly toward the space E, until it is completely filled. Thus one cannot conclude from this anything other than that the force with which they tend toward E is perhaps vibratory in nature and redoubles and relaxes in diverse small tremors as the parts change position. This seems to be a property quite suited to light.

Now, if you have understood all this sufficiently by supposing the spaces E and S and all the small angles between the parts of the heaven to be empty, you will understand it still better by supposing them filled with the matter of the first element. For the parts of that first element in the space E cannot impede those of the second between the lines AF and DG from advancing to fill it in just the same way as they would if it were void, because, being extremely subtle and extremely agitated, they are always as ready to leave the places where they are as any other body might be to enter them. And for this same reason, the parts of the first element that occupy the small angles between the parts of the heaven cede their place without resistance to

OU TRAITE' DE LA LUMIERE. 489

celles qui viennent de cét espace E, & qui se vont rendre vers le point S. Je dis plutost vers S, que vers aucun autre lieu, à cause que les autres corps, qui estant plus vnis & plus gros ont plus de force, tendent tous à s'en éloigner.

Mesmes il faut remarquer qu'elles passent d'E vers S entre les parties du second Element qui vont d'S vers E, sans s'empescher aucunement les vnes les autres. Ainsi que l'air qui est enfermé dans l'horloge X Y Z, monte de Z vers X au travers du sable Y, qui ne laisse pas pour cela de descendre cependant vers Z.

Enfin les parties de ce premier Element qui se trouvent en l'espace A B C D, où elles composent le corps du Soleil, y tournât en rond fort promptemét autour du point S, tendent à s'en éloigner de tous costez en ligne droite, suivant ce que je viens d'expliquer; & par ce moyé toutes celles qui sont en la ligne S D, poussent ensemble la

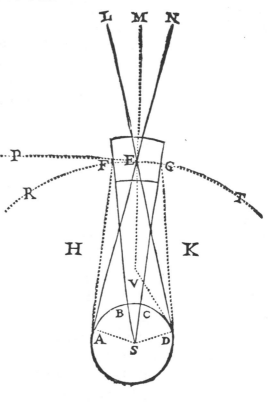

those coming from that space E and tending to go toward the point S. I say toward S rather than toward any other place because the other bodies which, being more united and larger, have more force all tend to move away from it.

Indeed, one should note that they pass from E toward S among the parts of the second element that go from S toward E, without the ones in any way impeding the others. Thus, the air enclosed in the sand clock XYZ rises from Z toward X through the sand Y, which does not for that reason cease to fall in the meantime toward Z.

Finally, the parts of that first element that are in the space ABCD, where they compose the body of the sun and there turn very rapidly in a circle about point S, tend to move away from it in all directions in a straight line, in accordance with what I have just set out. By this means, all those in line SD together push the

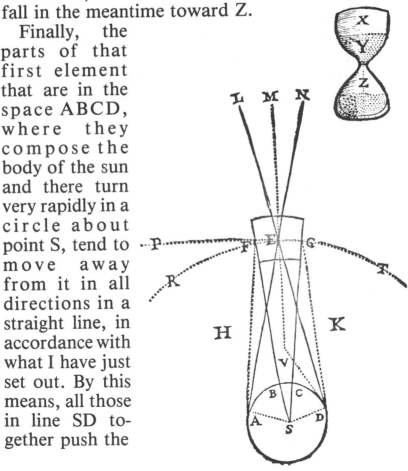

490   LE MONDE DE RENE' DESCARTES,
partie du fecond Element qui eft au point D ; & toutes
celles qui font en la ligne S A , pouffent celle qui eft au
point A , & ainfi des autres ; En telle forte que cela feul
fuffiroit pour faire que toutes celles de ces parties du fecond Element qui font entre les lignes A F, D G, s'avan-
çaffent vers l'efpace E, encore qu'elles n'y euffent aucune
inclination d'elles-mefmes.

Au refte , puis qu'elles doivent ainfi s'avancer vers cét
efpace E, lors qu'il n'eft occupé que par la matiere du
premier Element , il eft certain qu'elles tendent auffi à y
aller , encore mefme qu'il foit remply de quelqu'autre
corps ; & par confequent qu'elles pouffent , & font effort
contre ce corps , comme pour le chaffer hors de fa place.
En forte que fi c'eftoit l'œil d'vn homme qui fuft au point
E, il feroit pouffé actuellement , tant par le Soleil , que
par toute la matiere du Ciel qui eft entre les lignes
A F, D G.

Or il faut fçavoir que les hommes de ce nouveau Monde feront de telle nature , que lors que leurs yeux feront
pouffez en cette façon, ils en auront vn fentiment tout
femblable à celuy que nous avons de la Lumiere, ainfi
que je diray cy-aprés plus amplement.

CHAPITRE XIV.

Des Proprietez de la Lumiere.

MAIS je me veux arrefter encore vn peu en cét endroit à expliquer les Proprietez de l'action dont
leurs yeux peuvent ainfi eftre pouffez. Car elles fe rap-
portent toutes fi parfaitement à celles que nous remarquons en la Lumiere, que lors que vous les aurez confi-

part of the second element that is at point D, and all those in line SA push that which is at point A, and so on. And they do so in such a way that this alone suffices to cause all those parts of the second element between the lines AF and DG to advance toward the space E, even though they might have no inclination themselves to do so.

Moreover since they must thus advance toward that space E when it is occupied only by the matter of the first element, it is certain that they also tend to go there even though it is filled by some other body and, consequently, that they push and make an effort against that body as if to drive it out of its place. Thus, if it were the eye of a man that was at the point E, it would actually be pushed, both by the sun and by all the matter of the heaven between the lines AF and DG.

Now one must know that the men of this new world will be of such a nature that, when their eyes are pushed in this manner, they will have from it a sensation very much like that which we have of light, as I will say more fully below.

CHAPTER 14

On the Properties of Light

But I want to stop a while at this point to set out the properties of the action by which their eyes can be thus pushed. For they all agree so perfectly with those that we note in light that, when you have consid-

OU TRAITE' DE LA LUMIERE.

derées, je m'affure que vous avoüerez comme moy, qu'il n'eft pas befoin d'imaginer dans les Aftres ny dans les Cieux d'autre qualité que cette action, qui s'appelle du nom de Lumiere.

Les principales proprietez de la Lumiere font 1. qu'el-le s'eftend en rond de tous coftez autour des corps qu'on nomme Lumineux. 2. Et à toute forte de diftance. 3. Et en vn inftant. 4. Et pour l'ordinaire en lignes droites, qui doivent eftre prifes pour les rayons de la Lumiere. 5. Et que plufieurs de ces rayons venant de divers points, peu-vent s'affembler en vn mefme point. 6. Où venant d'vn mefme point, peuvent s'aller rendre en divers points. 7. Où venant de divers points, & allant vers divers points, peuvent paffer par vn mefme point, fans s'empefcher les vns les autres. 8. Et qu'ils peuvent auffi quelquefois s'em-pefcher les vns les autres, à fçavoir quand leur force eft fort inégale, & que celle des vns eft beaucoup plus gran-de que celle des autres. 9. Et enfin, qu'ils peuvent eftre détournez par reflexion. 10. ou par refraction. 11. Et que leur force peut eftre augmentée, 12. ou diminuée, par les diverfes difpofitions ou qualitez de la Matiere qui les re-çoit. Voila les principales qualitez qu'on obferve en la Lumiere, qui conviennent toutes à cette action, ainfi que vous allez voir.

1. Que cette action fe doive eftendre de tous coftez au-tour des corps Lumineux, la raifon en eft évidente, à cau-fe que c'eft du mouvemant circulaire de leurs parties qu'elle procede.

2. Il eft évident auffi qu'elle peut s'eftendre à toute forte de diftance : Car par exemple, fuppofant que les parties du Ciel qui fe trouvent entre A F, & D G, font déja d'elles-mefmes difpofées à s'avancer vers E, comme

Voyez la figure precedente.

Qqq ij

ered them, I am sure you will admit, as do I, that there is no need to imagine in the stars or in the heavens any other quality but this action that is called by the name of "light."

The principal properties of light are: (1) that it extends in all directions about bodies one calls "luminous," (2) to any distance, (3) and in an instant, (4) and ordinarily in straight lines, which must be taken to be the rays of light; (5) and that several of these rays coming from diverse points can come together at the same point, (6) or, coming from the same point, can go out toward different points, (7) or, coming from diverse points and going toward diverse points, can pass through the same point without impeding one another; (8) and that they can also sometimes impede one another, to wit, when their force is very unequal and that of some of the rays is much greater than that of the others; (9) and, finally, that they can be diverted by reflection, (10) or by refraction, (11) and that their force can be increased, (12) or diminished, by the diverse dispositions or qualities of the matter that receives them. These are the principal qualities that one observes in light and all agree with this action, as you are about to see.

1. The reason is evident why this action should extend in all directions around luminous bodies, because it proceeds from the circular motion of their parts.

2. It is also evident that it can extend to any distance. For example, supposing that the parts of the heaven between AF and DG are already themselves disposed to advance toward E, as

492   LE MONDE DE RENE' DESCARTES;

nous avons dit qu'elles font, on ne peut pas douter non plus que la force dont le Soleil pouſſe celles qui font vers A B C D, ne ſe doive auſſi eſtendre juſques à E, encore meſme qu'il y euſt plus de diſtance des vnes aux autres, qu'il n'y en a depuis les plus hautes Etoiles du Firmament juſques à nous.

3. Et ſçachant que les parties du ſecond Element qui font entre A F, & D G, ſe touchent & preſſent toutes l'vne l'autre autant qu'il eſt poſſible, on ne peut pas auſſi douter que l'action, dont les premieres font pouſſées, ne doive paſſer en vn inſtant juſques aux dernieres; Tout de meſme que celle dont on pouſſe l'vn des bouts d'vn bâton, paſſe juſques à l'autre bout au meſme inſtant; ou plutoſt, afin que vous ne faſſiez point de difficulté ſur ce que ces parties ne font point attachées l'vne à l'autre ainſi que le font celles d'vn bâton, tout de meſme qu'en la neufiéme figure la petite boule marquée 50 deſcendant vers 6, les autres marquées 10. deſcendent auſſi vers là au meſme inſtant.

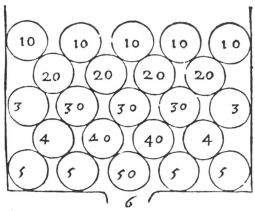

4. Quant à ce qui eſt des lignes ſuivant leſquelles ſe communique cette action, & qui font proprement les rayons de la Lumiere, il faut remarquer qu'elles different

we have said they are, one can no longer doubt that the force with which the sun pushes those at ABCD should also extend out to E, even though there is a greater distance from the one to the other than there is from the highest stars of the firmament down to us.

3. And knowing that the parts of the second element between AF and DG all touch and press one another as much as possible, one also cannot doubt that the action by which the first ones are pushed must pass in an instant out to the last, in just the same way that the force with which one pushes one end of a stick passes to the other end in the same instant; or rather (so you make no difficulty on the basis that the parts of the heaven are not attached to one another as are those of a stick) in just the same way that, as the small ball marked 50 falls toward 6, the others marked 10 also fall toward 6 at the same instant.

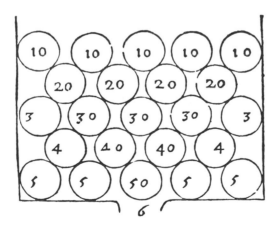

4. Regarding the lines along with this action is communicated and which are properly the rays of light, one must note that they differ

OU TRAITE' DE LA LUMIERE. 493

des parties du fecond Element par l'entremife defquelles
cette mefme action fe communique; & qu'elles ne font
rien de materiel dans le milieu par où elles paffent, mais
qu'elles defignent feulement en quel fens, & fuivant
quelle détermination le corps Lumineux agit contre celuy qu'il illumine; & ainfi qu'on ne doit pas laiffer de les
concevoir exactement droites, encore que les parties du
fecond Element qui fervent à tranfmettre cette action,
ou la Lumiere, ne puiffent prefque jamais eftre fi directement pofées l'vne fur l'autre, qu'elles compofent des lignes toutes droites. Tout de mefme que
vous pouvez aifément concevoir que la
main A pouffe le corps E fuivant la ligne
droite A E, encore qu'elle ne le pouffe
que par l'entremife du bâton B C D, qui
eft tortu. Et tout de mefme auffi que
la boule marquée 1, pouffe celle qui eft
marquée 7, par l'entremife des deux
marquées 5.5. auffi directement que par
l'entremife des autres 2. 3 4. 6.

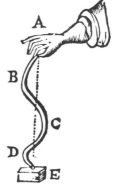

5. 6 Vous pouvez auffi aifément concevoir comment plufieurs de ces rayons venant de divers points,
s'affemblent en vn mefme point, où venant
d'vn mefme point, fe vont rendre en divers
points, fans s'empefcher, ny dépendre les
vns des autres. Comme vous voyez en la fixiéme figure qu'il en vient plufieurs des points
A B C D, qui s'affemblent au point E, & qu'il en
vient plufieurs du feul point D, qui s'eftendent
l'vn vers E, l'autre vers K, & ainfi vers vne infinité d'autres lieux; Tout de mefme que les diverfes forces
dont on tire les cordes 1. 2. 3. 4. 5. s'affemblent toutes en

Voyez la
figure pag.
489.

Qqq iij

from the parts of the second element through the intermediary of which this same action is communicated, and that they are nothing material in the medium through which they pass, but they designate only in what direction and according to what determination the luminous body acts on the body it is illuminating. Thus, one should not cease to conceive of them as exactly straight even though the parts of the second element that serve to transmit this action, i.e., light, can almost never be placed so directly one on the other that they compose completely straight lines.

In just the same way, you can easily conceive that the hand A pushes the body E along the straight line AE even though it pushes it only through the intermediary of the stick BCD, which is twisted. And in just the same way, you can conceive that the ball marked 1 pushes that marked 7 through the intermediary of the two marked 5 and 5 as directly as through the intermediary of the others, 2, 3, 4, and 6.

5, 6. You can also easily conceive how several of these rays, coming from diverse points, come together at the same point (or, coming from the same point, go out toward different points) without impeding or depending on one another. As you see in Figure 6, several of them come from the points A, B, C, D and come together at point E, and several come from the single point D and extend, one toward E, another toward K, and thus toward an infinity of other places. In just the same way, the diverse forces with which one pulls the cords 1, 2, 3, 4, and 5 all come together in

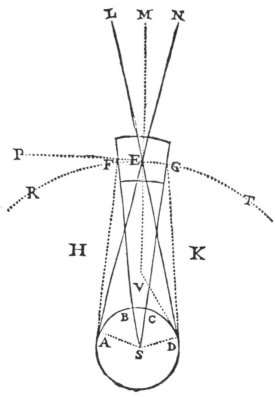

494   LE MONDE DE RENE' DESCARTES,

la poulie, & que la refiftance de cet-te poulie s'eftend à toutes les diver-fes mains qui tirent ces cordes.

7. Mais pour conceuoir comment plufieurs de ces rayons venant de di-vers points, & allát vers divers points, peuvent paffer par vn mefme point, fans s'empefcher les vns les autres, comme en cette fixiéme figure, les deux rayons A N, & D L, paffent par le point E, il faut confiderer que chacu-ne des parties du fecond Element eft capable de recevoir plufieurs divers mouvemens en mefme téps : En forte que celle qui eft par exemple au point E, peut tout pouf-fée enfemble eftre vers L , par l'a-ction qui vient de l'endroit du Soleil marqué D, & en mefme téps vers N, par celle qui vient de l'en-droit marqué A. Ce que vous en-tendrez encore mieux , fi vous confiderez qu'on peut pouffer l'air en mefme temps d'F vers G , d'H vers I , & de K

the pulley, and the resistance of this pulley extends to all the diverse hands that are pulling those cords.

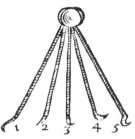

7. But to conceive how several of those rays, coming from diverse points and going toward diverse points, can pass through the same point without impeding one another, just as in Figure 6 the two rays AN and DL pass through point E, one must consider that each of the parts of the second element is capable of receiving several diverse motions at the same time. Thus, the part at, say, point E can be pushed as a whole toward L by the action coming from the place on the sun marked D and, at the same time, toward N by that coming from the place marked A. You will understand this still better if you consider that one can push the air at the same time from F toward G, from H toward I, and from K

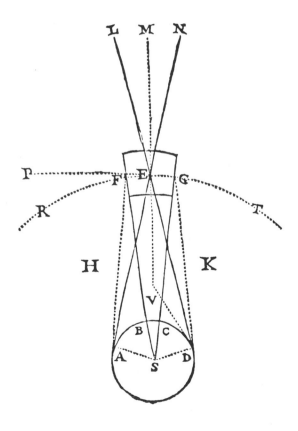

OU TRAITE' DE LA LUMIERE.

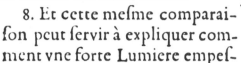

vers L , par les trois tuyaux F G, H I, K L, bien que ces tuyaux ſoient tellement vnis au point N, que tout l'air qui paſſe par le milieu de chacun d'eux , doit neceſſairement paſſer auſſi par le milieu des deux autres.

8. Et cette meſme comparai-ſon peut ſervir à expliquer com-ment vne forte Lumiere empeſ-che l'effet de celles qui ſont plus foibles : Car ſi l'on pouſ-ſe l'air beaucoup plus fort par F, que par H, ny par K, il ne tendra point du tout vers I, ny vers L , mais ſeule-ment vers G.

9. 10. Pour la reflexion & la refraction , je les ay déja ailleurs ſuffiſamment expliquées. Toutesfois parce que je me ſuis ſervy pour lors de l'exemple du mouvement d'vne bale , au lieu de parler des rayons de la Lumiere, afin de rendre par ce moyen mon diſcours plus intelligi-ble , il me reſte encore icy à vous faire conſiderer, que l'action ou l'inclination à ſe mouvoir, qui eſt tranſmiſe d'vn lieu en vn autre , par le moyen de pluſieurs corps qui s'entretouchent , & qui ſe trouvent ſans interruption en tout l'eſpace qui eſt entre deux , ſuit exactement la meſme voye , par où cette meſme action pourroit faire mouvoir le premier de ces corps, ſi les autres n'eſtoient point en ſon chemin ; ſans qu'il y ait aucune autre diffe-rence , ſinon qu'il faudroit du temps à ce corps pour ſe mouvoir , au lieu que l'action qui eſt en luy peut par l'en-tremiſe de ceux qui le touchent s'eſtendre juſques à tou-tes ſortes de diſtances en vn inſtant. D'où il ſuit que com-me vne bale ſe refléchit quand elle donne contre la mu-

toward L, through the three tubes FG, HI, and KL, even if those tubes are so joined at point N that all the air that passes through the middle of each of them must necessarily also pass through the middle of the other two.

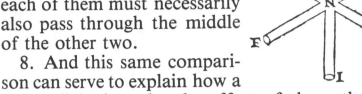

8. And this same comparison can serve to explain how a strong light impedes the effect of those that are weaker. For, if one pushes the air much more strongly through F than through H or through K, it will not tend at all toward I or toward L, but only toward G.

9, 10. As for reflection and refraction, I have already explained them sufficiently elsewhere.[63] Nevertheless, because I then used the example of the motion of a ball instead of speaking of rays of light, in order by this means to render my discourse more intelligible, it still remains for me here to have you consider that the action, or the inclination to move, that is transmitted from one place to another by means of several bodies that touch one another and that continuously fill all the space between the places follows exactly the same path along which this same action could cause the first of those bodies to move if the others were not in its way.[64] The only difference is that it requires time for that body to move, whereas the action that is in it can, through the intermediary of those touching it, extend to all sorts of distances in an instant. Whence it follows that, just as a ball is reflected when it strikes against the

496 LE MONDE DE RENE' DESCARTES;
raille d'vn jeu de paume , & qu'elle fouffre refraction
quand elle entre obliquement dans de l'eau, ou qu'elle
en fort; de mefme auffi quand les rayons de la Lumiere
rencontrent vn corps qui ne leur permet pas de paffer outre , ils doivent fe refléchir ; & quand ils entrent obliquement en quelque lieu par où ils peuvent s'eftendre plus
ou moins aifément que par celuy d'où ils fortent , ils doivent auffi au point de ce changement fe détourner &
fouffrir refraction.

11. 12. Enfin la force de la Lumiere eft non feulement
plus ou moins grande en chaque lieu, felon la quantité
des rayons qui s'y affemblent, mais elle peut auffi eftre
augmentée ou diminuée par les diverfes difpofitions des
corps qui fe trouvent aux lieux par où elle paffe ; Ainfi
que la viteffe d'vne bale ou d'vne pierre qu'on pouffe dans
l'air, peut-eftre augmentée par les vents qui foufflent vers
le mefme cofté qu'elle fe meut, & diminuée par leurs con-
traires.

CHAPITRE XV.

Que la face du Ciel de ce nouveau Monde doit
paroiftre à fes Habitans toute femblable à celle
du Noftre.

AYANT ainfi expliqué la Nature & les Proprietez
de l'action que j'ay prife pour la Lumiere, Il faut
auffi que j'explique comment par fon moyen les Habitans de la Planete que j'ay fupofée pour la Terre , peuvent voir la face de leur Ciel toute femblable à celle du
noftre.

Premierement, il n'y a point de doute qu'ils ne doivent

wall of a tennis court and undergoes refraction when it enters or leaves a body of water obliquely, so too, when the rays of light meet a body that does not permit them to pass beyond, they must be reflected, and when they enter obliquely some place through which they can extend more or less easily than they can through that from which they are coming, they must also be diverted and undergo refraction at the point of that change.

11, 12. Finally, the force of light is not only more or less great in each place according to the quantity of the rays that come together there, but it can also be increased or diminished by the diverse dispositions of the bodies in the places through which it passes. In the same way, the speed of a ball or a stone one is pushing in the air can be increased by winds blowing in the same direction that it is moving and diminished by their contraries.

CHAPTER 15

That the Face of the Heaven of That New World Must Appear to Its Inhabitants Completely like That of Our World

Having thus explained the nature and the properties of the action I have taken to be light, I must also explain how, by its means, the inhabitants of the planet I have supposed to be the earth can see the face of their heaven as wholly like that of ours.

First, there is no doubt that they

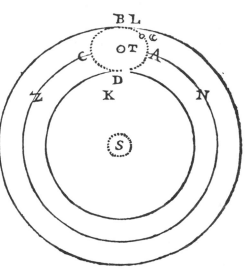

vent voir le corps marqué S tout plein de Lumiere, & femblable à noſtre Soleil ; veu que ce corps envoye des rayons de tous les points de ſa ſuperficie vers leurs yeux : Et parce qu'il eſt beaucoup plus proche d'eux que les Etoiles, il leur doit paroiſtre beaucoup plus grand. Il eſt vray que les parties du petit Ciel A B C D, qui tourne autour de la Terre, font quelque reſiſtance à ces rayons ; mais parce que toutes celles du grand Ciel qui ſont depuis S juſques à D, les fortifient, celles qui ſont depuis D juſques à T, n'eſtant à comparaiſon qu'en petit nombre, ne leur peuvent oſter que peu de leur force : Et meſme toute l'action des parties du grand Ciel F G G F, ne ſuffit pas pour empeſcher que les rayons de pluſieurs Etoiles fixes ne parviennent juſques à la Terre, du coſté qu'elle n'eſt point éclairée par le Soleil.

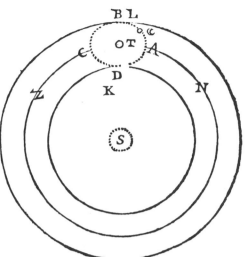

must see the body marked S as completely full of light and like our sun, given that that body sends rays from all points of its surface toward their eyes. And, because it is much closer to them than the stars, it must appear much greater to them. It is true that the parts of the small heaven ABCD that turns about the earth offer some resistance to those rays; but, because all the parts of the great heaven that are between S and D strengthen the rays, those that are between D and T, being comparatively small in number, can take away only very little of their force from them. And even all the action of the parts of the large heaven FGGF does not suffice to impede the rays of many fixed stars from reaching to the earth from the side on which it is not illuminated by the sun.

498 LE MONDE DE RENE' DESCARTES,

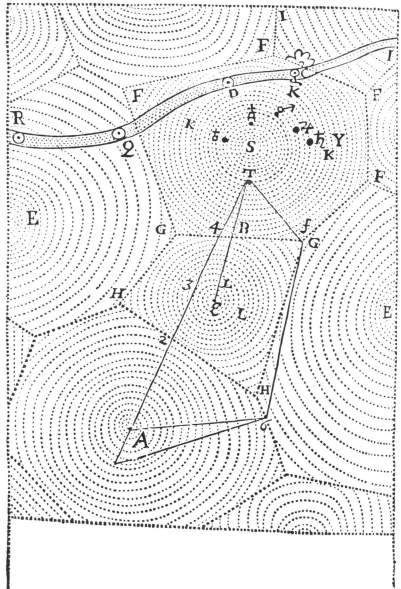

Car il faut fçavoir que les grands Cieux , c'eſt à dire
ceux qui ont vne Etoile fixe ou le Soleil pour leur centre,

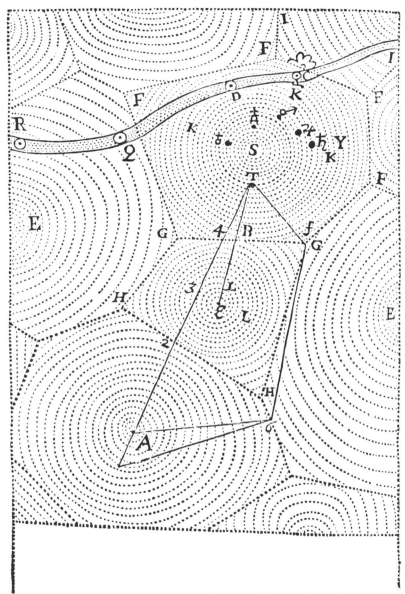

For one must know that, although the large heavens (i.e., those that have a fixed star or the sun for their center)

187

OU TRAITE' DE LA LUMIERE. 499

quoy que peut-eſtre aſſez inégaux en grandeur, doivent
eſtre toujours exactement d'égale force ; En ſorte que
toute la matiere qui eſt par exemple en la ligne S B, doit
tendre auſſi fort vers ε, que celle qui eſt en la ligne ε B,
tend vers S : Car s'ils n'avoient entr'eux cette égalité, ils
ſe détruiroient infailliblement dans peu de temps, ou du
moins ſe changeroient juſques à ce qu'ils l'euſſent acquiſe.

Or puis que toute la force du rayon S B par exemple,
n'eſt que juſtement égale à celle du rayon ε B, il eſt
manifeſte que celle du rayon T B, qui eſt moindre, ne
peut empeſcher la force du rayon ε B de s'eſtendre juſques à T. Et tout de meſme il eſt évident que l'Etoile A
peut eſtendre ſes rayons juſques à la terre T ; dautant
que la matiere du Ciel qui eſt depuis A juſques à 2, leur
ayde plus, que celle qui eſt depuis 4 juſques à T ne leur
reſiſte ; & avec cela que celle qui eſt depuis 3 juſques à 4,
ne leur ayde pas moins, que leur reſiſte celle qui eſt depuis 3 juſques à 2. Et ainſi, jugeant des autres à proportion, vous pouvez entendre que ces Etoiles ne doivent
pas paroiſtre moins confuſément arrangées, ny moindres en nombre, ny moins inégales entr'elles, que font
celles que nous voyons dans le vray Monde.

Mais il faut encore que vous conſideriez, touchant
leur arrangement, qu'elles ne peuvent quaſi jamais paroiſtre dans le vray lieu où elles ſont. Car par exemple,
celle qui eſt marquée ε, paroiſt comme ſi elle eſtoit en la
ligne droite T B, & l'autre marquée A, comme ſi elle
eſtoit en la ligne droite T 4 ; dont la raiſon eſt, que les
Cieux eſtant inégaux en grandeur, les ſuperficies qui les
ſeparent, ne ſe trouvent quaſi jamais tellement diſpo-
ſées, que les rayons qui paſſent au travers, pour aller de

Rrr ij

188

may perhaps be rather unequal in size, they must always be exactly of the same force, so that all the matter that is, say, in the line SB must tend as strongly toward Ɛ as that which is in the line Ɛ B tends toward S. For, if they do not have that equality among them, they will most certainly be destroyed in a short time, or at least they will change until they have acquired it.

Now, since the whole force of the ray SB, for example, is just exactly equal to that of the ray ƐB, it is manifest that that of the ray TB (which is less) cannot impede the force of the ray Ɛ B to extend to T. And in the same way, it is evident that the star A can extend its rays to the earth T, inasmuch as the matter of the heaven between A and 2 aids them more than that between 4 and T resists them, and in addition inasmuch as that between 3 and 4 aids them no less than that between 3 and 2 resists them. And thus, judging others proportionately, you can understand that those stars must appear no less confusedly arranged, nor less in number, nor less unequal to one another, than do those we see in the real world.

But you must still consider in regard to their arrangement that they can just about never appear in the true place where they are. For example, that marked Ɛ appears as if it were in the straight line TB, and the other marked A as if it were in the straight line T4. The reason for this is that, since the heavens are unequal in size, the surfaces that separate them are just about never so disposed that the rays that pass through them to go from

500 LE MONDE DE RENE' DESCARTES;

ces Etoiles vers la Terre, les rencontrent à angles droits:
Et lors qu'ils les rencontrent obliquement, il eſt certain, ſuivant ce qui a eſté demontré en la Dioptrique,
qu'ils doivent s'y courber, & ſouffrir beaucoup de refraction, dautant qu'ils paſſent beaucoup plus aiſément
par l'vn des coſtez de cette ſuperficie, que par l'autre.
Et il faut ſuppoſer ces lignes T B, T 4, & ſemblables, ſi
extremement longues, à comparaiſon du diametre du
cercle que la Terre décrit autour du Soleil, qu'en quelque endroit de ce cercle qu'elle ſe trouve, les hommes
qu'elle ſouſtient voyent toujours les Etoiles comme fixes,
& attachées aux meſmes endroits du Firmament; c'eſt à
dire, pour vſer des termes des Aſtronomes, qu'ils ne
peuvent remarquer en elles de paralaxes.

   Conſiderez auſſi, touchant le nombre de ces Etoiles,
que ſouvent vne meſme peut paroiſtre en divers lieux, à
cauſe des diverſes ſuperficies qui détournent ſes rayons
vers la Terre; Comme icy celle qui eſt marquée A, paroiſt en la ligne T 4, par le moyen du rayon A 2 4 T, &
enſemble en la ligne T f, par le moyen du rayon A 6 f T;
ainſi que ſe multiplient les objets qu'on regarde au travers des verres ou autres corps tranſparens qui ſont tail-
lez à pluſieurs faces.

   Deplus conſiderez touchant leur grandeur, qu'encore qu'elles doivent paroiſtre beaucoup plus petites qu'elles ne ſont à cauſe de leur extréme éloignement; & meſme qu'il y en ait la plus grande partie, qui pour cette
raiſon ne doivent point paroiſtre du tout; & d'autres qui
ne paroiſſent qu'entant que les rayons de pluſieurs joints
enſemble rendent les parties du Firmament par où ils
paſſent vn peu plus blanches, & ſemblables à certaines
Etoiles que les Aſtronomes appellent Nubileuſes, ou à

the stars toward the earth meet them at right angles. And when the rays meet them obliquely, it is certain, according to what has been demonstrated in the *Dioptrics,* [65] that there they must bend and undergo a great deal of refraction, inasmuch as they pass much more easily through one side of this surface than through the other. And one must suppose those lines TB, T4, and ones like them to be so extremely long in comparison with the diameter of the circle the earth describes about the sun that, wherever the earth is on that circle, the men on it always see the stars as fixed and attached to the same places in the firmament; that is, to use the terms of the astronomers, they cannot observe parallax in the stars. [66]

Regarding the number of those stars, consider also that the same star can often appear in different places because of the different surfaces that divert its rays toward the earth. Here, for example, that marked A appears in the line T4 by means of the ray A24T and simultaneously in the line Tf by means of the ray A6fT. In the same way are the objects multiplied that one looks at through glasses or other transparent bodies cut along several faces.

Moreover, regarding their size, consider that they must appear much smaller than they are, because of their extreme distance; for this reason the greater part of them must not appear at all, and others appear only insofar as the rays of several joined together render the parts of the firmament through which they pass a bit whiter and similar to certain stars the astronomers call "nebulous," or to

191

Our World

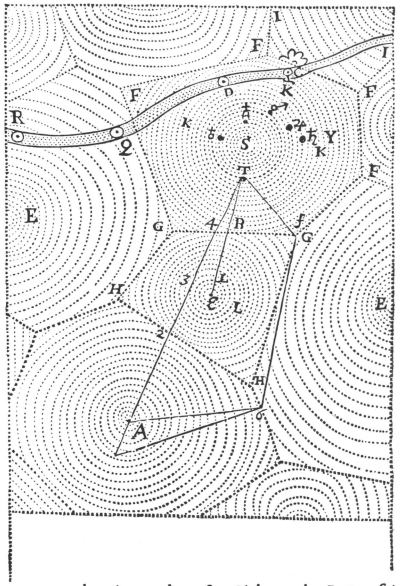

cette grande ceinture de noſtre Ciel, que les Poëtes fei-
gnent eſtre blanchie du lait de Junon : Toutesfois, pour

Rrr iij

192

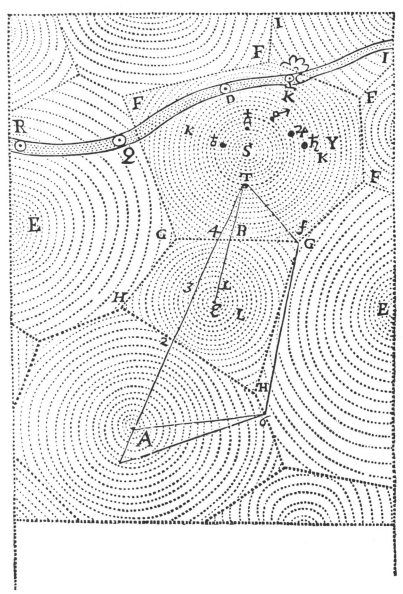

that great belt of our heaven that the poets pretend to be whitened by the milk of Juno.[67] Despite this, it nevertheless suffices to suppose

502   LE MONDE DE RENE' DESCARTES,
celles qui font les moins éloignées, il fuffit de les fuppofer environ égales à noftre Soleil, pour juger qu'elles
peuvent paroiftre aussi grandes que font les plus grandes
de noftre Monde.

Car outre que generalement tous les corps qui en-
voyent de plus forts rayons contre les yeux des regardans, que ne font ceux qui les environnent, paroissent
aussi plus grands qu'eux à proportion ; & par confequent
que ces Etoiles doivent toujours fembler plus grandes
que les parties de leurs Cieux égales à elles, & qui les
avoifinent, ainfi que j'expliqueray cy-aprés, les fuperficies F G, G G, G F, & femblables, où fe font les refractions de leurs rayons, peuvent eftre courbées de telle
façon, qu'elles augmentent beaucoup leur grandeur ; &
mefme eftant feulement toutes plates elles l'augmentent.

Outre cela il eft fort vray-femblable que ces fuperficies eftant en vne matiere tres fluide, & qui ne ceffe jamais de fe mouvoir, doivent branler & ondoyer toujours
quelque peu ; & par confequent que les Etoiles qu'on
voit au travers, doivent paroiftre étincelantes & comme
tremblantes, ainfi que font les noftres, & mefme à caufe de leur tremblement vn peu plus groffes ; ainfi que
fait l'image de la Lune, au fond d'vn lac dont la furface
n'eft pas fort troublée ny agitée, mais feulement vn peu
crefpée par le fouffle de quelque vent.

Et enfin il fe peut faire que par fucceffion de temps ces
fuperficies fe changent vn peu, ou mefme aussi que quelques-vnes fe courbent affez notablement en peu de téps,
quand ce ne feroit qu'à l'occafion d'vne Comete qui s'en
approche, & par ce moyen que plufieurs Etoiles femblent aprés vn long-temps eftre vn peu changées de place fans l'eftre de grandeur, ou vn peu changées de gran-

194

the less distant stars to be about equal to our sun, in order to judge that they can appear as large as the largest of our world.

For, generally, all the bodies that send out stronger rays against the eyes of onlookers than do the bodies surrounding them appear proportionately that much greater than they, and consequently those stars must always seem larger than the parts of their heavens that are equal to them and that border them, as I will explain below. In addition to this, however, the surfaces FG, GG, GF and ones like them, where the refractions of [the stars'] rays take place, can be curved in such a way that they greatly increase [the stars'] size; indeed, even when completely flat, they increase it.

Moreover, it is very probable that those surfaces, being in a matter that is very fluid and that never ceases to move, should always shake and quiver somewhat, and consequently that the stars one sees through them should appear to scintillate and vibrate, just as ours do, and even, because of their vibration, appear a bit larger. In this way, the image of the moon appears larger when viewed from the bottom of a lake of which the surface is not very stirred up or agitated, but merely a bit rippled by the breath of some wind.

And, finally, it can happen that, over the course of time, those surfaces change a bit, or indeed even that some of them bend rather noticeably in a short time, even if this is only on the occasion of a comet's approaching them. By this means, several stars seem after a long time to change a bit in place without changing in size, or to change a bit in

OU TRAITE' DE LA LUMIERE.

deur fans l'eftre de place ; & mefme que quelques-vnes
commencent affez fubitement à paroiftre ou à difpa-
roiftre, ainfi qu'on l'a vû arriver dans le vray Monde.

Pour les Planetes & les Cometes qui font dans le mefme Ciel que le Soleil, fçachant que les parties du troifiéme Element dont elles font compofées, font fi groffes, ou
tellement jointes plufieurs enfemble, qu'elles peuvent
refifter à l'action de la Lumiere, il eft aifé à entendre
qu'elles doivent paroiftre par le moyen des rayons que
le Soleil envoye vers elles, & qui fe refléchiffent de là vers
la Terre ; ainfi que les objets opaques ou obfcurs qui font
dans vne chambre, y peuvent eftre vûs par le moyen des
rayons que le flambeau qui y éclaire, envoye vers eux, &
qui retournent de là vers les yeux des regardans. Et avec
cela les rayons du Soleil ont vn avantage fort remarquable pardeffus ceux d'vn flambeau; qui confifte en ce que
leur force fe conferve, ou mefme s'augmente de plus en
plus, à mefure qu'ils s'éloignent du Soleil, jufques à ce
qu'ils foient parvenus à la fuperficie exterieure de fon
Ciel, à caufe que toute la matiere de ce Ciel tend vers là:
au lieu que les rayons d'vn flambeau s'affoibliffent en s'é-
loignant, à raifon de la grandeur des fuperficies fpheri-
ques qu'ils illuminent, & mefme encore quelque peu
plus, à caufe de la refiftance de l'air par où ils paffent.
D'où vient que les objets qui font proches de ce flambeau, en font notablement plus éclairez que ceux qui en
font loin ; & que les plus baffes Planetes ne font pas à mefme proportion plus éclairées par le Soleil que les plus
hautes, ny mefme que les Cometes, qui en font fans comparaifon plus éloignées.

Or l'experience nous montre que le femblable arrive
auffi dans le vray Monde ; Et toutesfois je ne croy pas

size without changing in place. Indeed, some even begin rather suddenly to appear or to disappear, just as one has seen happen in the real world.[68]

As for the planets and the comets that are in the same heaven as the sun, knowing that the parts of the third element of which they are composed are so large or so joined severally together that they can resist the action of light, it is easy to understand that they must appear by means of the rays that the sun sends toward them and that are reflected from there toward the earth, just as the opaque or obscure objects that are in a room can be seen there by means of the rays that the lamp shining there sends toward them and that return from them toward the eyes of the onlookers. In addition, the rays of the sun have a quite noteworthy advantage over those of a lamp. It consists in their forces' being conserved, or even being increasingly strengthened to the degree that they move away from the sun, until they have reached the exterior surface of its heaven, because all the matter of that heaven tends there. By contrast, the rays of a lamp are weakened as they move away, in proportion to the size of the spherical surfaces they illuminate and, indeed, still somewhat more because of the resistance of the air through which they pass. Whence it is that the objects close to that lamp are noticeably more lighted by it than those far from it, and that the lowest planets are not, in the same proportion, more lighted by the sun than the highest, nor even more than the comets, which are incomparably more distant.

Now, experience shows us that the same thing also happens in the real world. I do not believe, however,

504   LE MONDE DE RENE' DESCARTES,

qu'il foit poffible d'en rendre raifon, fi on fuppofe que
la Lumiere y foit autre chofe dans les objets, qu'vne
action ou difpofition telle que je l'ay expliquée. Je dis
vne action ou difpofition: Car fi vous avez bien pris garde à ce que j'ay tantoft demontré, que fi l'efpace où eft
le Soleil eftoit tout vuide, les parties de fon Ciel ne laifferoient pas de tendre vers les yeux des regardans en mefme façon que lors qu'elles font pouffées par fa matiere, &
mefme avec prefque autant de force, vous pouvez bien juger qu'il n'a quafi pas befoin d'avoir en foy aucune action,
ny quafi mefme d'eftre autre chofe qu'vn pur efpace, pour
paroiftre tel que nous le voyons; ce que vous euffiez peut-
eftre pris auparavant pour vne propofition fort para-
doxe. Au refte, le mouvement qu'ont ces Planetes autour de leur centre eft caufe qu'elles étincellent, mais
beaucoup moins fort & d'vne autre façon que ne font les
Etoiles fixes; & parce que la Lune eft privée de ce mouvement, elle n'étincelle point du tout.

Pour les Cometes qui ne font pas dans le mefme Ciel
que le Soleil, elles ne peuvent pas à beaucoup prés en-
voyer tant de rayons vers la Terre que fi elles y eftoient,
non pas mefme lors qu'elles font toutes preftes à y entrer; & par confequent elles ne peuvent pas eftre veuës
par les hommes, fi ce n'eft peut-eftre quelque peu, lors
que leur grandeur eft extraordinaire. Dont la raifon eft,
que la plufpart des rayons que le Soleil envoye vers elles,
font écartez çà & là, & comme diffipez par la refraction
qu'ils fouffrent en la partie du Firmament par où ils paffent. Car par exemple, au lieu que la Comete C D, reçoit du Soleil, marqué S, tous les rayons qui font entre les lignes S C, S D, & renvoye vers la Terre tous
ceux qui font entre les lignes C T, D T, il faut penfer

que

that it is possible to give a reason for it if one supposes that light is anything in the objects other than an action or disposition such as I have set forth. I say an action or disposition; for, if you have attended well to what I have just demonstrated, to wit, that, if the space where the sun is were totally void, the parts of its heaven would not cease to tend toward the eyes of onlookers in the same way as when they are pushed by its matter (and even with almost as much force), you can well judge that there is just about no need to have any action in the sun itself nor even for it to be anything other than pure space in order to appear as we see it. This is something you would perhaps earlier have taken to be a quite paradoxical proposition. Furthermore, the motion those planets have about their center is the reason why they twinkle, though much less strongly and in another way than do the fixed stars; because the moon is deprived of that motion, it does not twinkle at all.

As for the comets that are not in the same heaven as the sun, they are far from being able to send out as many rays toward the earth as they could if they were in the same heaven, not even when they are all ready to enter it. Consequently, they cannot be seen by men, unless perhaps when their size is extraordinary. The reason for this is that most of the rays that the sun sends out toward them are borne away here and there and effectively dissipated by the refraction they undergo in the part of the firmament through which they pass. For example, whereas the comet CD receives from the sun, marked S, all the rays between the lines SC and SD and sends back toward the earth all those between the lines CT and DT, [69] one must imagine that the

199

OU TRAITE' DE LA LUMIERE.

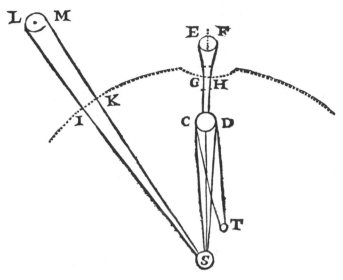

que la Comete E F, ne reçoit du mefme Soleil que les rayons qui font entre les lignes S G E, S H F, à caufe que paffant beaucoup plus aifément depuis S jufques à la fuperficie G H , que je prens pour vne partie du Firmament, qu'ils ne peuvent paffer au delà, leur refraction y doit eftre fort grande, & fort en dehors ; ce qui en détourne plufieurs d'aller vers la Comete E F : Veu principalement que cette fuperficie eft courbée en dedans vers le Soleil, ainfi que vous fçavez qu'elle doit fe courber, lors qu'vne Comete s'en approche. Mais encore qu'elle fuft toute plate, ou mefme courbée de l'autre cofté, la plufpart des rayons que le Soleil luy envoyeroit, ne laifferoient pas d'eftre empefchez par la refraction, finon d'aller jufques à elle, au moins de retourner de là jufques à la Terre. Comme par exemple, fuppofant la partie du Firmament I K, eftre vne portion de Sphere , dont le centre foit au point S, les rayons S I L, S K M, ne s'y doivent point du tout courber en allant vers la Comete

S ff

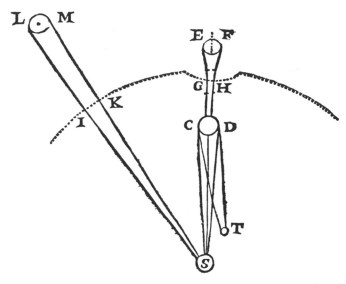

comet EF receives from the same sun only the rays between the lines SGE and SHF because, since they pass much more easily from S to the surface GH (which I take to be a part of the firmament that they cannot pass beyond), their refraction there must be very great and very much outward. This diverts many of them from going toward the comet EF, given first of all that this surface is curved inward toward the sun, just as you know it should curve when a comet approaches it. But, even if it were completely flat, or even curved in the other direction, most of the rays that the sun sent out to it would not cease to be impeded by the refraction, if not from going up to it, at least from returning from there to the earth. For example, if one supposes the part IK of the firmament to be a portion of a sphere of which the center is at S, the rays SIL and SKM should not bend there at all in going toward the comet

L M; mais en revanche, ils ſe doivent beaucoup courber en retournant de là vers la Terre; en ſorte qu'ils n'y peuvent parvenir que fort foibles, & en fort petite quantité. Outre que cecy ne pouvant arriver que lors que la Comete eſt encore aſſez loin du Ciel qui contient le Soleil, (car autrement, ſi elle en eſtoit proche, elle feroit courber en dedans ſa ſuperficie) ſon éloignement empeſche auſſi qu'elle n'en reçoive tant de rayons que lors qu'elle eſt preſte à y entrer. Et pour les rayons qu'elle reçoit de l'Etoile fixe qui eſt au centre du Ciel qui la contient, elle ne peut pas les renvoyer vers la Terre, non plus que la Lune eſtant nouvelle n'y renvoye pas ceux du Soleil.

Mais ce qu'il y a de plus remarquable touchant ces Cometes, c'eſt vne certaine refraction de leurs rayons, qui eſt ordinairement cauſe qu'il en paroiſt quelques-vns en forme de queuë ou de chevelure autour d'elles; Ainſi que vous entendrez facilement, ſi vous jettez les yeux ſur cette figure; Où S eſt le Soleil, C vne Comete, E B G la Sphere qui ſuivant ce qui a eſté dit cy-deſſus eſt compoſée des parties du ſecond Element qui ſont les plus groſſes & les moins agitées de toutes, & D A le cercle qui eſt décrit par le mouvement annuel de la Terre; & que vous penſiez que le rayon qui vient de C vers B, paſſe bien tout droit juſques au point A, mais qu'outre cela il commence au point B à s'élargir, & à ſe diviſer en pluſieurs autres rayons, qui s'eſtendent çà & là de tous coſtez; en telle ſorte que chacun d'eux ſe trouve d'autant plus foible, qu'il s'écarte davantage de celuy du milieu B A, qui eſt le principal de tous, & le plus fort. Puis auſſi que le rayon C E, commence eſtant au point E à s'élargir, & à ſe diviſer auſſi en pluſieurs autres, comme E H, E Y, E S, mais que le principal & le plus fort de ceux-cy,

LM; by the same token, however, they should bend greatly in returning from the comet toward the earth, so that they can reach the earth only very feebly and in very small quantity. Beyond that, since this can happen when the comet is still rather far from the heaven that contains the sun (for otherwise, if it were close to that heaven, it would cause the heaven's surface to curve inward), its distance also impedes it from receiving as many rays as when it is ready to enter the heaven. As for the rays it receives from the fixed star at the center of the heaven containing it, it cannot send them back toward the earth any more than the moon, being new, can send back those of the sun.

But what is even more noteworthy regarding those comets is a certain refraction of their rays, which is ordinarily the reason why some of them appear around [the comets] in the form of a tail or of a curl.[70] You will easily understand this if you cast your eyes on this figure, where S is the sun, C a comet, EBG the sphere that (according to what has been said above) is composed of those parts of the second element that are the largest and least agitated of all, and DA the circle described by the annual motion of the earth. Imagine further that the ray coming from C toward B passes straight-away to point A, but that in addition it begins at point B to grow larger and to be divided into many other rays, which extend every which way in all directions. Thus, each of them is that much weaker as it is carried farther away from the one in the middle, BA, which is the principal ray of all and the strongest. Then, too, when the ray CE is at point E, it begins to grow larger and also to be divided into many others, such as EH, EY, ES; the principal and strongest of these, however,

OU TRAITE' DE LA LUMIERE.

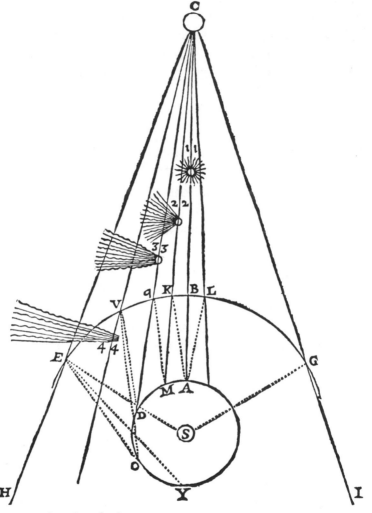

eſt E H, & le plus foible E S ; & tout de meſme que C G
paſſe principalement de G vers I , mais qu'outre cela il
s'écarte auſſi vers S, & vers tous les eſpaces qui ſont entre
G I & G S ; & enfin que tous les autres rayons qui peuvent eſtre imaginez entre ces trois C E, C B, C G, tiennent plus ou moins de la nature de chacun d'eux , ſelon

S ſ ſ ij

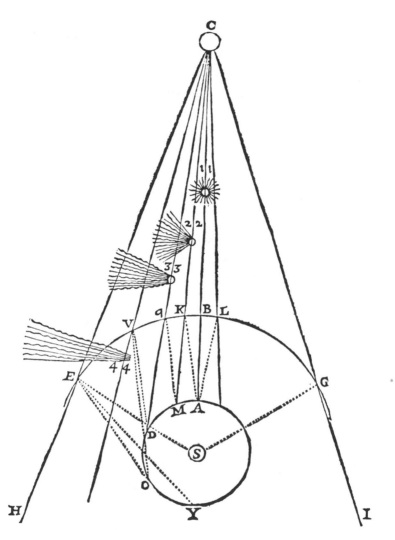

is EH, and the feeblest is ES. In the same way, CG passes principally from G toward I, but in addition it is also carried away from S and toward all the spaces between GI and GS. Finally, all the other rays that can be imagined between those three rays CE, CB, and CG hold more or less to the nature of each of them, according

508   LE MONDE DE RENE' DESCARTES,

qu'ils en font plus ou moins proches. A quoy je pourrois adjouter qu'ils doivent eftre vn peu courbez vers le Soleil : mais cela n'eft pas tout à fait neceffaire à mon fujet, & j'obmets fouvent beaucoup de chofes, afin de rendre celles que j'explique d'autant plus fimples & plus aifées.

Or cette refraction eftant fupofée, il eft manifefte que lors que la Terre eft vers A, non feulement le rayon B A doit faire voir aux hommes qu'elle fouftient le corps de la Comete C; mais auffi que les rayons L A, K A, & femblables, qui font plus foibles que B A, venant vers leurs yeux, leur doivent faire paroiftre vne couronne, ou chevelure de Lumiere, éparfe également de tous coftez autour d'elle (comme vous voyez à l'endroit marqué 11.) au moins s'ils font affez forts pour eftre fentis ; ainfi qu'ils le peuvent eftre fouvent venant des Cometes, que nous fupofons eftre fort groffes, mais non pas venant des Planetes, ny mefme des Etoiles fixes, qu'il faut imaginer plus petites.

Il eft manifefte auffi que lors que la Terre eft vers M, & que la Comete paroift par le moyen du rayon C K M, fa chevelure doit paroiftre par le moyen de Q M, & de tous les autres qui tendent vers M ; en forte qu'elle s'efted plus loin qu'auparavant vers la partie oppofée au Soleil, & moins, ou point du tout, vers celle qui le regarde, comme vous voyez icy 22. Et ainfi paroiffant toujours de plus en plus longue vers le cofté qui eft oppofé au Soleil, à mefure que la Terre eft plus éloignée du point A, elle perd peu à peu la figure d'vne chevelure, & fe transforme en vne longue queuë, que la Comete traifne aprés elle. Comme par exemple, la Terre eftant vers D, les rayons Q D, V D, la font paroiftre femblable à 33. Et la Terre eftant vers o, les rayons V o, E o, & femblables, la font

as they are more or less close. To this I might add that they should be a bit bent toward the sun; but that is in fact not necessary for my purposes, and I often omit many things in order to render those I do explain that much simpler and easier.

Now, this refraction having been supposed, it is manifest that, when the earth is at A, not only should the ray BA cause men on it to see the body of comet C, but also the rays LA, KA, and others like them, which come to their eyes more feebly than BA, should cause to appear to them a crown or curl of light uniformly spread out in all directions around the comet (as you see at the place marked 11), at least if they are strong enough to be perceived. They can often be strong enough coming from comets, which we suppose to be very large, but not coming from planets, or even from fixed stars, which one must imagine to be smaller.

It is also manifest that, when the earth is at M and the comet appears by means of the ray CKM, its curl should appear by means of QM and all the other rays tending toward M, so that it extends farther than before in the direction opposite to the sun, and less far or not at all toward the person looking at it, as you can see here at 22. And thus appearing longer and longer on the side opposite the sun, to the degree that the earth is farther away from point A, it little by little loses the shape of a curl and is transformed into a long tail, which the comet trails behind it. For example, when the earth is at D, the rays QD and VD make it appear like 33. And, when the earth is at O, the rays VO, EO, and others like them make it

OU TRAITE' DE LA LUMIERE. 509

paroiſtre encore plus longue ; Et enfin la Terre eſtant
vers Y, on ne peut plus voir la Comete à cauſe de l'inter-
poſition du Soleil, mais les rayons V Y, E Y, & ſemblables, ne laiſſent pas de faire encore paroiſtre ſa queuë, en
forme d'vn chevron ou d'vne lance de feu, telle qu'eſt
icy 44. Et il eſt à remarquer que la ſphere E B G, n'eſtant
point toujours exactement ronde, ny auſſi toutes les autres qu'elle contient, ainſi qu'il eſt aiſé à juger de ce que
nous avons expliqué, ces queuës ou lances de feu ne doivent point toujours paroiſtre exactement droites, ny tout
à fait en meſme plan que le Soleil.

    Pour la refraction qui eſt cauſe de tout cecy, je confeſſe
qu'elle eſt d'vne nature fort particuliere, & fort differente
de toutes celles qui ſe remarquent communement ailleurs. Mais vous ne laiſſerez pas de voir clairement qu'elle ſe doit faire en la façon que je viens de vous décrire, ſi
vous conſiderez que la boule H, eſtant pouſſée vers I,

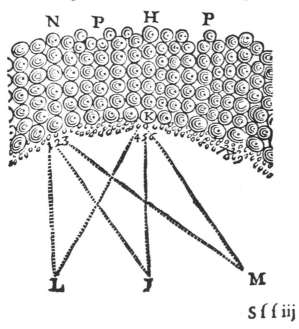

appear still longer. And, finally, when the earth is at Y, one can no longer see the comet because of the interposition of the sun; however, the rays VY, EY, and others like them do not cease to cause its tail still to appear in the shape of a chevron or of a torch, such as here at 44. And one should note that, since the sphere EBG is not always exactly round, nor also any of the others it contains (as is easy to judge from what we have set out), those tails or torches should not always appear exactly straight, nor in fact in the same plane as the sun.

As for the refraction that is the cause of all this, I confess that it is of a nature very special and very different from all those commonly observed elsewhere. But you will not fail to see clearly that it should take place in the manner I have just described to you if you consider that the ball H, being pushed toward I,

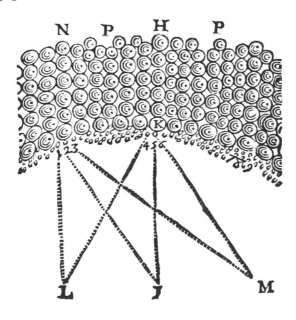

510 LE MONDE DE RENE' DESCARTES,
pousse aussi vers là toutes celles qui font au deßous juſques à K; mais que celle-cy eſtant environnée de pluſieurs autres plus petites, comme 456, ne pouſſe que 5
vers I; & cependant qu'elle pouſſe 4 vers L, & 6 vers M,
& ainſi des autres: En ſorte pourtát qu'elle pouſſe celle du
milieu 5. beaucoup plus fort que les autres 4,6, & ſemblables, qui ſont vers les coſtez. Et tout de meſme que la
boule N eſtant pouſſée vers L, pouſſe les petites boules 1.
2. 3, l'vne vers L, l'autre vers I, & l'autre vers M. Mais avec
cette difference, que c'eſt 1. qu'elle pouſſe le plus fort de
toutes, & non pas celle du milieu 2. Et de plus que les petites boules 1. 2. 3. 4. &c. eſtant ainſi en meſme temps toutes
pouſſées par les autres boules N. P. H. P. s'empeſchent les
vnes les autres de pouvoir aller vers les coſtez L. & M. ſi
facilemét que vers le milieu I. En ſorte que ſi tout l'eſpace
L I M eſtoit plein de pareilles petites boules, les rayons de
leur action s'y diſtribueroiét en meſme façon que j'ay dit
que font ceux des Cometes au dedans de la Sphere E B G.

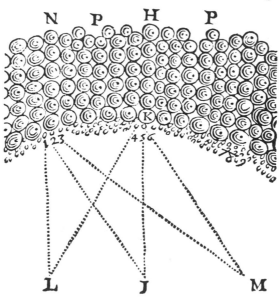

also pushes toward I all those below it down to K, but that the latter, K, being surrounded by many other smaller balls, such as 4, 5, and 6, only pushes 5 toward I, and meanwhile pushes 4 toward L and 6 toward M, and so on. Nevertheless, it does so in such a way that it pushes the middle one, 5, much more strongly than the others, 4, 6, and those like them which are on the sides. In the same way, the ball N, being pushed toward L, pushes the small balls 1, 2, and 3, one toward L, the other toward I, and the other toward M; but with this difference, that it pushes 1 the most strongly of all, and not the middle one, 2. Moreover, the small balls 1, 2, 3, 4, etc., being thus all pushed at the same time by the other balls N, P, H, P, impede one another from being able to go in the directions L and M as easily as toward the middle, I. Thus, if the whole space LIM were full of similar small balls, the rays of their action would be distributed there in the same manner as I have said are those of the comets within the sphere EBG.

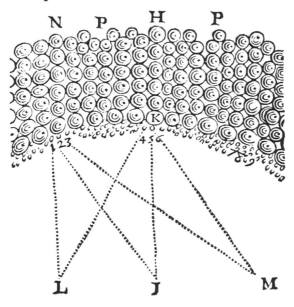

OU TRAITE' DE LA LUMIERE. 511

A quoy si vous m'objectez que l'inégalité qui est entre les boules N. P. H. P. & 1. 2. 3. 4. est beaucoup plus grande que celle que j'ay supposée entre les parties du second Element qui composent la Sphere E B G, & celles qui sont immediatement au dessous vers le Soleil, Je répons qu'on ne peut tirer de cecy autre consequence, sinon qu'il ne se doit pas tant faire de refraction en cette Sphere E B G. qu'en celle que composent les boules 1. 2. 3. 4. &c. Mais qu'y ayant derechef de l'inégalité entre les parties du second Element qui sont immediatement au dessous de cette Sphere E B G, & celles qui sont encore plus bas vers le Soleil, cette refraction s'augmente de plus en plus, à mesure que les rayons penetrent plus avant; En sorte qu'elle peut bien estre aussi grande, ou mesme plus grande, lors qu'ils parviennent à la Sphere de la Terre D A F, que celle de l'action dont les petites boules 1. 2. 3. 4. &c. sont poussées. Car il est bien vray-semblable, que les parties du second Element qui sont vers cette Sphere de la Terre D A F, ne sont pas moins petites à comparaison de celles qui sont vers la Sphere E B G, que le sont ces boules 1. 2. 3. 4. &c. à comparaison des autres boules N. P. H. P.

F I N.

If to this you object that the inequality between the balls N, P, H, P and 1, 2, 3, 4, etc., is much greater than that which I have supposed between the parts of the second element that compose the sphere EBG and those that are immediately below them toward the sun, I respond that one can draw no other consequence from this than that there should not take place as much refraction in the sphere EBG as in that composed by the balls 1, 2, 3, 4, etc. However, since there is in turn some inequality between the parts of the second element that are immediately below this sphere EBG and those that are still lower toward the sun, this refraction increases more and more as the rays penetrate farther. Thus, when the rays reach to the sphere of the earth DAF, the refraction can well be as great as, or even greater than, that of the action by which the small balls 1, 2, 3, 4, etc. are pushed. For it is very likely that the parts of the second element toward this sphere of the earth DAF arc no less small in comparison with those toward the sphere EBG than are those balls 1, 2, 3, 4, etc. in comparison with the other balls N, P, H, P.

THE END

Notes

1. *sentiment*. It is difficult to render this word into English with full precision. Descartes's own parenthetical explication—"idea that is formed in our imagination through the intermediary of our eyes"—is of limited help, since at the time of writing *The World* he had not yet worked out the details of his metaphysics or theory of mind. But it does place *sentiments* in the mind and makes them more than merely the sensory data connoted by "sensations." Moreover, in *Man* the brain has *sentiments* not only of heat and of the color red (note the judgment involved), but also of pain, tickling, and taste. Hence, the term covers both sensations caused by external objects and feelings originating within the body; in an example soon to follow, a soldier who mistakenly thinks himself wounded in battle "senses" (*sent*) both pain and a strap. The mind's involvement in a *sentiment* tempts one to translate it by "perception," especially since the French cognate does not appear either in *The World* or in *Man*. However, it does occur in the *Principles of Philosophy* and in the *Passions of the Soul*. The latter includes *sentiment* among several different sorts of *perception*. Perception in a general sense is any thought that does not result from the action or will of the soul, and in a restricted sense is "evident knowledge"; *sentiment* is "what is received in the soul in the same way as objects of the external senses and is not otherwise known by the soul" (*Passions,* I, 28; AT.XI.349). Perceptions may arise in the imagination, in which case their objects do not really exist. *Sentiments* arise in the body by the intermediary of the nervous system and, whether really or only apparently, involve the body's external senses. Since here in *The World* it is the external senses and their relation to the external world that Descartes is discussing, "sensation" seems the best English equivalent.

2. Like all university-educated people of his day, Descartes was as fluent in Latin as he was in his native tongue. Not having to translate Latin discourse to understand it, he might well have been unable later to recall in what language he had heard or read something.

3. For the theory of mind underlying this argument, see Rule XII of *Rules for the Direction of the Mind* and *Man* (AT.XI.170ff.).

4. Galileo used this example of the feather drawn lightly over the skin to make roughly the same point about sensory data; see his *Assayer* (1624), chapter 48.

5. In Discourse I of the *Dioptrics,* Descartes adds to this list of light sources the eyes of cats and other animals that can see in the dark.

6. I have added quotation marks here to reflect Descartes's belief that these Aristotelian terms are merely names signifying nothing real.

7. See Aristotle, *Physics,* III, 2, 202a, where in addition the mover must be in contact with the moved.

8. Here Descartes hints for the first time that the measure of force in his world is the product of size and speed. The hint never becomes an explicit statement, however, and "size" is later used ambiguously; see below, page 462, note 50.

9. Discourse II, "Of Refraction": "It is only necessary to note that the power, whatever it be, which causes the movement of this ball to continue is different from that which determines it to move in one direction rather than in another.. . . " (*Descartes: Discourse on Method, Optics, Geometry, and Meteorology,* trans. P.J. Olscamp [Indianapolis, 1965], p. 75). On the distinction, which Descartes discusses in more detail in chapters 7 and 13 below, see the analyses of M.S. Mahoney, *The Mathematical Career of Pierre de Fermat* (Princeton, 1973), App. II, and A.I. Sabra, *Theories of Light from Descartes to Newton* (London, 1967), chapters I-IV.

10. Here Descartes invokes for the first of several times a principle of natural economy for which he provides no justification. He states it most clearly below, page 482: "When nature has many ways of arriving at the same effect, she most certainly always follows the shortest." Neither the nature of matter nor the conserving action of God, both soon to be introduced as the basic principles of the physical universe, seems to imply that nature always takes the most direct path.

11. Descartes develops the mechanism for these sensations in *Man;* see AT.XI.143-144.

12. *en action de. Action* acquires a technical meaning in chapter 7, where Descartes introduces and explains the laws of motion; cf. below, note 37. But the phrase as used here seems to mean no more than that the balls are in continuing contact and not, as in the next paragraph, touching one another only in passing, i.e., in contact for an instant and no more.

13. *eaux fortes;* F. Alquié, *Descartes: Oeuvres philosophiques* (Paris, 1963ff), I:328, note 3, identifies these "strong waters" as nitric acid, used at the time especially for etching copper plates.

14. This removal of any upper limit to the size of a part, combined with the absence of any lower limit (see chapter 5 on the first element), distinguishes Descartes's theory of matter from other atomist and corpuscularist theories, all of which posited a finite but imperceptibly small size for the ultimate constituents of matter.

14a. See Rule XII of *Rules for the Direction of the Mind,* AT.X.424.

15. For examples of such "experiments" from the works of the fourteenth-century philosophers Albert of Saxony, Jean Buridan, and Marsilius of Inghen, see Edward Grant, ed, *Source Book in Medieval Science* (Cambridge, Mass., 1974), 324-328. For later writers, see Charles B. Schmitt, "Experimental Evidence for and against a Void: The Sixteenth-Century Arguments," *Isis* 58 (1967): 352-366.

16. The argument here employs unstated premises to achieve a *reductio ad absurdum* of the theory that vacua exist but that nature "abhors" them. First, it is argued that machines lift great weights before breaking because for, say, a beam to break would require the creation (at least for an instant) of a vacuum between its ruptured parts. But, if so, how could air contain interstitial vacua and still have any body at all (which its resistance to motion through it shows it does)? Why would it not simply dissipate? Second, it is argued that in pumps the water rises against its natural inclination in order to prevent the formation of a vacuum as the piston is withdrawn. But, if so, then why would the water not fall naturally from the clouds to fill interstitial vacua in the air below?

17. This motion of mutual replacement is quite reminiscent of Aristotle's *antiperistasis,* mentioned in *Physics* IV, 8, 215a, as one possible mechanism for the continued motion of projectiles. Aristotle uses it, however, not to account for motion in a plenum, but to argue against the existence of a vacuum.

18. Descartes here again posits a principle of natural economy for which he offers no independent justification; see above, note 10. Its application here contravenes the results of his earl.. ..searches in hydrostatics while conforming to arguments to be made later (below, chapter 13) about the propagation of light through the second element.

19. Here the first element assumes the properties of the mathematical continuum. There are no atoms in Descartes's world, just a fragmented continuous space. See above, note 14.

20. In traditional Aristotelian cosmology, the four elements were themselves compounds of the terms, taken two at a time, of two pairs of contrary "principles" or qualities: hot ≠ cold and wet ≠ dry. Fire was hot and dry, air hot and wet, water cold and wet, and earth cold and dry. The compositions were often displayed schematically in the following form:

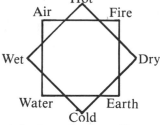

Reference to the principles here leads to Descartes's statement of his mechanistic program and emphasizes what a radically different approach that program represents. Rather than serving as explanatory constituents of the elements, the principal qualities must be explained in terms of the nature and behavior of those elements.

21. Hence, differing only by size and speed, all elements are transformable into one another merely by change of size or speed.

22. Descartes retains here some vestige of the Aristotelian doctrine of natural place. It is no less justified by his argument so far than is his assumption of three elementary states of matter.

23. It would seem to follow from Descartes's principles that mixed bodies exist along the surfaces of all the planets. In restricting his claim to the surface of the earth, he may have been reflecting his uncertainty about the theological acceptability of a plurality of (possibly inhabited) worlds.

24. See Edward Grant, "Medieval and Seventeenth-Century Conceptions of an Infinite Void Space beyond the Cosmos," *Isis* 60 (1969): 39-60.

25. It is perhaps worth asking here whether Descartes might be hinting at the distinction between a boundless space and an infinite one. On an ocean-covered spherical earth the surface water, though finite in area, nonetheless appears endless through the absence of any boundaries.

26. Descartes here appeals without further explication to his doctrine of clear and evident ideas.

27. See below, page 433, for some elucidation of this remark. There Descartes insists on at least half of the identification of space and matter, i.e., that the essential property of matter is to take up space. Although the arguments just presented against the void would seem to complete the identification, note that God creates matter in an already existing space of indefinite extent.

28. Here cosmogony and cosmology are reduced to the same mechanism.

29. But, "[We cannot be sure] . . . that He cannot do what we cannot understand; for it would be temerity to think that our imagination is as extensive as His power." Descartes to Mersenne, 15.IV.30, AT.I.146.

30. Descartes set out the "others" in the *Principles of Philosophy;* see below, note 38.

31. Descartes repeats here in somewhat different terms the critique he made in Rule XII of *Rules for the Direction of the Mind.*

32. Aristotle, *Physics* III, 1, 201a.

33. Although Descartes here places rest and motion on the same ontological level, it is not until the *Principles of Philosophy* that he argues the relative nature of motion; see *Principles,* Part II, pars. 24 and 25.

34. Since Descartes has nowhere given quantitative meaning to "motion," it must remain unclear what is being transferred here and what governs that transfer.

35. When finally published in the *Principles,* the rules of impact derived from the laws of motion were indeed "manifestly contrary" to empirical data, as critics immediately pointed out. Descartes anticipated the criticism in Part II, par. 53 by noting how difficult it was to single out the bodies involved in any real exchange of motion. He expanded this defense in a letter to Clerselier in February 1645 (AT.IV.183-188) and added to it another version of his principle of economy: "When two bodies, which have in them incompatible modes [of motion], collide, some change must certainly take place in these modes to render them compatible, but . . . this change is always the least possible." True to his word in *The World,* Descartes steadfastly refused to accept empirical evidence against his laws of motion, and several of his followers took an equally stubborn stance after his death.

36. Note the determinative role of mathematics in this argument.

37. See above, note 12; here the phrase *en action de* seems to preserve its meaning, although *action* has picked up (page 440) the technical sense of "inclination to move." So later, for example, light is an *action;* chapter 14 sets out "the properties of the *action* by which [men's] eyes can be thus pushed [to see light]," but it establishes no parameters by which it might be measured.

38. The rules are contained in pars. 45-52 of Part II of the *Principles.* For a handy schematic presentation, see E.J. Aiton, *The Vortex Theory of Planetary Motions* (New York, 1972), 36.

39. *Sapientia,* VIII, 21. The statement was a commonplace of medieval thought and was encountered by every schoolboy in the opening line of Johannes de Sacrobosco's *Algorismus vulgaris,* the standard arithmetic textbook from the mid-thirteenth to the mid-sixteenth century.

40. To compound the vagueness of the measure of "motion," Descartes here seems to suggest a non-linear gradient of motion in the vortex, though he offers no reason for it.

41. Here again is the non-linear variation of orbital speed with respect to radial distance.

42. Descartes shifts here from explication of the mechanism to illustration of it by analogy with more familiar phenomena.

43. Compare this explanation with Descartes's theory of the tides, below, chapter 12.

44. The nature and location of the three comets observed in 1618 became the focal issues in an acrid debate between Galileo and the Jesuit astronomer Orazio Grassi. The debate triggered Galileo's masterful *Assayer* (1624), in which he defended empirical investigation and the use of mathematics and the telescope at the same time that he argued that comets were little more than atmospheric optical illusions. For the central texts of that debate, see S. Drake and C.D. O'Malley (trans.), *The Controversy on the Comets of 1618* (Philadelphia, 1960).

45. Saturn.

46. Jupiter.

47. Mars.

48. In order: Saturn, Jupiter, Mars, Earth, Venus, Mercury.

49. This shift from volume to surface as a measure of a body's magnitude only further confuses the question of the parameters of "motion" or "force."

50. The surface varies as the square of the ball's radius, the volume of its cube; hence, the ratio of surface to volume varies inversely to the radius and so decreases with increasing radius.

51. Moon.

52. Here again a principle of natural economy substitutes for a missing mechanism; see above, note 10.

53. Foremost among the new astronomers, of course, was Galileo, who first reported the moons of Jupiter in his *Starry Messenger* (1610). Later that year he observed what he thought were satellites about Saturn; he mentioned them in the dedication of his *Floating Bodies* (1611) to Cosimo II of Tuscany.

54. Descartes here introduces the void as a counterfactual hypothesis. He employs the same device later in explicating his theory of light; see below, chapter 13, page 482.

55. Descartes had clearly never been down to any depth himself nor talked to anyone who had. Nonetheless, one would think that his hydrostatical investigations and his knowledge of those of Stevin and Beeckman would have compensated for the absence of direct experience. The replacement principle just invoked here is the obverse of Archimedes' famous principle that a body immersed in a fluid loses as much weight as the weight of the fluid displaced.

56. This paragraph in particular shows the necessity of the earth's motion in Descartes's universe.

57. Compare this and the following chapter to Discourses I and II of the *Dioptrics,* for which they supply the real model of light.

58. It is important to follow the construction of the diagram here, and

hence to modify it. Strictly speaking E is a point, the apex of the visual cone EAD. By taking a neighborhood of points about E, Descartes generates a space, which he also calls E. The light coming to that space is the light contained in all the visual cones having a vertex in the space and a base in the sun, i.e., it is the light contained in the truncated cone FADG, where F and G should lie at the upper corners of the space, as shown in the following figure:

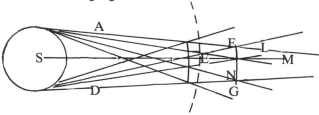

The whole argument seems motivated solely by the need to have a person's eye at E see the whole disk of the sun.

59. Here again the counterfactual use of the void introduced above; see note 54.

60. The principle of economy again; see note 10.

61. Compare the "packing" argument to follow with the analogy of the wine vat in Discourse I of the *Dioptrics.*

62. Note the virtue of conceiving of light as a *force* or *tendency to move* rather than as a motion.

63. Discourse II of the *Dioptrics.*

64. On the relation of the real model of light (an impulse propagated instantaneously through a medium) and the heuristic model used in the *Dioptrics* (a tennis ball moving through empty space), see M.S. Mahoney, *The Mathematical Career of Pierre de Fermat* (Princeton, 1973), Appendix II.

65. Discourse I.

66. Thus Descartes removes perhaps the strongest empirical argument against the Copernican system. If, that is, the earth makes an annual circuit about the sun at a distance sufficient to account for observed planetary phenomena, observations of the fixed stars made from opposite sides of the orbit ought to differ by some amount. No one had

been able to ascertain any difference, nor would anyone do so until the nineteenth century. Descartes joined Galileo and other defenders by arguing away the point with reference to the immense distance of the fixed stars.

67. Among the startling telescopic discoveries announced by Galileo in his Copernican works of the 1610s was the composition of the Milky Way; magnification revealed it to consist of a huge number of separate stars.

68. The *novae* or "new stars" observed in 1572 and 1604 had much to do with the spread of Copernicanism and of opposition to it.

69. Note the sloppiness of Descartes's mathematics here. C and D cannot be common points of tangency unless T coincides with S. The error makes clear how little of Descartes's argument in fact rested on mathematical reasoning.

70. In the *Assayer* (translated by Drake in Drake and O'Malley, *Controversy,* p. 190; see note 44 above), Galileo describes the phenomenon as a "curl" (*chioma*); Descartes's term is *chevelure,* which literally means "head of hair."

Fautes principales à corriger.

Pag. 428. l. 19. *liſez* qui s'eſt.
Pag. 440. l. 4. *liſez* ſe meut.
Pag. 494. l. 15. *liſez* peut tout enſemble eſtre pouſſée.

An S. Karabel Production